Jim Gash has brought forth a book that might just cause you to sing. *Divine Collision* reminds you of the great worth of a seemingly obscure life, and how a little decision can have ripple effects into eternity. It's about saying YES to the God who sees the broken places—and doesn't look away. This gripping true story of redemption and beauty deserves a wide audience of thrill-seekers and those who want to discover new ways to love God, even when He calls us to what seems impossible.

—Sara Hagerty, Author of *Every Bitter Thing Is Sweet*

What happens when God calls a Southern California law professor to serve "the least of these" in Uganda? *Divine Collision* is the riveting story of God at work in two families on two continents. It is a roller coaster of faith, perseverance, disappointments, and ultimately triumph—not only for a falsely convicted Ugandan youth, but the transformation of the justice system of an entire nation. You will be inspired by how God can use normal, everyday people to accomplish His purposes!

—Terry Fahy, Vice President of Salem Media Group, Los Angeles

Jim Gash is a quiet hero. He is a brilliant justice fighter, and his life is marked by humility. His story, told in *Divine Collision*, is courageous and inspiring. Read this book!

—John Sowers, Author of *The Heroic Path*

Divine Collision is a thrilling story of how an American law professor driven by faith, compassion, and love made sacrifices for himself and his family in order to secure justice and freedom through Uganda's judicial system for many children, including Henry, who had been convicted of murder. The story is written against the background of the successful collaboration between the Pepperdine University School of Law and the Ugandan Judiciary, which has promoted exchange programs between the two institutions and made a significant contribution to the transformation of the justice system. Because of Jim Gash's commitment and historical contribution to the Ugandan Judiciary, which is clearly evident in this book, he was named Specialist Advisor to the Ugandan High Court and became the first American ever to argue a case in the Ugandan Court of Appeals. Indeed, his frequent visits to Uganda have made Uganda his second home.

—Dr. Benjamin J. Odoki, Retired Chief Justice of Uganda (2001–13)

There is no greater love than laying down your life for a friend. This profound love seeps through every page of Jim and Henry's story, like a healing balm. Over the last several years I have had the great privilege of witnessing Jim's passion for Ugandan people and his willingness to lay down his own life for others. *Divine Collision* will remind you once again how one small gesture of love can make a monumental impact on a person for eternity.

—Katie Davis, Author of the *New York Times* Bestseller *Kisses from Katie*

A beautiful and riveting story, *Divine Collision* is an emotional roller-coaster ride illustrating how a life of service is not only personally satisfying but also an avenue for our own liberation. With tears in my eyes as I read along, this story powerfully reminded me that the most satisfying life is a life of service. Jim Gash humbly chronicles how he, through tireless and devoted work to free a wrongly accused teenager, gained his own freedom by discovering his true purpose in life.

—Monty Moran, Esq., Co-CEO of Chipotle Mexican Grill

Divine Collision is an encouragement to those of us who walk daily in the corridors of law and order, believing that if you persist and follow the divine blueprint, it is possible to extract justice from the very jaws of injustice. The story of Jim and Henry illustrates further that justice knows no color, no jurisdiction, no age, and no boundaries. Justice is without borders.

—Justice Mike J. Chibita, Director of Public Prosecutions, Uganda

With great courage and conviction, Jim Gash provides an extraordinary glimpse into the power of obedience, prayer, and hope in transforming not only one life—or even one community—but an entire justice system. *Divine Collision* speaks to what is at the heart of our Christian calling: "Learn to do right; seek justice. Defend the oppressed. Take up the cause of the fatherless; plead the case of the widow" (Isaiah 1:17).

—Gary A. Haugen, President & CEO of International Justice Mission
and author of *The Locust Effect*

Divine Collision weaves together a compelling narrative of Jim Gash's passion to protect children forgotten within the web of the Ugandan justice system and his desire to obey the biblical command to act justly, love mercy, and walk humbly. Jim's story inspires all of us to "remember the poor" and to serve "the least of these."

—Ken Starr, President of Baylor University

I first heard Jim Gash speak years ago when giving a sermon in place of our pastor who was on hiatus. It was something I will never forget and changed the way I look at chance meetings forever. He said there is no such thing as a coincidence, only "God-scheduled opportunities." Thanks to that shared wisdom, my life has been greatly blessed. Jim is a man like no other, and I know this story will touch and inspire you. You picking up this book is more than chance curiosity—it's an example of a "God-scheduled opportunity." Enjoy!

—Scott Hamilton, Olympic Gold Medalist and Author

Divine Collision is about justice and the heart of a Christian lawyer. I encourage anyone who thinks God cannot use them to make a difference in the world: read this book! Jim Gash did a simple thing—he followed where God called him. And in the end, Jim was a part of God's plan for justice in lives stretching from California to Uganda.

—David Nammo, Executive Director and CEO
of the Christian Legal Society

Divine Collision is an incredible story of faith, determination, brotherhood and, finally, sweet victory for the good guys. Jim Gash, a professor at Pepperdine Law School, tells of his friendship with Henry, a Ugandan teenager falsely accused of a crime, and their battle with the Ugandan courts to introduce due process and basic fairness. While this book does tell how they changed the system, Jim and Henry's story is more about how anyone can accomplish great things when they see a wrong and simply decide its time to correct it.

—Roger Cossack, ESPN Legal Analyst and
Adjunct Professor at Pepperdine University School of Law

There is a moment of sober acceptance when vocation and training intersect urgently with avocation and a deep and personal need to do what is right. *Divine Collision* is the true story of a man fit perfectly to a mountain. In an age when the practice of law feels sometimes as much like business as it is profession, this remarkable story cannot help but restore faith in the nobility of the law and its humble, respectful practitioners. This is a story about nothing less than a hero's journey in service to justice.

—Andrew K. Benton, President of Pepperdine University

A remarkable story of what happens when you follow God's commandments to love the Lord your God with all your heart, with all your soul, and with all your mind and then to love your neighbor as you love yourself—you get a divine collision, and your life and the lives of those around you are changed forever! Jim Gash, in his book *Divine Collision*, shows us what the true meaning of humanity is and how it leads to justice, peace, and fulfillment.

—Justice Geoffrey Kiryabwire, Justice of the Court of Appeal
for the Constitutional Court of Uganda

In challenging times, the world needs reminders of hope and justice. *Divine Collision* delivers that message clearly and with a clarion call to action: we can all do our part to heal a broken world.

—Jay Milbrandt, Professor at Bethel University (MN) and
Author of *The Daring Heart of David Livingstone* and *Go and Do*

A compelling and joyous story of the transformation of a legal system—and of the individuals who brought it about. A must-read for anyone committed to the proposition that law is a calling to serve others.

—Jeffrey Brauch, Dean of Regent University School of Law

Divine Collision is the extraordinary story of the dedicated work done in Uganda by Professor Jim Gash of the Pepperdine University School of Law. Professor Gash responded to his own faith calling and to the desperate needs of hundreds of young people in remand homes in Uganda, imprisoned for long periods of time without any semblance of what we know as due process. Through this journey, Professor Gash not only forged a bond with Henry, the African hero of the story, but he helped change the practices of the entire Ugandan criminal justice system. His significant contributions stand as models for bringing fairness and the rule of law to people around the globe. It is a privilege to be a colleague of Professor Gash and to be part of the home of the Global Justice Program, which he directs.

—Deanell Reece Tacha, Duane & Kelly Roberts Dean of
Pepperdine University School of Law

Find out what happens when a sharp, self-effacing California lawyer without any penchant for mission trips goes to Africa and befriends a sharp, self-effacing Ugandan teenager who has suffered a grave injustice. He gives the boy his cell phone number . . . and nothing will ever be the same for either of them. Part legal thriller, part spiritual memoir, this book will remind you what wonderful surprises are in store when a person says yes to God—even an initially hesitant yes.

—Rick Hamlin, Executive Editor of *Guideposts* magazine
and Author of *10 Prayers You Can't Live Without*

Divine Collision tells the extraordinary and compelling story of the friendship between Jim and Henry, separated by thousands of miles and a cultural gap wider still. It is the story of deep and sacrificial friendship, of the relentless pursuit of justice, of a dramatic and unexpected divine collision. Gash lovingly and beautifully shares his story with Henry's help, drawing us in and exposing us to the transforming power of living in response to God's call on our lives. Inspiring and encouraging, you will not be the same after reading *Divine Collision*.

—L. Timothy Perrin, President of Lubbock Christian University

Despite all the bad news from Africa—and his book hides none of that— Jim Gash offers some good news about how individuals can make a transformational difference in others' lives, regardless of where they are in this world. *Divine Collision* is a well-told and inspiring story of love, hope, and mercy one life at a time.

—Edward Larson, Pulitzer Prize–Winning Author of *Summer for the Gods*

We all desire to live lives of meaning. We all long to know we've helped make the world a better place. *Divine Collision* is an inspiring, heartwarming story that chronicles Jim Gash's cross-continental journey to unlock a lifetime of meaning and possibility for a young African boy named Henry. It's a powerful reminder of God's desire for us to love one another and to boldly follow the passion he places in our hearts. Uplifting and inspiring!

—Phil Schubert, President of Abilene Christian University

Jim Gash's account of Henry's journey through the Ugandan judicial system is riveting, colorful, and emotional. Jesus said, "I am the door," and Jim walked through the door to answer Henry's prayer for help. In the process, he's helped catalyze the juvenile judicial system in Uganda. Among its many inspirational lessons, *Divine Collision* shows how empathetic and sustained service bear fruit in foreign missionary efforts.

—Edith H. Jones, Judge for U.S. Court of Appeals for the Fifth Circuit

Divine Collision is a captivating book! Jesus calls us to visit the prisoner, proclaim justice for the oppressed, and set the captive free. Too often we've forgotten that He really meant it. Jim Gash didn't forget, and his book reminds us this is Jesus' call for us too.

—Richard Stearns, President of World Vision U.S.
and Author of *The Hole in Our Gospel* and *Unfinished*

DIVINE COLLISION

DIVINE COLLISION

An African Boy, An American Lawyer, *and*
Their Remarkable Battle *for* Freedom

JIM GASH

WORTHY®
PUBLISHING

Published by Worthy Books, an imprint of Worthy Publishing Group, a division of Worthy Media, Inc., One Franklin Park, 6100 Tower Circle, Suite 210, Franklin, TN 37067.

WORTHY is a registered trademark of Worthy Media, Inc.

HELPING PEOPLE EXPERIENCE THE HEART OF GOD

eBook available wherever digital books are sold.

———————————————————————

Library of Congress Control Number: 2015952292

———————————————————————

For foreign and subsidiary rights, contact rights@worthypublishing.com

Scripture quotations are from THE HOLY BIBLE, NEW INTERNATIONAL VERSION®, NIV® Copyright © 1973, 1978, 1984, 2011 by Biblica, Inc.® Used by permission. All rights reserved worldwide.

Published in association with Yates & Yates, www.Yates2.com

ISBN: 978-1-61795-671-3 (Hardcover w/ Jacket)

Cover Design: Matt Smart / Smartt Guys design
Cover Images: Craig Detweiler (top) and Jay Milbrandt (bottom)

Printed in the United States of America
16 17 18 19 20 LBM 8 7 6 5 4 3 2 1

To Joline, who has unfailingly loved,
encouraged, and believed in me
for more than a quarter of a century.

CONTENTS

PART FOUR

FOREWORD BY BOB GOFF

JIM GASH IS A GOOD FRIEND of mine. He's many things. A father, a lawyer, an advocate, a professor at Pepperdine Law School. He's too humble to let on, but those of us who have been around him for a while know he could be running a small country. Instead, he's devoted his life to his family, his friends, his students, and Jesus. Doing this is more complicated than it sounds at first, because Jim assumes everyone is his friend. He also takes Jesus literally. Jesus told His friends when they did something for the lost and hurting, they were doing it for Him. This book is about what Jim did next, because he actually believes what Jesus said is true.

He also doesn't think loving his neighbor means just loving the person across the street from him. He's gone around the world loving people. You'll meet a couple of them in this book. While I've learned a lot of things from Jim over the years, he's never thought he was my teacher; he just thought he was my friend. There are a lot of people who feel this way about Jim. You'll know why, before you turn the last page of this book.

Jim knew I didn't have a place to stay one night, so he gave me a key to his house and said I could stay there every night. People who know how to love extravagantly do these things. I've spent more than a few nights at Jim's house since then, and he's a man of habits. He makes the same breakfast every morning. An egg. A piece of toast. A slice of meat.

The same way. Every day. No exceptions. He loves the people he meets the same way. Everybody. Every day. No exceptions. He started loving people in Uganda this way, and you'll read in this book how he helped to change a country.

Jim prepares for his day at Pepperdine Law School the way most people study for the bar exam. He memorizes the cases, the rules, and the outcomes. Even though he knows the cases better than any of the students, he makes them feel as though they're teaching him. Humble people make a habit of loving people this way. Jim also memorizes the name of every student in his class. Perhaps this could work for some of us if we had a class of a dozen or less. Jim has hundreds of students in his classes. On the first day of class, he calls on them by name. He knows where each student went to school, what their ambitions are, and where they lived before they came to law school. He could probably tell them their favorite color. This isn't a parlor room trick. You see, Jim cares for everyone he meets this way. Ferociously. Purposefully. Intensely. He's memorized the way Jesus loved people, and Jim knows he can't love people the way Jesus did if he doesn't know them. So Jim set out many years ago to get to know as many people as he can. He treats the chief justice of Uganda's Supreme Court and his many friends in the judiciary the same way he treats his students. With tremendous love and respect.

It won't take you long to figure out Jim doesn't walk; he leaps. People light up when he springs into a room. He does life with a boyish charm, which is irresistible even to his most imposing adversary. He doesn't just put his toe in the water, he grabs his knees and does a cannonball. And without knowing what just happened, most of us have felt Jim grab us by the wrist a time or two and take us along with him.

When Jim let his love off the chain in Uganda many years ago, he visited many times and did tremendous things, but he knew he could accomplish more if he moved there with his family—so he did. Who loves people that way? I have a school in Northern Uganda and have been at the receiving end of Jim's audacious brand of love. I've watched him hope for other people what they've been hoping for themselves. He must have done a Jedi move on me once, as I found myself enrolling students into my school he'd freed from a prison in Uganda. I didn't even know what Jim had done until much later. Typical Jim! Love isn't a spell that is cast; it's a habit that is practiced. Jim has practiced love a lot, and it's cost him more than a little.

As a young man, Jim landed a job with a huge law firm—which is the envy of most lawyers—but Jim didn't want to just do things he was able to do; he wanted to do things he was *created* to do. He knows there's no justice without love and no love without justice, so Jim started doing a lot of both. To be sure, he's one of the world's best cheerleaders, but Jim loves people like a linebacker. The last place I'd want to be in the world is standing in between him and injustice. This is because Jim doesn't see people as issues; he sees them as people.

If what I believe is true, one day each of us is going to wrap up our time here on earth and we'll sit with God. Jesus said on that day He'll want to talk to us about how we treated hungry people, thirsty people, strange people, sick people, naked people, and imprisoned people. Some of those conversations will be brief, and some of those conversations will be long. I'm betting Jesus will have a long conversation with Jim about the people who were hurting and somehow got inside the blast radius of his love.

Jim is a lot like Jesus—they both went after the ones who were on society's fringe. Jim doesn't let many people know what he does for others. He's old fashioned that way and thinks love doesn't need to be televised for it to matter. Or even put in a book for the masses to read. But he wanted to tell his story to draw more attention to others, including an African boy named Henry. In these pages, you're going to get a peek through a knothole and learn more than a little from a guy who's been doing a lot more than just talking about love and justice.

It's a delight to introduce you to my friend Jim Gash.

PART
ONE

CHAPTER 1
THE CATALYST

"IS THAT REALLY AFRICA, DAD?" Jessica asked.

My thoughts floated across the water stretching out before us as my family and I stood at the cliff's edge in the early summer of 2008.

"Dad? DAD? Are you even listening to me?" my inquisitive thirteen-year-old daughter, Jessica, persisted.

"What, sweetie?" I said, snapping back into the moment.

"Is . . . that . . . Africa?" She was pointing at a smudge of brown on the horizon separating the water from the sky.

"Yes, that's Morocco, and that's the Strait of Gibraltar in front of it. We're standing on the southernmost tip of Europe."

"Are we going there?"

"No, sweetie. We're going to drive around Spain for a while before we go to London." We were en route to the UK, where we would live for six months while I worked at Pepperdine's London Program during the summer and fall terms.

My eight-year-old, Jennifer, took off her rainbow-rimmed sunglasses and sighed. "When can we get some ice cream?"

"I want some too," my burr-headed middle child, Joshua, added.

"No, Dad." Jessica stood on her tiptoes until she and her furrowed brow were centered in my field of view. "I mean, are we *ever* going to Africa?"

"Nope. I have no plans to go to Africa. Ever."

"Why not?"

All she got in reply was a shrug. I turned her shoulders around to face the horizon and placed her head under my chin. *What would we ever do in Africa?*

"Hey, Jim, let me get a photo," my wife, Joline, said as she lined us up against the rail and we squeezed together to fit in the frame of the picture.

This was the only memory of Africa I expected our family ever to share.

Had Joline's camera lens been able to focus over my shoulder on a small village 3,358 miles south of Gibraltar, it would have captured a deceptively innocuous scene—a dusty peasant farmer hiring an itinerant herdsman to tend his nine cows.

✻   ✻   ✻

A red sun peeked expectantly over the rolling hills as the herdsman shuffled onto the bustling road. His dew-drenched shirt clung to his stiff back, and his alcohol-soaked head hammered from his three-day binge. He was no stranger to sleeping on the ground, but his aching joints reminded him he wasn't getting any younger.

He pulled a hat over his weathered face and blinked at the red dirt swimming beneath his bare feet. The sputtering cough of a *boda boda* drew his glance to the driver and then to the middle-aged man seated behind him on the motorcycle. The passenger wore a faded Manchester United T-shirt and a scowl. *That isn't him*, the herdsman thought. *But better to be safe.*

He quickened his pace and ambled unsteadily into Hoima's outdoor market, seeking anonymity among the merchants propping up crude wooden stalls and setting out their merchandise—tomatoes, pineapples, secondhand clothing, and other necessities for life in rural East Africa.

Are they still hunting me? the herdsman wondered, carefully avoiding any eye contact. *Why didn't I take a bus south to Kampala? They wouldn't have looked for me two hundred kilometers away. Why did I steal from them in the first place? They gave me a job and treated me well.*

He cursed himself for squandering the money on alcohol. Now it was too late. *I can't even afford a* matatu *to Masindi!*

As he ducked under a yellow Uganda Cranes soccer jersey dangling over the narrow path leading into the market, his stomach growled. He could afford little more than some bread and something to drink while he hid yet another day. More than hunger, though, he felt fear. It wasn't fear of the police; they only cared about more serious crimes. It was the boda drivers.

He shuddered as he remembered the beatings he'd witnessed, and sometimes participated in during his younger days, when thieves were caught red-handed.

"Two *chapattis*," he said to the woman laboring over an iron skillet.

"One thousand shillings," came the reply in broken English as she slipped the circular pieces of flat bread into a plastic bag.

As he pocketed his change, an unfamiliar voice startled him from behind. "Imanriho?"

The herdsman turned slowly and found himself staring into the eyes of a boda driver twice his size and half his age—the one who had zoomed past minutes earlier.

"My passenger told me you are the thief called Imanriho," the hulking man growled.

He weighed his options. He could run, but with his shaky legs, his odds of escaping were razor thin. He could offer his remaining money as a bribe, but the boda driver would earn that amount on a few fares over the next hour. Or he could play dumb.

"Eh? Who are you looking for?"

"Imanriho—the herdsman who stole money from his employer three days ago."

"That is not me." He shook his head vigorously.

"Then you should not be worried!" The boda driver seized his arm and forcefully escorted him back through the market.

"I am not a thief, I am not a thief!"

His trembling protests drew a crowd, their experience telling them a boda driver dragging a suspected thief meant violence was imminent. By the time captive and captor reached the road, about twenty onlookers had convened, many of whom were also boda drivers. His captor yanked off his hat and turned his chin toward the man in the Manchester United shirt. The man spat. "He is the one. Make him pay."

The first blow landed behind Imanriho's right ear, knocking him to his knees. A kick to his left ribcage emptied his lungs. As he wretched and gasped for air, he felt himself being hoisted onto a motorcycle behind a boda driver. Another man scrambled on behind him, the jeering crowd trailing them as the motorcycle eased out of the market. Imanriho instantly recognized the route—they were heading toward his employer's home.

The crowd's insults gradually intensified into death threats, which sharpened Imanriho's focus. As the motorcycle slowed near a school, Imanriho lunged sideways and escaped while a chorus of female voices pierced the morning air in alarm. Imanriho's adrenaline surged as he darted around trees, vaulted over ditches, and zigzagged between houses like a gazelle being chased by lions. He'd never run so fast.

But it wasn't fast enough.

Imanriho was glancing back at his pursuers when an agile young man leapt from his doorway and sent the escapee sprawling. Before Imanriho could regain his feet, the crowd was upon him, dragging him and showering him with punches and kicks until he'd lost several teeth and could hear only ringing in his ears.

The pain was excruciating. Was this the end?

Through swollen eyes, he saw his employer's neighbors emerging from their shanties. As they joined in the pummeling, Imanriho recognized his boss's deep voice. "Stop! That is enough!"

A moment passed. Then another. No more blows.

"Someone bring my herdsman some water."

Imanriho rolled onto his side and tried to sit up. His mouth fumbled for words of remorse, but only mumbles emerged. He scanned the crowd in vain for his employer's kindhearted wife.

Suddenly a towering figure approached from behind him, blocking out the sun. Imanriho turned and squinted, trying to identify the object the man held above his head.

He heard his employer scream, "Nooo!" as the heavy stone tile crashed down on his skull.

Everything went dark.

CHAPTER 2
IHUNGU

"THIS IS YOUR NEW HOME. It is called Ihungu. You will stay here until you are released. Understand?"

Henry and Joseph nodded. The woman said she was called Rose, though her stocky figure, wrinkled face, and graying temples suggested her bloom had long since wilted.

"I am in charge, and you will do as I say. Understand?"

The boys nodded again. Henry's joints throbbed from the jarring ride to Ihungu.

"Which of you is called Henry?" Rose snarled, squinting in the fading light of day at a document the Hoima police officer had handed her.

"I am the one," said the older yet smaller of the two. "And this is my brother Joseph."

Rose's unflinching stare bore into Henry until he had to divert his eyes. Henry had honed his submissive posture during his two-month stay in the Hoima jail in the summer of 2008, where he and five other boys had been detained while awaiting word about their court cases.

Both brothers kept their heads bowed until Rose whipped her sharp-tipped umbrella upward toward the truck they'd just arrived on. "What are you waiting for?" Rose shouted to the driver in Swahili. "Leave!"

As the truck drove away, Rose calmed a bit. "This is the custody," she said flatly, pointing her umbrella javelin at the concrete building directly in front of them. "You will stay there with the others."

"Dinner is in one hour," she said, gesturing to her right at a boy inside a detached kitchen structure. He was stirring the contents of a blackened pot on a roaring fire. Two months ago was the last time Henry had cooked directly over a fire. It was the day his world had burst into flames.

✷ ✷ ✷

Henry's phone alarm buzzed on his pillow at 5:00 a.m. as usual. He raised his mosquito net in the darkness—taking care not to awaken his younger brothers, Joseph and Herbert, next to him—and felt the dirt floor for his flip-flops. The events of the past three days had replayed in his mind all night long. Trudging out the back door of his family's small concrete dwelling, fifteen-year-old Henry's troubles weighed on him like a lead robe.

"Good morning," Henry said groggily.

His mother knelt on the floor of the detached kitchen and added chunks of wood to a small fire. "Good morning, son." She sat up and studied Henry's expressive eyes. She could see trouble swimming in them this morning. "Are you too tired today? You know you don't need to help me every morning, don't you?"

"I am okay, and two work faster than one. I will have enough time to prepare for school when we finish." Henry lifted a boiling pot of water from the fire.

"Okay, but if this takes away from your studies, you must stop."

He shook a plain white bag of wheat flour into the pot and began the ten-minute mingling process. "I will keep my scholarship if I stay on top. I will not fail to do so."

"Your father and I are so proud of you. We want you to finish secondary school so God can give you opportunities we did not have."

Henry paused his stirring. "Do you still believe that is possible? Even after what has happened?"

10

"Is that what is bothering you? Always remember, God's plans are better than ours. Even when bad things happen, Henry, things outside our control, God will use them for good."

"Your mother is as wise as she is beautiful." The voice behind Henry was authoritative yet kind. Henry's father ducked under the doorway and set a fresh bag of wood chunks next to the fire.

Henry saw his mother blush and hoped he would someday love his own wife as much as his father loved his mother after twenty-plus years of marriage.

"Your mother and I had to go to work before we completed secondary school. You must finish. Do not worry about the family; God will provide. Just trust in Him and He will make your dream come true."

Henry wanted to believe this—that his dream of being the first in his family to go to university and become a doctor was possible. But he knew only one in twenty Ugandans attend university. His older brother, Kegan, had dropped out of school after Senior Four and now worked cutting hair and burning CDs. His older sister was also trapped in a menial job in Hoima even though she had completed Senior Six. Her national exam scores fell short of those necessary to earn a government scholarship, and the family couldn't afford to pay her university tuition.

Deep down, Henry knew his family couldn't afford to send *him* to university either. In fact, he feared that if he lost his scholarship, he would have to drop out of secondary school midway through Senior Three.

As Henry stirred the chapatti dough, his memories of three days ago were also stirred.

Henry's phone had vibrated in his pocket during geography class. "Henry, come home right now," his mom had pleaded.

Her desperate tone had set Henry's heart racing. "Is everything okay? Should Joseph come?"

"Leave Joseph. No one is hurt, but I need you." Then the line had suddenly gone dead.

Henry had sprinted the two hundred meters home, where his frazzled mother ushered him into his parents' bedroom. The mattress had been overturned and cast to one side.

"It is gone, Henry. It is all gone!" she had said while sobbing.

Each day his mother made hundreds of chapattis and sold them to local restaurants, and his father cut, folded, and glued rolls of paper into homemade envelopes and sold them to Hoima drugstores for packaging pills. The family's savings were kept under his parents' mattress.

"Who did this?" Henry had asked.

"Imanriho. Your father was in town delivering envelopes, so I asked the herdsman to go buy some new scissors to surprise your father. Imanriho waited in the front room while I went to get the money. We both walked out together, and he started to leave but said he forgot his coat inside. After tending to the chickens, I came inside and found this." She had swept her arm across the scene and said, "We have been saving for two years. It is all gone. All we have now are the animals."

Henry's father had been upset but more concerned with getting back the money than casting blame. Father, son, and some neighbors had fanned out across Hoima to search for Imanriho the rest of that day. After two more days had passed with no sign of him, everyone assumed he had caught a bus to Kampala or a matatu to Masindi.

"It has been three days," Henry's father declared while Henry was packaging chapattis with his mother, jarring him back to the present. "What is gone is gone."

"Everything happens for a reason," Henry's mother said. "In time, God will show us why."

As Henry walked to school, he tried to imagine what good could come from the loss of his family's savings. Though nothing came to him, a faint smile creased Henry's lips as his mother's words echoed in his head. He marveled at her faith and wondered if he would ever trust God as much as she did.

✶　✶　✶

"What are you waiting for? Into the custody!" Rose snapped at Henry. The memory of his mother's unshakable faith seemed so distant and unattainable now.

The wooden doorway to the custody was centered on the shorter side of a rectangular, V-roofed building. Carved into the concrete above the door was "1962." Henry surmised this was when the custody was built— the same year Uganda gained its independence from Great Britain.

Behind him were rows of corn and a mango tree. To his right were two more buildings, both much smaller than the custody, with more corn and another mango tree beyond them—but surprisingly, no fence in sight. The boy Rose had pointed out earlier was cooking something in the smaller building on the far right. A rusting drum of water sat in front of the other building.

As Henry and Joseph approached the custody, a hand plunged through a rectangular hole in the door and deftly removed a golden padlock. The door slowly opened inward. Henry's heart thundered as he and Joseph nervously ascended the three steps into the dark entrance.

Rose watched the door close behind them with satisfaction. Ihungu's warden allotted her a monthly food allowance based on the number of inmates. More inmates meant more money. Because the corn grown on Ihungu's ten acres produced more flour than the inmates needed, Rose could "redirect" the portion of the allowance otherwise allocated to corn flour.

She walked up the crumbling steps of the U-shaped building next to the custody and opened the door, dropping Henry's and Joseph's court documents onto the disorganized pile of papers between sacks of beans, corn flour, and cassava on one side, and stacks of hoes, shovels, and machetes on the other. Heaped in one corner of this storeroom was a mound of T-shirts and flip-flops.

As she closed the door behind her, she yelled, "Two more bowls— twenty-one to feed tonight! Smaller portions for everyone."

"Yes, ma'am," replied the shirtless, shoeless boy in the kitchen. He knew this actually meant twenty smaller portions for the juveniles and one large portion for Rose. He'd been warned not to talk back to her . . . and not to get between her and food.

Sweat streaked his face and smoke clouded his eyes as he gingerly slid another piece of firewood between two stone supports. Recalling his own arrival at Ihungu a month ago, he hoped the two new boys wouldn't make the same mistake he'd made by resisting what was about to happen.

Henry and Joseph crept inside the custody like it was haunted. As the door creaked to a close behind them, their pupils strained to capture the light trickling in through slits high on the walls. Henry scanned the length of the room, barely able to see a few dozen water jugs scattered along the walls near the back. Closer to the door lay blanket-covered mats in two evenly spaced rows of six—some with two boys on them; some with one. Most boys leaned against the side walls.

As their faces came into focus, none of the silent, penetrating stares conveyed even a hint of welcome. But in their eyes, Henry detected more apprehension than hatred. Henry finally exhaled.

Suddenly, one boy stood right up in Henry's face. Like the others, his hair was trimmed short. He wore a faded-red Arsenal soccer jersey and was almost six feet—eight inches taller than Henry. "I am Jamil, the Chairman. Remove your shoes and shirts," he menacingly instructed in Swahili.

Henry and Joseph glanced at each other, back at the Chairman, and then at everyone else leaning forward in anticipation. *Chairman of what?* Henry wondered.

"Take off your shoes and shirts, now!" The Chairman puffed his chest like a prizefighter at a press conference. His flashing eyes, clenched teeth, and tight fists punctuated the urgency in his voice.

Henry and Joseph complied. Another boy darted forward, scooped up their things, and disappeared through the custody's doorway, returning empty-handed moments later. Their simple act of obedience released the tension in the room.

Jamil returned to his mat adjacent to the door, mildly disappointed he wouldn't need to subdue them as he had the previous arrival, who had learned the hard way that the shoes and shirt were coming off. The others had also been reminded that insubordination came at a cost.

Another boy rose from a mat on the other side of the door. "I am called Sam. I am the *Katikkiro*." His countenance was stern but noticeably less intimidating than Jamil's.

Henry knew Katikkiro (Kah-tee-kee-roh) means "prime minister" in Swahili, which meant Sam was in charge. Aiming for an appropriate balance of deference and confidence, Henry looked Sam in the face and stretched out his hand. "Nice to meet you. I am called Henry, and this is my brother Joseph."

Sam paused. Henry's hand didn't move. No one breathed.

Henry swallowed hard, wondering whether to drop his eyes and withdraw his hand. Suddenly, Sam flashed a toothy smile and shook Henry's hand.

"Nice to meet you too. Welcome to Ihungu. With you, we are now nineteen. We have only twelve beds, so you will share with others. There is also one girl, but she stays with Rose in the store—the building between the custody and the kitchen."

Sam assigned Henry and Joseph mats and said, "We will eat soon, so sit quietly and wait. At nine o'clock you will be told the Rules."

Henry wondered what the Katikkiro meant by "the Rules" but knew he would learn soon enough.

All the boys appeared clean and healthy, though thin. Many of them looked Munyoro, like Henry and Joseph, but several appeared to be from different tribes. Oddly, none of the conversations among any of the boys were in the Munyoro language of Runyoro—all were in Swahili.

Some of the prisoners had small boxes of personal effects; some just had small piles of playing cards and clothing items. Even through the crusted paint on the walls, Henry could read dozens of carved messages, many of which were simply names. Others were phone numbers. Still others were pleas for help.

Thin slats near the top of the walls let in slender rays of light—as well as malaria-carrying mosquitos, yet there were no mosquito nets in sight. The boys' mats were thin, deteriorating foam or piles of reeds. A threadbare blanket covered each one, and there were no additional blankets to cover them. Between the mats were one-gallon white or yellow plastic jugs filled with drinking water. The back wall of the custody opened into a small room with a floor that sloped down to a drain. Near the entry point hung a clothesline.

At dinner inside the custody, each boy received a small bowl of corn-based *posho*, beans, and potato-like cassava root—food that Henry was served nearly every day at school. Henry wondered if he'd ever eat with his classmates again.

After sunset, with no electricity nearby and the closest streetlights two hundred kilometers away in Kampala, a curtain of inky darkness draped Ihungu. At precisely 9:00 p.m., an excited hush settled over the room. The Katikkiro stood and lit the only candle lamp in the custody. "Henry and Joseph, please come to me." The boys obeyed.

Sam walked them from mat to mat to introduce them to each prisoner. With the lamp in each boy's face, Sam asked, "Do you know Henry or Joseph?" Most were from Masindi or the surrounding villages. None was from Hoima, fifty kilometers away. No one recognized either of them.

Then Jamil, the Chairman, took the lamp and began the meeting. "We have rules at Ihungu. Violating these rules will result in punishment."

He cleared his throat and addressed the entire room as if he were Moses returning from Mount Sinai with the stone tablets. Proceeding from memory, he announced:

- Rule #1: Cruelty to others will be punished.
- Rule #2: Escape is forbidden. If a prisoner attempts to escape, he will be caught, brought back, and punished.
- Rule #3: Talking about escape is forbidden. To make sure no one speaks of it, prisoners may speak only Swahili. We took your shoes and shirts so you would not try to escape. You will get them back after three months if you do not attempt escape.
- Rule #4: No stealing. Prisoners who steal will be severely punished.
- Rule #5: No walking at night. Once this lamp is put out, prisoners must stay on their mats. If a prisoner has to get up, he must first tell the Katikkiro, who will light the lamp. Walking at night without permission will result in punishment.
- Rule #6: No rumor mongering. Prisoners who talk about others or repeat what they hear will be punished.
- Rule #7: Prisoners must carry their gardening tools in front of them when going to work. Those who carry their tools on their shoulder will be punished.

"Those are the Rules of Ihungu. Do you have any questions?"
Henry had several, but decided this wasn't the time to ask.

JULY 18, 2008

The boy next to me fell asleep right after the Katikkiro put out the lamp. I did not. I had not seen two of my brothers and my sister for two months. I had not seen my father for one month. I wondered how my mother would survive without the income from the envelope business. She would soon have to start selling the animals.

I wondered how long Joseph and I would be here. I missed school, and I knew the third term of Senior Three would be starting soon. Would the headmaster let me rejoin the class in the middle of the term? Or would I have to wait a year? It felt like my dream of attending university was slipping away.

I heard two or three boys crying softly. One of them sounded like Joseph. When Joseph cried in the Hoima jail, I could comfort him. I thought about going over to his bed, but that was against the Rules.

I imagined what my mom would say if she were here. She would tell me God is in control and that He uses even the bad things to make good. I tried to remind myself of this. I wanted to believe it very much.

I did not know what else to do, so I prayed very hard, like I had been praying every night for two months.

I asked God to help Joseph go to sleep so he would not be sad. I asked Him to protect my mom and brothers and sister at home. I asked Him for my father's release so he could take care of my family. I asked Him to help Joseph and me be released soon. I asked Him to help me get back in school.

But most of all, I asked God to help me keep believing He was hearing my prayers.

CHAPTER 3
THE GOVERNMENT

DURING THE NIGHT, Henry had awakened often, whenever the boy sharing his mat moved, coughed, or snored. Each time, Henry found himself momentarily disoriented as he scanned the room for something familiar, only to be filled with despair as the reality of his nightmare confronted him.

Whenever he closed his eyes, images from that fateful day replayed all over again.

✴ ✴ ✴

The morning Henry's family gave up searching for Imanriho—three days after the theft—a warbling, high-pitched sound rang out in front of Henry's school, signaling that someone was hurt . . . or about to be. All forty students in Henry's Senior Three class rushed to the open windows overlooking the main road from town.

"Back to your seats, students! This instant!"

The students grudgingly returned to their rickety desks while their teacher lingered at the window a bit longer, until the din and dust of a throng of villagers dissipated. His countenance betrayed the seriousness of the situation. "Get back to work," he sighed. "I am sure you will find out what happened after school."

A few minutes later, the headmaster strode into their classroom.

"Students, I do not know why the crowd assembled or why the alarm sounded. It is not important you know either. You will focus on your studies and ignore the commotion. No students or staff may leave today without my permission. Is that understood?"

His drill-sergeant delivery made clear this was a directive, not a question. This scenario played out in each classroom, including Joseph's Senior One class. Though Henry would have to wait to learn who had sounded the alarm and why, deep in the pit of his stomach he feared he already knew the answer.

The rest of the day Henry kept recalling his father's words from earlier that morning: *"What is gone is gone."*

But Henry now couldn't help wondering if what was gone . . . had returned.

MAY 29, 2008

Each day I attended school from 8:00 a.m. to 5:00 p.m. After class, I stayed until 9:00 p.m. to study with those who boarded at school. Because I was first in my class, I could eat supper with the boarding students for free. On this day, which was near the end of the second of three terms, I went home before supper because I could not stop thinking about the alarm that morning.

When I got home, my youngest brother, Herbert, was waiting outside. He told me what had happened. He was talking very fast and loud. I could not believe what he was telling me.

The Chairman's voice jerked Henry back to Ihungu at 5:30 a.m. The Katikkiro's candle lamp hurled shadows around the room, allowing just enough light for Henry to see Joseph's puffy red eyes as they locked on his own. The brothers carried on a wordless conversation: *We are okay. We are together. Stay strong.*

The boy sharing Henry's mat had told him the night before that Ihungu had two sets of toilets—one behind the custody and the other in the field where they occasionally played soccer.

When Henry's turn came to relieve himself, he was more than ready—he'd been holding it since he'd arrived at Ihungu. Stepping into one of the three plastic outhouses behind the custody, he found only a jagged twelve-inch hole in the cement floor. What was underneath was not far below; Henry's eyes burned from the stench.

Back in the custody, Henry was allowed to rest for a few more minutes until a thunderclap startled him out of a light doze. When two more claps followed in rapid succession, he realized it wasn't thunder at all but a heavy fist pounding on the custody door.

"Everyone out! We should have left five minutes ago!" Rose barked.

Henry and Joseph groggily followed the others out of the custody. The Chairman brought up the rear to ensure everyone exited. Two boys distributed shovels while the prisoners lined up. The morning chill bit into Henry's bare chest and back, and moist ground coated his bare feet. It had been years since Henry had walked any appreciable distance without shoes.

As the prisoners marched in a tight line, Rose imprinted her work rules on the new arrivals:

1. March in a single line. If someone gets out of line, I will assume he is trying to escape.
2. Carry the gardening tool in front of you, not on your shoulder, so you don't poke the boy behind you.
3. Do not talk while walking to the farm.
4. Upon reaching the farm, spread out and work in a line.
5. Work hard and fast or you will be punished.
6. Whoever finishes first must help the one farthest behind. In return, the helper gets a portion of the helped one's breakfast.
7. No eating or drinking anything until all the work is finished.

Twenty minutes later, they arrived at a square patch of cleared land. Rose ordered them to spread out two arms' lengths apart and to each prepare a row of sweet potato heaps. Henry's family had a small farm where they raised chickens, cows, and pigs, and on which they grew crops, so he knew what to do. Each boy mounded the red dirt into two-foot-high piles and jammed sweet potato branches into them.

The act of shoveling this dirt transported Henry back to when his youngest brother, Herbert, had shown him another mound of fresh dirt just months ago.

✱ ✱ ✱

Herbert talked so fast, Henry could only catch pieces of his words: ". . . thief found . . . villagers beat him . . . buried in our field."

"What? There is a dead man buried *here*?" Henry had heard about mob killings before, but never had one happened so close to home.

"Around eight thirty this morning, a neighbor spotted Imanriho in the market," Henry's father told the family over their usual dinner of rice and beans. "Some boda drivers brought him to the house. I was working in the field when I heard an alarm and saw the crowd coming up the road with Imanriho. He had been beaten very badly, and they were still beating him in front of our house."

"We heard the alarm at school," Joseph said.

"Was he dead?" Henry asked.

"Not quite. He was bleeding and seriously injured, but he was alive. I ordered them to stop, and they did. But then a boda driver from town picked up a stone and smashed his head."

"The crowd buried him in our field!" Herbert blurted with the misplaced enthusiasm of a ten-year-old.

"No. The crowd went home when they saw he was dead," his father said. "I do not know his relatives, so *I* buried him in the field."

"Did you call the police?" Henry asked.

"They are corrupt and useless," Henry's father scoffed.

The next morning, the headmaster strode into Henry's entrepreneurship class and motioned for Henry to follow him. As Henry turned a corner near the school's main office, a police officer stepped out, spun the boy around, and forced him against a wall, cuffing Henry's hands behind him. Henry's classmates watched through the window as Henry was loaded into the bed of an idling truck where Joseph and their mother were waiting, also in handcuffs.

"What is happening, Mom?" Henry asked.

The bravery in her voice defied the tears in her eyes as she knelt next to her boys. "They have not told me. But do not worry; everything will be okay. Whatever happens, remember God loves you and He will take care of you."

At the police station, Henry and Joseph were separated from their mother and led to a holding cell with seven adult men, one of whom was their father.

MAY 30, 2008

I looked around the cell and saw there were no beds—just a cement floor and a plastic jug in the corner for a toilet. It was almost full and it smelled very bad.

We stayed there with our father on Friday, Saturday, and Sunday. Every afternoon, a guard gave us each a small bowl of posho and a cup of water. We were not allowed to see anyone else.

On Monday, Joseph and I were brought into Magistrate Court and charged with murdering Imanriho. I tried to tell the magistrate we were in school when the man died, but he told me to be quiet. Because we were under eighteen, we were not taken back to the adult cell. Instead, we were moved to a larger cell with a movable divider. One side was for juveniles; the other side was for women. Our mother was there, and we were so happy she was okay. On the juvenile side there were four sets of bunk beds, a flush toilet, and a water faucet. Joseph and I were the only juveniles there.

After one week, my mother was released. She visited each day and brought us more food and water. She also brought us playing cards, but they were taken away by the guards.

After two weeks in this room, we were taken again to the Magistrate Court, where we waited for eight hours without any food or water. On that day, Wednesday, June 18, 2008, the magistrate told us our case was committed to the High Court in Masindi. No one explained what this meant. The next month we spent in the juvenile room passed very slowly because we had nothing to do but wait.

On July 18, Joseph and I were again brought to court. The judge told us we were being sent to a juvenile remand home in Masindi to wait for our trial. I was encouraged that we were moving out of jail and into what we thought was a home. Joseph and I had been praying very hard, so we thought our prayers were being answered and we would be released soon.

Now, while Henry dug into the dirt, he watched as Sam paced in front of them carrying a stick three feet long and a half inch thick. Rose lounged in the shade and periodically yelled at the boys to work faster. Henry piled sweet potato heaps as fast as he could. Exhaustion threatened to overtake him as he finished his final mound three hours later, but he didn't finish last. Fortunately, neither did Joseph.

Later that afternoon, while resting inside the custody, Henry heard the rumble of an approaching motorcycle. "Mr. William is here," Sam announced. The boys bounced to their feet and anxiously congregated at the door. Sam let everyone out except for Henry and Joseph.

"Mr. William is the warden and probation officer," Sam said. "As warden, he is responsible for our safety and well-being. As probation officer, he makes sure we appear in court when scheduled, and he prepares our court documents. He checks on us every day at this time, except for Saturdays, when he is in Kampala.

"He will want to talk to you alone," Sam continued. "He is not like Rose. He is a good man, and he cares about us. Do not tell him about working in the mornings because Rose will get very angry and punish us all."

The boys gathered around Mr. William as he shook their hands and talked with them. Henry saw the female prisoner for the first time. Her head was shaved like the boys', and she wore a torn and oversized dress. She lingered away from the others, her downward gaze and hunched shoulders conveying fear and loneliness.

"I am called Henry. What is your name?"

"I am called Beatrice." She spoke softly without looking up.

"My brother is Joseph, and we arrived yesterday. How long have you been here?"

"Two months. Or maybe four. I don't know."

"Nice to meet you, Beatrice," Henry said. She gave a barely perceptible nod and turned away.

Henry sized up Mr. William as he moved through the crowd. He looked to be in his early thirties, was slim, and had a receding hairline and a wispy mustache. But what Henry noticed most was his kind smile when he saw the newcomers.

"You are welcome!" His sincere eyes matched his warm handshake. "Come walk with me so we can get to know each other."

Henry and Joseph learned that Mr. William's office was next to the courthouse and that he took a bus to Kampala every Friday afternoon to attend university classes in social work all day Saturday. He came to Ihungu after arriving home on Sundays.

Mr. William did his best to answer their questions, compassionately telling Henry and his brother, "I am sorry, but I do not know how long you will be here. Yesterday I read your indictment, so I know you have been charged with a capital offense. This means it is in the High Court and not the Magistrate Court. The resident High Court judge for Masindi is a good man, but he has too much work. I do not know when he will be able to schedule a juvenile session. The last one was almost a year ago. I hope the next one will happen within six months."

Henry's shoulders slumped. *Six months? I will not be able to resume school until the first term starts in February.*

No doubt sensing their disappointment, Mr. William changed the subject. "You are allowed to have visitors as often as you like. Just tell me in advance who is coming and when."

"Our father is in prison also, but our mom can come," Joseph said as his eyes welled up.

"Does she have a mobile phone? I can call her and tell her where you are."

"Can we call her now?"

"Yes, but it will have to be short because I do not have much airtime left."

When their mother answered, Joseph struggled to maintain his composure as tears streamed down his cheeks. When he was done, Joseph handed Henry the phone.

"We are okay. How are you and the others?" Henry asked.

"They are okay. Joseph says I can visit. I can sell another cow so I have money for transport. I will come next month."

"Wait, *another* cow? How many have you sold?"

"Do not worry, Henry. We can talk about that when I see you. Where is the prison?"

"The warden can tell you. I will give him the phone. I love you, Mom."

"I love you too. I am praying hard for you boys and for your father. Remember, God is good."

The rest of the day crawled by as Henry sat on his mat and anguished about his mother. *How long can she survive without our father?*

The next morning, only five minutes into the trek to their worksite, Henry absentmindedly switched his shovel from his side onto his shoulder. After a few steps, he realized his error and hastily brought it back in front of him.

Too late. Rose had seen him.

When they arrived at the farm, Henry took his place in line and tried to avoid eye contact with Rose, but it was no use. Rose strode out in front of the line.

"One of you violated my rules and must be punished!"

A line of heads swiveled amid murmurs as the boys tried to determine who was Rose's target.

"Tell me your name," she demanded, menacingly pointing her umbrella. The murmuring instantly ceased as all eyes trained on Henry.

When he answered, she hissed, "Well, *Henry*, you broke my rules and now you must be punished."

As she approached him, brandishing the umbrella like a spear, Henry nervously eyed her, wondering if she was about to puncture him with it. Instead, she ordered Jamil to give Henry five strokes with the Katikkiro's stick. Jamil didn't hesitate to follow Rose's directive.

Whack. Whack. Whack. Whack. Whack.

Acutely aware that nineteen pairs of eyes were studying him for any sign of weakness, Henry clenched his teeth in silence under the stinging blows. After the fifth, he stood and stoically gripped his shovel. It certainly smarted, but his father's occasional disciplinary "canings" had carried more force.

The pain in Henry's buttocks soon faded, but pain in his hands grew and intensified. Eventually, a few of his blisters started to bleed. But he pressed on, determined not to add insult to the day's injury by finishing last.

Back at Ihungu, as the boys ate outside for a change, Henry noticed Sam, Jamil, and three others conferring in hushed whispers. After breakfast, Sam signaled to those four and announced, "The Cabinet will meet in the custody with Henry. The rest of you remain here until we come out."

Everyone except Joseph backed away from Henry as if he'd contracted a contagious disease.

Once they were all inside, Sam instructed Henry to sit on the nearest unoccupied mat. Jamil took over. "At Ihungu, it is very important for the prisoners to be disciplined and to obey those in charge. The Rules must be respected and followed. The warden, Mr. William, is first in command. Mr. William has a family so he does not stay with us. He has appointed Sam as Katikkiro of Ihungu," Jamil continued.

"And as Katikkiro," Sam broke in, "I must maintain discipline. So when Mr. William is not around, I am in charge. It is my responsibility to make sure no one escapes. You have seen there are no fences or walls, so the prisoners must be watched very closely.

"The Chairman carries out most of the punishment for rule violations. I have appointed him and the rest of the Cabinet you see here to help me keep order. We are the Ihungu government. For some violations, I must administer the punishment. But when a prisoner tries to escape, only Mr. William can punish."

Jamil interjected, "He makes them slash all the grass at Ihungu with a machete. It takes the whole day."

"When there is a problem, I call Mr. William at once," Sam said as he proudly displayed a mobile phone. "Mr. William allows only the Katikkiro to have a phone. When someone is sick, I call Mr. William. He comes here, and I go with him and the sick one to the hospital.

"When I am away from Ihungu, the Assistant Katikkiro is in charge. He is called Obed." To Sam's left, a very dark-skinned boy nodded. "As you know, Jamil is the Chairman. He is responsible for informing new prisoners of the Rules. The Chairman must be strong and willing to enforce discipline. He delivers most of the strokes that are necessary."

Jamil puffed his chest in what appeared to be both a show of strength and a touch of pride at Sam's words.

"When Jamil is not around, the Assistant Chairman takes his place. He is called Buhanga." A muscular boy to Jamil's right nodded. "The final member of the Cabinet is the RP. He is called Mubisha. He supervises the daily cleaning of the custody, makes sure we have enough food in the store for the week, and assigns the boys to cooking duty."

"What does RP stand for?" Henry inquired.

The others all looked at each other and laughed. "We do not know," Sam finally admitted. "That is what it was called when we arrived. The RP cannot punish anyone. Any violations he sees, he reports to the Chairman. The Chairman decides guilt or innocence and then punishes the guilty. If the violation is serious, or if one of the Cabinet members is accused, the Chairman takes the matter to me. If I find him guilty, I carry out the punishment. Do you understand?"

"I do," Henry replied. "But what about Rose? How is she involved?"

"Mr. William told me he hired her two years ago, when a girl was first brought to Ihungu. He hired Rose to cook and to stay here with the girl, but Rose locks her in the room on the back side of the store where she sleeps and then walks home at night after we go to bed. She does not think we know, but I have seen her leave many times."

"She also does not cook!" added the RP resentfully.

"Mr. William says we must do what she says when he is not around," Sam said with evident frustration. "She makes us work every morning except Sunday, and sometimes in the evenings also. We are always here in the afternoon because Mr. William comes then to see us. On Sundays, Mr. William arrives from Kampala at different times. That is why we do not work on Sundays."

"Why does it matter if Mr. William knows we are working?" Henry asked.

"Juvenile prisoners are not allowed to work, and Rose would get in trouble if we told," Sam said. "The farmers pay her well, so she would be very angry to lose that money. She would make our lives miserable if Mr. William found out."

"She has a very bad temper," Jamil broke in. "On my third day at Ihungu, she got very mad at a boy while we were making sweet potato heaps and ordered two boys to bury him alive."

Henry was aghast. "Why?"

"He was working too slowly, and he did not work faster after she warned him."

"Did he die?"

"No. He was only buried up to his neck. He cried for fifteen minutes and promised to work harder, so Rose let him be uncovered. It scared us all very much, and no one has worked slowly since then."

"Thank you for telling me. I will also tell Joseph. Are we finished?"

A momentary pause hung in the air as Jamil and Sam looked at each other. "Not yet," Sam said. "Today you violated one of our Rules. So you need to be punished by us."

Confusion registered on Henry's face.

"You were given five strokes at the farm today," Sam clarified, "but that punishment was ordered by *Rose*. We must give our own punishment for violation of *our* Rules."

"I understand," Henry said, though he didn't.

He rolled onto his stomach, and Jamil gave Henry three more strokes. Jamil's earlier strokes had been harder, but the tenderness in Henry's buttocks caused these to hurt more. Sam also ordered Henry to mop the custody for the next three days.

Henry left with more than a little respect for the members of the government—it seemed like they had the prison under control and were fair in their dealings. Henry also made a mental note to keep his distance from Rose. She seemed capable of making his life even more miserable than it already was.

CHAPTER 4
LIFE AT IHUNGU

PERIODIC DOWNPOURS carved pits in the uneven natural terrain of the winding dirt road between Hoima and Masindi, stretching a thirty-mile matatu journey to more than two hours. A month had passed since her boys had been taken to Ihungu, and Henry and Joseph's mother was missing them terribly. She prayed most of the way there. In truth, she could have done little else because she was wedged in among fourteen other passengers in a thirty-year-old Toyota van meant for twelve.

She walked the twenty minutes it took to reach Ihungu from the matatu stop, checking with locals a few times along the way to ensure she was heading in the right direction. The last person she asked pointed to an open field and a group of buildings set back from the road. She had arrived.

✱   ✱   ✱

Henry and Joseph were adapting to the daily routine: up before dawn to work, usually back in time for a late breakfast. The shirtless prisoners were confined to the custody the rest of the day, except for an afternoon toilet break. The others could mingle outside under the Cabinet's supervision. Henry and Joseph had heard about afternoon soccer matches, but the ball had been flat since they arrived.

Henry hadn't heard his brother crying since the first night, but he knew that didn't prove anything. Henry had silently dampened the

31

blanket next to his head with his own tears several nights; he was certain Joseph had also.

Mr. William had told the brothers their mother was planning to come on Saturday, August 23. A three-year-old calendar from 2005 taped to the wall above the Katikkiro's mat provided the only means of tracking days. Each morning Sam announced both the day and date. Together, Henry and Joseph had counted down the days to their mother's first visit.

"When she arrives, you may come out to greet her," Sam said. "You can sit under the mango tree behind the custody until she leaves."

Henry and Joseph played cards inside the custody with the other shirtless prisoners to pass the time. Every few minutes, one or the other would walk over to the doorway and peer through the mailbox-sized cutout in the door.

Two minutes after Joseph's latest turn, "Visitor coming" rang out—Jamil's voice first, then a chorus.

Joseph beat Henry to the doorway. He couldn't get his entire head through the opening, but it seemed like he was trying.

"Mom is here!" Joseph whispered.

"How is she? Does she look well?" Henry asked.

"She is okay. She is in her Sunday dress. She is looking for us." Joseph could hardly contain his excitement.

"Let me see, let me see!" Henry's gentle nudges to let him look escalated into a hard shove.

Joseph finally relented, allowing the top half of Henry's face to frame the opening. As it did, his eyes locked on his mother's.

✳ ✳ ✳

From birth, Henry had the most penetrating eyes. Wherever he went as a boy, people told him how beautiful his eyes were. But they were never as beautiful as now. There they were, smiling at her through the hole in the door.

She shrieked with delight and scurried toward the custody. One of the boys blocked her passage. "Visitors are not allowed inside." He pointed to some plastic chairs underneath a mango tree. "They will meet you there."

She hurried over to the chairs but couldn't sit. She was too excited, too relieved, too eager to hug them. She didn't have to wait long.

When her boys appeared, she involuntarily clapped her hands over her mouth. Then the floodgates opened, washing away her resolve not to make a scene. Her wet kisses and flowing tears glazed their cheeks. Henry fought back his own tears. Joseph didn't even try.

"I am sorry I could not come before now," she said as she gripped each boy's hand. "There is so much for me to do without your father around."

"We are okay," Henry assured her. "We have enough food, and these boys are our friends. How is Father?"

"He is okay. He is still at the Hoima jail. I see him each Sunday after church. He misses you very much. He told me to tell you to stay strong."

"And how are the others?"

"They are okay. They miss you also. They send their greetings. They wanted to come with me, but . . ." Her voice trailed off as she struggled to maintain her composure. "When I was in jail for two weeks, Herbert, Kegan, and Doreen stayed with relatives. When I came home, most of our chickens were dead or gone. Only twenty remained."

Henry and Joseph were stunned. She hadn't told them about the chickens when she visited them at the Hoima jail.

"I did not want to worry you before," she said, anticipating their next question. "The pigs were okay, and the neighbor's herdsman made sure our cows were fed, so they were also okay."

"On the phone, you mentioned selling the cows. How many have you sold?"

She averted their gaze. "I have sold two. I sold one last month to buy food and to pay Herbert's school fees. I sold another last week so I could afford to come here."

"What is going to happen, Mom? Will we lose everything?" Joseph asked nervously.

"No, Joseph, God will provide. But even if we do, God will restore it to us again someday. I believe that. We still have seven cows, and one is pregnant. I will try not to sell any more before you and your father are released."

"Do you know when that will be?" Joseph asked.

She scoffed. "No. The police in Hoima say they are still investigating, but they have done nothing. No one at the police station knows when your father will go to court."

✱　✱　✱

For the next hour, they talked about life at Ihungu. Their mother asked how they got the calluses on their hands. Mothers don't miss much. Rose wasn't around, so they told her.

As she was preparing to leave, Mr. William rode up on his motorcycle. Squashed in behind him were Rose and one of the boys who had been at Ihungu for nearly a year.

Henry introduced his mother to the adults. Mr. William was warm and friendly. But as was her custom with visitors, Rose couldn't have been less interested.

Mr. William explained they had been at the Magistrate Court. The boy had pled guilty to a petty offense and would be released as soon as the paperwork could be completed.

AUGUST 23, 2008

Joseph and I were so happy to see our mom. We missed her very much, but her visit encouraged us. She reminded us to be patient with God and to never give up hope. "Nothing lasts forever, except the word of God," she said.

When I heard that a boy had gone to court and was being

released, I had more hope. Joseph and I decided we would pray to-gether every day. We started to believe we would also be released soon.

Days passed into weeks, and the weeks piled up. At the end of the eighth week, Sam took Henry aside. Holding Henry's shirt and flip-flops, he said, "I have watched you at work and with the other prisoners. I have also seen you reading the books your mom brought during her last visit. You are a leader. When there is an open position on the Cabinet, I will appoint you. For now, I am giving you your shirt and shoes one month early."

"Thank you, Sam. I will accept the appointment if I am still here, but I hope I will be released before that happens."

Sam paused, choosing his words carefully. "Henry, no one whose case is at the High Court has been released. Only those charged with petty offenses have been to court. The magistrate hears those cases, and he is not as busy as the High Court judge."

Until now, Henry hadn't realized that none of the juveniles Mr. William periodically retrieved for court appearances had been charged with capital offenses.

"I am sorry to tell you, Henry, but you will probably be here a long time."

✶ ✶ ✶

At the three-month mark, Joseph received his shirt and shoes. A few weeks later, Sam shuffled the Cabinet and promoted Henry from RP (his first post in Sam's cabinet) to Assistant Katikkiro.

Meanwhile, Henry attempted to cultivate a good relationship with Rose, going out of his way to be friendly and deferential. He'd success-fully stayed out of her crosshairs since his second day at Ihungu. In fact, Henry started wondering whether Rose's temper had been overstated.

That all changed in a brain-etching instant.

In the early afternoon of a day in late October 2008, the police dropped off a boy named Tafureka. It was clear Tafureka was going to be trouble when his shoes and shirt had to be forcibly removed. Over the next few days, Tafureka also tangled with Rose. It all came to a frothing head when he refused to work one morning. Rose ordered Jamil to give him five strokes.

When Tafureka still refused to work, Rose flew into a rage and pummeled him with her umbrella on his legs and back. When this also failed to achieve its desired effect, Rose shoved him to the ground between two heaps of dirt. "Bury him alive!" she ordered as if issuing a presidential proclamation.

Henry's mind flashed back to the story Jamil had relayed about Rose ordering such a burial previously, so this barbarism didn't catch Henry completely off guard, though he would never forget the fear and panic imprinted on Tafureka's face as he was covered up to his neck. He cried hysterically for fifteen minutes and pledged his unwavering obedience if Rose would uncover him.

But before she issued her reprieve, Rose gathered the prisoners together. "This is what happens when you disobey me! Do you understand?" They nodded in petrified unison.

Tafureka was a model prisoner from that day forward.

✶　✶　✶

In mid-January of 2009, Mr. William brought Sam to court. When they returned, Sam was jubilant. "The magistrate said I will be released next week!" Everyone gathered around him to offer congratulations. Meanwhile, Mr. William gently led Henry by the elbow around behind the custody.

"Sam will be leaving next week. The others need a strong leader they like and trust. That is you. I can see it, and Sam agrees you are the one."

"I will do it. But I have been here six months. When will *my* case go to court? How long will *I* have to stay here? I did *not* do what I am accused of doing."

"I believe you, Henry. But I do not know when the High Court will have a juvenile session again. The judge is very busy, and the registrar says there is no money for a session."

"How long do you *think* it will be?" Henry asked more forcefully.

With regret coating his words, Mr. William responded softly, "From what I am hearing, I think it will be at least one more year. Please do not tell the others; they might all run away."

Henry nodded, but inwardly he crumbled as he faced the bitter reality that he wouldn't be returning to school that year. And perhaps not ever. His dream of going to university was flat-lining, and he was powerless to resuscitate it.

Over the next few weeks, Henry sank into depression. He stopped praying. What was the point? The tattered Bible Sam had passed down when he left remained unopened.

★　★　★

Joseph recognized Henry's nosedive. At first, Henry couldn't bring himself to share Mr. William's prediction with Joseph, but eventually he came clean. Privately, Joseph told his brother, "You are our leader. The boys depend on you for discipline. They depend on you for hope. *I* depend on you, Henry. How can I have hope if you do not?"

Joseph's words hit hard. Henry's initial instinct was to hit back. But rather than lashing out, Henry simply said, "I need to be alone for a while."

As Katikkiro, Henry was permitted to leave Ihungu temporarily. So he did. He set off walking toward town. Then he ran. And cried. And cursed. And prayed. *Where are You, God? Are You even listening to my prayers?*

Deep down, he knew Joseph was right, but it was difficult not to think of his own shattered dreams. Still, he dug deep and resolved to be the leader and friend the prisoners needed.

The next day Henry called a Cabinet meeting, which now included his brother as the Assistant Chairman. Henry laid out his plan to improve the morale of the prisoners. For starters, they would play soccer every day from now on with the ball Henry had repaired with a needle and thread his mother had brought him. Next, Henry announced he was appointing Bo to be the Ihungu pastor, to lead the prisoners in a time of worship each evening. Lastly, they would start a school.

✴ ✴ ✴

Since they'd arrived, Henry had been sporadically giving Joseph math, science, and history lessons, trying to ensure his brother didn't fall behind the rest of his Senior One classmates. In addition to the fresh chapatti she brought on her now bi-weekly visits, Henry's mother also brought Henry's textbooks and notes from his Senior One classes.

Periodically, other prisoners would sit in, but they never lasted long because many of the boys had either never gone to school or had completed only a few of the seven years of primary school. The fact that the textbooks and Henry's notes were written in English created an additional barrier.

The Ihungu school Henry sought to establish sputtered to a halt like a boda boda with an empty fuel tank, largely because it took so long to secure a chalkboard for the lessons. Fortunately, the soccer initiative met with much greater success.

The first order of business was to construct proper goal posts—the piles of shoes and shirts they'd used to mark the goals in their infrequent matches failed to conjure up the images of the English Premier League Henry envisioned. He commissioned the others to locate and strip six reasonably straight tree limbs. He'd previously seen a long nail on the ground next to the custody and concluded it had come from the sheet metal roofing. With Jamil's help, Henry strategically removed three other nails without compromising the integrity of the roof, and with these he completed the goalposts and then lowered them into the holes he had dug.

The final task was to clear the field of as many obstacles as possible. Accustomed to working a field shoulder to shoulder, the boys sifted out the big rocks and pried out the clumps of vegetation. When they finished, the whole group beamed from the pride of their workmanship.

To top it off, Mr. William brought them a new soccer ball, which Henry suspected he bought with his own money.

From that day forward, the prisoners played every afternoon. Although they were tired from working, the daily games improved their physical conditioning. Henry captained one team, and Joseph captained the other. Each day they prepared lineup cards for the one-hour match.

Rose occasionally watched with the female prisoner and never objected to the soccer matches. Good morale among the prisoners meant good work from her chain gang.

At 9:00 p.m. each evening, Bo led the prisoners in a few songs he'd learned growing up in church. Most of the kids already knew the songs, and even the Muslim prisoners eventually joined in. Occasionally, Rose would hammer on the door and yell at them to be quiet. "God is not listening to you," she would scoff.

After Rose's interruptions, they would wait a few minutes and then resume singing more softly. Henry and Joseph often read from the Bible, and someone would close the night with a prayer.

As the months wore on, however, and the brothers "celebrated" one year at Ihungu in July of 2009, Henry's faith began to waver again. He still sang, read from the Bible, and prayed, but it was more rote than real. Every week or two, Henry asked Mr. William if he had any updates. He never did.

The mobile phone the Katikkiro was permitted to have allowed Henry to stay in more frequent contact with his mother. His father still languished in the Hoima jail. Meanwhile, Henry's mom had sold all but three of the cows and was struggling mightily to make ends meet. She visited Henry and Joseph less often to save on transport costs, and there was even talk of Herbert dropping out of primary school for want of school fees.

Through it all, Henry's mother seemed unshakable in her faith. Henry wondered if it was all an act, but nothing suggested it was. As August became September, Henry felt the fog of depression rolling back in. By early October, Henry was barely clinging to his faith and was contemplating letting go entirely.

If only God would send a sign, Henry thought, he'd have a reason to maintain hope.

CHAPTER 5
MZUNGUS

Every month or two, Mr. William brought visitors to Ihungu. Some were students from a university in Kampala. I liked talking to them because it allowed me to imagine going to university like them. They asked us questions about the charges against us and how long we had been at Ihungu. I asked them questions too—where they had gone to secondary school, what they were studying, and what university was like. Most were studying social work, and they said they would come back to help us. At first, I believed them. But they never came back.

Some of the other visitors were from what Mr. William called "NGOs"—organizations from other countries who helped poor Ugandans. A few times I talked to these people. They also said they would come back and help us. They never did.

Earlier this month, Mr. William brought some visitors from an NGO. One of the boys told me two mzungus were with Mr. William. Mzungu means "white-skinned foreigner" in Swahili. I saw them through the hole in the door of the custody. One foreigner was about fifty, and one was about twenty-five. Both were very tall.

The mzungus walked around with Mr. William and talked to some of the prisoners. Mr. William translated for them when they asked questions. I did not go outside to talk to them. I believed these

41

mzungus were just like the others; they would say things to give us hope, but they would do nothing to help us.

After they left, Mr. William sat down with me on my mat. He knew I was sad and losing hope. He put his hand on my arm and looked into my eyes. He said, "The men who just left are lawyers from America. They said they had heard there were many juvenile prisoners here waiting a long time for a trial. I told them many have been waiting for more than one year. They said they would come back and help."

I reminded him about the others who said the same thing. "This is no different," I told him.

"No, Henry. You are wrong this time. These men are different. I can tell."

I could see in his eyes and hear in his voice that he believed them. My heart started beating very fast. "Do you really think they will come back?" I so wanted to believe this was true. I wanted to have hope again.

"I do, Henry. We must pray very hard."

I found Joseph, Jamil, and Bo and told them what Mr. William said. We prayed together that the mzungus would come back. We prayed every day, and we prayed very hard. We also fasted one day each week until the mzungus returned.

I called my mom and asked her to pray the mzungus would come and help us. She said she would ask everyone at church to pray also.

For the first time since I had arrived at Ihungu, I truly believed God was hearing my prayers. He had sent me a sign.

CHAPTER 6
DEATH AT IHUNGU

ONE DAY IN NOVEMBER, Mr. William drove up the path with two new prisoners on the back of his motorcycle. This made four additions since the beginning of the month. Henry greeted the new arrivals with Joseph—his newly appointed Chairman.

"This one is called Simeon, and this one is called Innocent," Mr. William said.

Simeon appeared older than seventeen and seemed in good health. By contrast, Innocent appeared weak and sickly, and heavy bandages adorned both wrists.

"Follow me to the custody," Joseph said to the newcomers.

That evening, Joseph told Simeon and Innocent the Rules and walked them around to the prisoners. Innocent and Jamil—now the Assistant Katikkiro—recognized each other, as both had grown up in Masindi. Jamil took Innocent aside. "You do not look well. Are you sick?"

"The men who caught me stealing beat me pretty badly. My wrists are also cut from the plastic the police used to tie me up for three days, and I do not have any more asthma medicine, so it is hard to breathe sometimes."

On the way to a local farm the next morning, Jamil told Henry about Innocent's condition. Once the work began, Innocent fell behind.

"You will work faster or I will order the Katikkiro to beat you," Rose snarled.

Innocent did not change his pace. After a few minutes, Rose demanded, "Cane him, Henry. Three strokes should get his attention."

"He is not well. He suffers from asthma," Henry tentatively responded.

"He is just lazy and deceiving you. Where is the proof he has asthma?" Rose said dismissively. She walked off under her umbrella but continued to yell at Innocent periodically to work faster. After a little while, Rose again ordered Henry to cane him. While Henry didn't want to create friction with Rose, neither did he carry out her order. He knew he couldn't punish Innocent for something he couldn't help. Though Rose was visibly upset, Henry had never challenged or disobeyed her before, and she did not press the matter.

The following morning, the prisoners trudged to a different farm owned by a local police officer who'd heard about Rose's workforce. When they arrived, Rose assigned the prisoners their own row and instructed them to make sweet potato heaps. After working alongside the others for three hours, Innocent stopped and sat down. He'd fallen far behind, but Rose had kept her cool. His refusal to continue working, however, pulled the pin from her emotional grenade. She exploded.

"Yesterday you worked slowly, and I told Henry to beat you. But he refused. Today you will see—I am going to beat you like a dog!"

"I am feeling very bad and cannot work," Innocent weakly protested.

"Either you get up and work, or I will have Henry beat you until you do!"

Innocent shook his head slowly in response.

To Henry's great surprise and relief, Rose again blinked. She must have sensed Henry's continued reluctance to punish Innocent and could clearly see he was much more fatigued than the others.

"We will be working over there tomorrow," she said, pointing to an adjacent field. "The land needs to be cleared of grass and sticks before you dig. Get up and go clear the field."

After a few anxious seconds, Innocent slowly stood and began this less-taxing task.

That afternoon Henry asked Innocent how he was doing.

"I have never had to work because of my asthma, and I am feeling very bad."

"You must try your best to work, and I will try my best to keep Rose from punishing you," Henry encouraged.

Because much of the work still remained unfinished on the farm, Rose rousted the prisoners even earlier the next morning. Predictably, Innocent worked slowly. After about two hours, Rose could no longer tolerate what she clearly perceived as insubordination. She stomped over to Innocent and roared, "I have been using my mouth to tell you what to do, and now I am going to use a stick. Katikkiro, I order you to give him three strokes. Now!"

All eyes turned to Henry. "But the boy is sick," Henry protested. After another tense moment, Henry opened his hand and let the stick drop to the ground by his side.

This simple act of defiance momentarily stunned Rose. She glared at him and then sauntered over to Henry, raising the stakes. "If you refuse, I will order each of the boys to beat *you*, Katikkiro."

The steely resolve in Rose's eyes and voice convinced Henry she wasn't bluffing. Henry drew in a deep breath. Disobeying Rose's order would force the other prisoners to choose between beating their leader and refusing a direct order from Rose. Concluding he had no choice, Henry silently collected his stick and gave Innocent three strokes. Making his own point, however, Henry eased up, ensuring they were softer than customary.

Rose noticed the leniency and lost it. She hustled over to Innocent and began beating him with her metal umbrella. Shaking and spitting as she screamed, she seized Innocent and dragged him between two sweet potato heaps.

"Bury him alive!" she half yelled and half laughed while threatening

Henry menacingly with her bayonet-like umbrella. The two boys who had made the heaps fearfully complied, careful not to cover Innocent's head. Within moments, Innocent was buried up to his neck. Some local kids playing nearby heard the yelling and came to watch. When they saw the prisoners shoveling dirt onto Innocent, they sprinted away to find help.

Thinking that letting the scene play out offered the best chance to de-escalate the situation, Henry kept a vigilant eye on Innocent, ready to intervene if he sensed the boy's life was in jeopardy. While Innocent seemed in no mortal danger, Henry had never witnessed Rose this angry. A few minutes later, some local villagers arrived and began shouting at Rose from a nearby road. She yelled back, threatening them with trespass if they intervened.

Every minute or so Henry made eye contact with Rose, silently asking whether this had gone far enough. Finally, Rose signaled to get him out.

"Get back to work now, Innocent," Henry called out. He breathed a heavy sigh of relief when Innocent stood without assistance and resumed working, albeit slowly. In the shadow of the agitated crowd, Rose decided it would be better to leave then and come back the next morning to finish, even though they didn't usually work on Sundays.

That evening Henry contemplated telling Mr. William how sick Innocent was, but ultimately decided against it because doing so would mean blowing the whistle on Rose's work details. Besides, it was a Saturday, and Henry didn't want to disturb Mr. William while he was taking classes. He'd be coming to Ihungu the next day, and if things went badly again on Sunday, he'd tell Mr. William in person. They just needed to make it through one more day.

✶ ✶ ✶

On Sunday, Innocent fell quickly behind yet again. After Innocent repeatedly bemoaned how terrible he felt, Rose ordered him to sit silently under a mango tree. She had decided to avoid another stand-off and presumed the dirt baptism the day before sufficiently vindicated her authority.

Innocent sat still for about five minutes, but when Henry and Rose looked the other way, he took off like a cheetah. Rose saw him first and ordered Henry and Jamil to hunt him down and bring him back. Even though Innocent had a sizeable head start, his asthma eventually slowed him enough for Henry and Jamil to catch him. The two boys escorted the heavily panting escapee back to Rose, who angrily instructed him to lay facedown. Even as he lay there, his back rose and fell in increasingly quick and shallow rhythms.

A seething Rose summoned the four most recent arrivals, including Simeon, who had come with Innocent a few days earlier. She glared at the four and hissed, "You must never try to escape. If you do, you will be brought back and punished." She scooped up four sticks of varying sizes and handed one to each of them. "Give him ten strokes each. Now!"

Each nervously complied, one after the other. The strokes were firm but not punitive. Innocent did not cry or call out. When the caning concluded, he struggled to his hands and knees and wobbled there for a few moments. Once back on his feet, he swayed unsteadily like the local drunks after a banana alcohol binge.

"I feel very bad," he said, his eyes distant and his lips blue. His voice rattled like a screen door in a windstorm.

Confident her message had been received, Rose sent him back to the shade of the mango tree. Innocent staggered over to the tree, dropped to his knees, then rolled onto his back.

"You may not lie down. You may sit or you may stand," she commanded. "If you lie down, you will be given more strokes."

Within a minute or so, Innocent started mumbling incoherently and then gradually attempted to shout, but the only discernible word was "water." Even while refusing his plea and threatening any boy who attempted to quench his thirst before all the work was done, Rose recognized Innocent's distress. She pulled out her mobile phone and called the owner of the farm. "Come right away. One of the boys is very sick and cannot walk back to Ihungu."

The owner arrived ten minutes later on a motorcycle. By this time Innocent had lain back down, his breathing coming in panicked, jagged gasps. Rose instructed Jamil and another boy to help Innocent onto the motorcycle and accompany him to the custody.

"Make sure he is bathed and ready to go to the hospital when I return," she said nervously.

The two boys placed him between them to keep him steady, and the four set off on the overloaded vehicle.

DECEMBER 6, 2009

I remember that day like it was yesterday. I could tell Innocent was very sick when they drove him away. When we returned, Innocent had already bathed and was lying on his mat.

I went in to check on him, saying his name as I walked toward him. He did not respond. I said it again. I bent down to touch his arm and said his name loudly once more. His lips were the wrong color, and he was not moving. I could tell he was dead.

Some of the boys walked into the custody behind me and saw what I saw. A few started crying, so I told everyone to go outside. I was very, very sad but needed to be strong. I walked outside to tell Rose, but the others had already told her. She was very scared and told me to take the boys away from the custody. Her hands were shaking as she called Mr. William.

Over the next few days, the police came to Ihungu many times and asked questions. They arrested Rose and took her away. Mr. William told me she would be charged with murder. He told me the prosecutor was considering charging me also. They said it was my responsibility as Katikkiro to keep Innocent safe. Mr. William asked me why I did not tell him Innocent was so sick and why I did not tell him Rose was making us work.

I asked myself those questions many times in the days after Innocent died. I spent Christmas of 2009 at Ihungu blaming myself for his death and wishing I had another chance to make different decisions.

I prayed for forgiveness. I prayed for Innocent's family. But most of all, I prayed the nightmares would stop.

PART TWO

CHAPTER 7
LOVE DOES

THE MOON HID ALL but a fraction of its face as if afraid to witness what was about to happen. With no electricity for thirty miles in any direction, only a thousand pinpricks in the inky sky and Mohamudu's headlights illuminated the crumbling strip of asphalt snaking out before us.

From my vantage point behind the front passenger in the minivan, I marveled at our hired driver's skills. I'd been observing Mohamudu's exploits since arriving in Uganda forty-eight hours earlier. He fixed his large brown eyes on the cramped road, gripped the steering wheel with his left hand, and pummeled the horn with his right as if he were a ham-fisted Morse code operator. And for good reason.

The Ugandan roads are difficult to capture in words. Imagine a narrow two-lane highway. Now take away the dividing stripe, and sub-tract a third of its width, such that oncoming cars can barely pass each other. Then add some serious "texture" to the road—bumps, dips, divots, breathtakingly large potholes, and randomly placed speed bumps. Now add scores of motorcycles, bicycles, and pedestrians, about half of whom are children. Finally, add slow-moving cattle with massive horns, fast-moving goats with no sense of danger, and scampering chickens with anxiety disorders.

"Someone could make a mint by designing a video game recreat-ing this experience," I had quipped to the other four American lawyers the day before, as Mohamudu drove us north from Kampala for some sightseeing at Murchison Falls National Park. Fortunately, Mohamudu traveled these roads often and deftly navigated the obstacle course. He honked more in one day than I had in twenty-seven years of driving. I yearned for a fistful of Valium to calm my nerves.

Each vehicle we encountered traveling the opposite direction at least equaled our speed of sixty miles per hour. The instinct to avoid oncoming traffic was so strong that I found myself jerking in my knee each time a car or truck sailed by so I wouldn't get clipped—even though I was riding inside the minivan, sitting on its left side as cars and trucks zoomed by us on the right. (Because cars were introduced while Uganda was under British control, Ugandans drive on the left side of the road like in Great Britain and steering wheels are on the right.)

Eventually, though, whether it was jetlag from the thirty-hour journey from Los Angeles or a psychological defense mechanism to block out this terrifying night ride, I fell asleep as we hurtled south toward Masindi. We had toured a displaced persons camp and the Restore Leadership Academy in the northern town of Gulu earlier that day.

Suddenly, I was jolted awake by a blaring car horn, panicked screaming, a bone-shattering impact, and what sounded like a shotgun blast, followed immediately by pellets ricocheting inside the van.

"What happened?" I yelled.

"We hit a guy on a bike, head-on!" Napier shouted from the seat directly in front of me.

Mohamudu slowed but didn't stop. Meanwhile, the five of us hurriedly inspected ourselves for injuries. The front side-view mirror rested in Napier's lap, and surface cuts laced his left arm. The window directly behind me next to Jay's head had exploded, showering him and the back of the van with glass. Miraculously, none had sprayed into his eyes, but his curly blond hair glittered like a tinseled Christmas tree, and a handful of slivers dusted the back of my head.

"We need to turn around," Napier said gravely to Mohamudu.

"He is dead. We must go," Mohamudu shot back.

"No, we must go back now!" Napier said, pointing behind us. The rest of us joined him in chorus.

"No. We must go!" Mohamudu yelled, pointing forward.

Just then, a matatu pulled up next to us on our right. The driver and the dozen passengers were yelling and pointing behind us.

"Yes, we are going back." Mohamudu waved and did a U-turn.

When we got within fifty yards of the accident site, he U-turned again. Mohamudu, Napier, and I hopped out. Because the minivan was facing the other direction, only an approaching car's headlights illuminated the motionless heap beside a crumpled bicycle in the middle of the road.

All three of us yelled and frantically jumping-jacked to warn the approaching car of the dead man in its path. When this failed, we leapt into the waist-high grass on the road's shoulder and braced for impact.

As the car barreled down on the body, the driver caught a glimpse of the carnage and swerved just in time, missing him by mere inches. Shockingly, the dead man rose and began mumbling incoherently.

"He's alive!" Napier shouted. "Praise God!"

Blood oozed from the side of his head, and his left leg elbowed grotesquely midway down his shin. Out of nowhere appeared another man who helped Mohamudu carry this modern-day Lazarus to the road's shoulder. To this day, Napier insists this other man was an angel sent to intervene. "Gabriel" urged us to hurry off and send an ambulance, promising to remain with "Lazarus" until help arrived.

Five miles ahead, we reached a roadside checkpoint manned by two police officers—a relic of the Joseph Kony war days. Mercifully, an aging concrete structure with a sign missing its *H*, though still recognizable as a hospital, sat fifty feet from the checkpoint. While one officer shined a flashlight on Mohamudu, the other shined his on the minivan.

"How are you tonight?"

Mohamudu just stared back blankly.

The other officer motioned to the damaged left front end. "What happened here?"

The stress of the accident had apparently robbed Mohamudu of his already limited English skills, so Napier took over. "Sir, we've been in an accident. A man on a bike swerved into our path ten kilometers back. Is there an ambulance at the hospital?"

One officer began dialing a mobile phone while the other gruffly said, "All of you, get out."

Jay mumbled, "Uganda 2010!" and flashed me a devious smile as I leaned my seat forward so he could crawl out. The phrase *What am I doing here?* hamster-wheeled through my head as we joined Mohamudu and our three American companions, now in police custody.

✶ ✶ ✶

Three months earlier, I had sat near the back of a crowded hotel ballroom at a Christian Legal Society Conference. The mesmerizing figure at the podium had the conference attendees alternately in stitches and in tears. I knew who Bob Goff was, but I didn't know him personally.

Bob had spoken to a student group at Pepperdine Law School two years earlier and invited them to join him for a judicial conference he was hosting in Uganda in the spring of 2007. The next day, two of these students came to me in my role as associate dean, seeking permission and funding to join Bob. From the time Ken Starr had taken over as dean at Pepperdine three years earlier, his vision for the law school had been global, so he immediately green-lighted my request on their behalf. These students returned wide-eyed with ideas of how Pepperdine could partner with the Ugandan judiciary to deliver justice and enforce the rule of law in this developing nation. Soon thereafter, the law school's Global Justice Program launched its first major project, under the leadership of Jay Milbrandt—a charismatic recent graduate who convinced Dean Starr to appoint him as director.

"Love does!" Bob boomed from the ballroom stage. "Love isn't just about praying for people or wishing them well. Jesus taught us real love actually does stuff."

With utmost humility, Bob told stories about visiting world leaders with his kids, rescuing girls trapped in Indian brothels through his Restore International organization, and starting a school in the war-torn northern region of Uganda. I knew precious little about Uganda, but felt irresistibly drawn to it as Bob spoke. Still, I wasn't looking for a new project, adventure, or cause.

Across the table from me in the ballroom, Jay whispered, "Hey, Jim, Uganda 2010!" and smiled impishly. I returned Jay's smile and shook my head, but with decidedly less conviction. For several months, Jay had been pestering me, gently at first, to join him and a group of Pepperdine students on a global justice trip. But over the past few weeks, Jay had stepped up his persistence, popping his head into my office at regular intervals to proclaim, "Uganda 2010!"

My consistent response to Jay mirrored the one I gave everyone who asked me to take on something else: my plate was full. I simply didn't have time to go to Uganda.

✷   ✷   ✷

When the police officers turned away from our group to confer, Napier inconspicuously separated himself and called his friend Dickson, who was not only a Ugandan lawyer but a former police officer and soldier. Moments later, Napier strode confidently toward one of the officers with his arm outstretched, insisting that a Ugandan lawyer needed to speak to him.

He took Napier's phone and contemptuously said, "Who are you?"

For the next two minutes, the officer listened intently, periodically injecting a "yes" here and an "I understand" there. Finally he said, "Thank you."

He handed the phone back to Napier with a warm smile and said, "Are you okay? Is anyone injured?"

"We're fine," Napier said, "but there's a man bleeding to death on the side of the road. An ambulance must be sent right away."

"My colleague has called for one, and it will go soon. We will release you soon as well."

In the meantime, the officers asked us to describe what had happened. All the eyewitnesses, which included everyone but me, agreed the bicyclist turned into us as we approached him. Mohamudu hit the horn, but not the brakes, before the collision. Mohamudu also insisted the man reeked of alcohol when he carried him to the side of the road.

"You should not have gone back," the officer declared matter-of-factly. "If something like that happens again, continue driving until you find someone to send for help."

"I *told* you we must go," Mohamudu agreed indignantly.

The officer explained that local villagers were known to pull drivers from their cars and beat them to death after they hit a pedestrian. Thankfully, we weren't near any villages when the collision happened or things could have turned out very differently.[1]

As we waited, we watched one officer inspect the car while the other took notes. The impact had been on the left front side of the minivan, taking out the headlight. The man or his bike then sheared off the side-view mirror. Blood spattered on the back windowsill suggested the man's head or leg struck the window that exploded onto Jay.

Upon completing this investigation, the police officers handcuffed Mohamudu and placed him into a police car.

"Good thing you didn't insist on driving this morning, dawg. You could've spent the night in a Ugandan jail," Jay snickered to me as Mohamudu was driven away.

He had a point.

Earlier that morning Mohamudu had showed up in a Toyota—Uganda imports nearly all of its cars from Japan. We had been surprised, however, that it had *not* been the Toyota minivan from the day before. Jay, Ray, David, and I had promised to pick up Napier in Gulu and bring him back with us to Masindi that evening. We'd clearly explained our requirements for a large vehicle to Mohamudu the day before.

"Four of you can ride in back," he had offered, motioning to the mid-sized Camry sedan he'd arrived in.

"No. Where's the minivan?" I had demanded.

"What?"

"The *other* car—the one you drove us here in *yesterday*."

He explained he'd rented that car from another rental company—not the one he worked for—and they needed it today. He then offered me the keys. "Okay, you drive and I will stay."

Determined not to abandon Napier, I had taken the keys. "Okay, that works."

Jay then shot me an incredulous look and burst out laughing. "You're *not* driving here in Uganda, Jim. Are you some kind of idiot?"

"I'll be fine," I had protested weakly, though I knew Jay was right. My blood pressure had tripled on the road from Kampala the day before, not to mention the wrong-side-of-the-road thing. During my family's seven-month stay in England in 2008, I hadn't dared to get behind the wheel, even though they have real roads, traffic signals, and no darting goats there.

Jay took over the negotiations. "Where can we find another minivan?"

After some prodding, Mohamudu then admitted his friend owned one. "But he does not hire it out."

"Call him anyway," Jay had prodded. "You're a good driver. What could go wrong?"

It turns out that for the right price, anything is for hire in Uganda. Fifteen minutes later, we had set off in the minivan on our fateful ride to Gulu.

Now, fifteen hours later, the officer informed us the minivan would need to be held for the next twenty-four hours. *Perfect. Our driver has been arrested, and our car has been impounded*, I thought. *What am I doing here?*

After conferring among ourselves, we called John Niemeyer, Restore International's Country Director whom we were planning to meet that night. He was thirty minutes south of Masindi driving north. We were forty minutes north of Masindi hoping to head south. We eventually decided it'd be faster for the officer to call for a matatu to take us back to Masindi rather than to wait for Niemeyer to come get us in his SUV.

We arranged to meet Niemeyer at the Masindi Hotel for breakfast the next morning before he took us out to begin the work we came to do—at a place Bob Goff in his "Love Does" conference speech had called Ihungu.

✳ ✳ ✳

Each time I told Jay to check back with me "later" about "Uganda 2010," we both knew I really meant, "Thanks, but no thanks." I'd grown up believing in missions work, praying for missionaries, and even financially supporting them. But the actual *doing* part was for other people.

A couple weeks before I had heard Bob Goff speak at the Christian Legal Society Conference, Baroness Caroline Cox, a leading humanitarian and member of the British House of Lords, had come to Pepperdine at Jay's invitation and challenged our students to think more globally in their service projects. She described her numerous trips to war zones and impoverished lands all over the world and how she felt called to go in person to help.

During the question-and-answer period afterward, a student asked Baroness Cox whether she recommended one visit a place in need or send the money that would otherwise have been spent getting there. *Good question. And a great excuse not to go*, I thought.

Her unequivocal answer caught me off guard:

> Please go. The fact that you visit . . . will be a great comfort for those people you do visit, because the kind of people we have been talking about, they often feel forgotten . . . and the fact that you care enough to go will be a blessing to them. . . . And when you come back, you'll be able to be an advocate for them.

. . . Other opportunities will open up which will show you your way forward through whatever door God may want you to go through in your life. . . . When you come back, you're going to have a massive ripple effect.[2]

Her response unsettled me, but I quickly suppressed the urge to respond personally. That is, until a couple weeks later when the call came again.

Near the end of his speech, Bob recounted his visit to a juvenile prison in Uganda's capital city of Kampala. He and a few other Americans had interviewed the kids, prepared summaries of their cases, hired some Ugandan defense lawyers, and paid the costs for these kids to have their day in court. "How cool is that?" he bellowed. "Love does stuff like that. Our God is a God of justice, and He's nuts about kids."

I know this sounds trite—it even *felt* trite at the time—but although there were five hundred others in the ballroom that evening, it seemed as if Bob were talking exclusively to me. By the time he finished, I was neck deep in one of *those* moments when you know things have instantly changed, when you see with uncommon clarity and feel compelled to life-changing action.

Up to that point in my life, I'd experienced only about a dozen such moments, one of which came in June of 1986 when I suddenly realized I wanted to marry Joline Oliver. Another was in 1999 when I decided to leave the practice of law to become a professor at Pepperdine. These moments, however, can vanish as quickly as they appear. Sadly, I had let many of them pass without having the fortitude to heed their call. In the midst of *this* moment, however, I was overcome with an overwhelming urge not to let this call go unmet.

I had no idea the extent to which my life would be forever changed, no idea the heights of joy and depths of sorrow this decision would bring. But when I leaned over to Jay at the end of Bob's talk and whispered, "Dude, we're going to Africa," there was no turning back.

✳ ✳ ✳

Just after the matatu summoned by the police officer arrived, Mohamudu called Jay's Ugandan cell phone and told him he'd been unexpectedly released. We picked him up near the police station and rode back to Masindi in stunned silence.

As I lay in bed that night, I again questioned, *What am I doing here? Though* I'm not at all in the habit of doing so, I even challenged God. *Why did You bring me here? This was Your idea, wasn't it?*

Wasn't it?

This was not the type of impact we'd hoped to make on the people of Uganda. If we'd stayed home, the man on the bike wouldn't be fighting for his life right now, Mohamudu wouldn't be facing legal charges, his friend's minivan wouldn't be banged up, and I wouldn't be away from Joline for seventeen days for only the second time in our twenty-year marriage.

CHAPTER 8
THROWING STARFISH

ALMOST EXACTLY eleven years earlier, in January of 1999, I had kissed Joline good-bye and left for another day of work, not knowing I wouldn't see her or our two kids again for more than two weeks. A couple hours later, the managing partner of Kirkland & Ellis's Los Angeles office and I were boarding the next plane to Dallas to fight a multibillion-dollar legal battle over ownership of a missile guidance system that had erupted only the day before between two major defense contractors. A taxi driver met me at the airport with a suitcase Joline had hurriedly packed for me with the help of our three-year-old, Jessica. The next seventeen days were the most exhausting of my six-year legal career.

While our client won, I lost the chance to be there when Joshua took his first steps just before his first birthday. Even now, I can't listen to Harry Chapin's "Cat's in the Cradle" without suffering pangs of remorse as I thought about the planes to catch, bills to pay, and my son learning to walk while I was away.

While the thrill of working on huge and complex cases satisfied my adrenaline appetite where competitive sports had left off, I wasn't the kind of husband, father, or friend my dad had been. And not the kind I wanted to be. As I looked down the road, I saw no way to continue excelling at my fast-paced, high-profile job and also be the man I needed to be.

I was out of control. *So I ran.*

I ran toward what I considered my dream job—where I could take back control of my life and where I could coach my kids' soccer teams, attend their school performances, and teach their Sunday school classes: a tenure-track teaching position at Pepperdine.

On my last day at Kirkland in the summer of 1999, I said good-bye to the managing partner—the best trial lawyer I've ever met. I liked and respected him very much, and we worked well together. He was kind and gracious, but I'll never forget what he said: "I really hate to lose you, Jim. You're a shoo-in to make partner four months from now. I tell you, it's hard to imagine leaving what we do, and how well we do it, in order to coach your kids' soccer teams. But I fully support your decision and I'm happy you have this opportunity."

His words confirmed that I'd made the right decision for me. Because trading work for the kind of family life I needed was precisely where I was headed.

I soon discovered the life of a law professor was quite different from that of a big-firm lawyer, offering freedom, flexibility, and control. In April of 2000, Joline and I had our third child, Jennifer. I helicoptered over her when she learned to walk and caught her when she fell. I coached each of my children's soccer teams. I was the husband I promised Joline I'd be when we married in June of 1990. I was the father my dad had been. Life was good.

Five years later, my mentor during my two-year stint in Kirkland's DC office was appointed dean of Pepperdine Law School. Ken Starr is indisputably one of the best appellate lawyers and legal scholars of his generation and one of the people I most admire. So when he asked me in the spring of 2005 to serve as associate dean for two years, I simply couldn't pass up the opportunity to work as his right-hand man in advancing a Christian law school. I soon discovered that the life of a law school administrator differs dramatically from that of a law school professor.

In no time at all, I resumed Kirkland hours. While Ken continually encouraged me to take more time off, there was so much to do, and he worked harder than anyone I'd ever met. I stopped coaching my kids' soccer teams and again winced when I heard "Cat's in the Cradle"—*When you coming home, Dad? / I don't know when, but we'll get together then.*

After the two years were up, I agreed to continue in this role as long as Ken remained dean. Being involved in the academic, social, and spiritual lives of Pepperdine law students truly fulfilled me. But all too often it consumed and controlled me too.

When my parents asked when we'd come visit, I told them we would once things slowed down a bit. They rarely did. When asked to teach a Bible class at church, I declined. When asked to chaperone one of my kids' field trips, I demurred. I'd lost control again.

So I ran again.

There was a need for an interim director of Pepperdine's London Program, so I raised my right hand at the right meeting and was offered the seven-month assignment for the summer and fall of 2008. This would allow me to step off the treadmill and regain some semblance of control, even if only temporarily.

That's how I ended up in the summer of 2008 standing on the southern tip of Europe gazing with my family at the northern coast of Africa and declaring I would never go to Africa. Ever.

✳ ✳ ✳

At the conclusion of Bob Goff's speech, Jay and I pushed through the crowd toward him. I knew from past experience I needed to be proactive in order to hold fast to the moment that had seized me. Fortunately, Jay had a verbal commitment from me, and this cat wasn't going to release the mouse he'd finally trapped under his paw.

"Hey, Bob, this is Professor Jim Gash," Jay said. "Can we schedule a call with you in the next few days to talk about a trip to Uganda?"

"Done. I can't wait to talk about this," Bob said excitedly. "It would be so fun to partner with you guys on an African caper."

Two days later, Bob called us. "Hey, guys, I have just the project for you. I went to visit a remand home a couple weeks ago in this little bush town called Masindi. At this juvenile prison, there are about twenty kids waiting for their day in court. Some have been there for almost two years. Can you believe it? My schedule won't allow me to get back to Uganda until March. Wouldn't it be cool if you guys put together a team of lawyers before then and helped those kids get access to justice?"

That sounded great to us.

Bob suggested we include in our planning efforts John Niemeyer, the Uganda Country Director of Restore International, Bob's nonprofit organization. Niemeyer was based at the school Bob had started in the war-torn north a couple years earlier called Restore Leadership Academy, only two hours from Masindi. Niemeyer had been with him when he'd visited Ihungu.

Soon Jay and I set to work assembling a team. We turned first to Pepperdine's Board of Visitors, comprised of forty prominent judges, lawyers, and entrepreneurs from around the country, many of whom are Pepperdine Law graduates. The first to express interest was Ray Boucher (Boo-shay).

To say Ray has enjoyed tremendous success as a trial lawyer is rather like saying LeBron James is good at basketball. After graduating from Pepperdine in 1983, Ray jumped directly into trial work on behalf of plaintiffs—those he calls "the underdogs." In a world where the size of one's verdicts and settlements dictates one's stature, Ray is a giant, though his bespectacled eyes and diminutive size disguise the brawn beneath the surface.

Ray's work as the lead lawyer in the priest abuse cases in Los Angeles catalyzed global change in the Catholic Church. As a lifelong Catholic himself, Ray anguished over the impact his representation of the abused children would have on the church as a whole. Nevertheless, he became convinced the victims wouldn't fully heal until their tragic stories were told. For years, Ray dreamed of impacting other parts of the world through international human rights work. This trip provided him the perfect avenue.

✱ ✱ ✱

I bolted awake at 4:00 a.m. to the unmistakable sounds of tribal chanting in the street directly in front of the Masindi Hotel. *Have the villagers come for revenge?*

I concede how ridiculous this sounds, but I'd been jarred from a deep slumber, was in a strange place, and at that point still thought we might have killed someone. My pulse raced as I frantically fumbled with the (nearly) idiot-proof mosquito net. After finally liberating myself, I reached for the light, then hesitated. An interior light would be visible from the road, giving away my location. So I stood statue-still and waited.

As the cacophony reached a fever pitch, my heart drumrolled. Just when it seemed the bloodthirsty throng was directly outside my door, the chanting began to fade. I climbed back into bed, relief washing over me. Sleep was elusive, so I pulled out my iPod and let Bon Jovi serenade me back to sleep.

A couple hours later, I rolled out of bed again and went exploring. The hotel where we'd spent our first night, the Kampala Sheraton, had essentially been like an American hotel—and its ten floors, elevators, and indoor room entrances made that apparent. The Masindi Hotel, in contrast, was more like a motel.

From my room at the northern end of the property, I ambled down the walkway separating the parking lot and each of the twenty-five rooms. Though renovated in 2000, the Masindi Hotel bills itself as "Uganda's oldest hotel," having been originally built in 1923 when the city served as an important rail transit point for goods moving from the Congo and Sudan to European markets in East Africa. Humphrey Bogart and Katharine Hepburn had stayed here while filming *The African Queen*.

"Good morning, sir," the clerk on duty said. "Breakfast will be served in the dining room beginning at seven. I believe one of your friends is already there."

I thanked her and walked through a library that doubled as a small lounge and into a spacious courtyard, where about twenty sets of wooden tables and chairs were scattered. A separate bar adjoined the restaurant.

Ray was inside the restaurant reading the Uganda Penal Code and other documents I'd given him in Los Angeles.

"Hey, Jim. I'm almost done with these materials. Thanks for putting the binder together," he said. "You hear those soldiers this morning?"

"Soldiers?"

"They marched by at about four o'clock on some sort of training routine. I stepped outside to watch them pass."

"No, I didn't see them," I said breezily. I opted not to burden him with my morning bout with cowardice.

"You a Hemingway fan?" he asked.

"I've heard of him, but I don't think I've read any of his books. Wasn't he British?"

Ray squinted over his spectacles at me. "Are you serious? Hemingway is one of the great *American* authors. He spent quite a bit of time at this hotel. In fact, he recuperated here after barely surviving two separate plane crashes in the same week. They've named the hotel bar after him."

"Good to know," I said, rather embarrassed I didn't know who Hemingway was. I thought about telling Ray I played college football and can throw and kick a ball really far, but that didn't seem pertinent to this discussion.

After breakfast, I told the others I'd meet them at the courthouse just down the road. I wanted to take one last walk before we commenced the work we came to do.

✷ ✷ ✷

A few days earlier, as we had waited in the Nairobi airport to board the last leg of our flight to Uganda, fellow attorney David Barrett and I pondered what we hoped to accomplish on this trip. Over the previous twenty-nine hours, we'd bonded as we discovered our families, backgrounds, and priorities mirrored one another's.

After graduating from Pepperdine in 1991 (two years before me), David practiced law for a number of years in both the New York and San Diego offices of a top-flight firm, Latham & Watkins. He rose to the level of partner in the environmental practice group before leaving Latham to join the legal department at one of his San Diego clients', where he manages a segment of the company's environmental legal issues in Southern California. He'd never been to Africa and felt called to put his legal training to good use. His wife and children had strongly encouraged him to join the team.

We stood shoulder-to-shoulder watching planes take off and land. As David stroked his goatee, he said, "Doesn't this trip remind you of 'The Starfish Story' we've all heard in church?"

He said "The Starfish Story" the same way I'd say "David and Goliath" or "Jonah and the Whale"—like it was an account any self-respecting churchgoer would know. A keyword search in my memory banks yielded exactly zero results. Not wanting to appear biblically ignorant, I nodded thoughtfully and responded, "Hmm." That's all I had.

"I really hope we can throw a few starfish on this trip," he said.

"Mmm-hmm," I grunted in assent. After a few beats, my conscience teamed up with my curiosity and goaded me into confessing, "Actually, I'm drawing a blank. 'The Starfish Story'?"

He graciously apologized for being cryptic and told me the story:

A man was walking down a long stretch of a nearly deserted beach in the early afternoon one day when he saw a figure off in the distance periodically bending down and standing up. As the man approached, he saw that the figure was a young boy and that he was picking up starfish from the sand and throwing them into the ocean. When the man asked what he was doing, the boy replied that the tide had gone out and that the starfish on the beach would die in the afternoon sun if he didn't throw them into the ocean. The man said to the boy, "There are starfish stranded on the beach in both directions as far as the eye can see. How can you possibly make a difference?" The boy simply bent over, picked up a starfish, and threw it into the ocean. He then looked defiantly at the man and said, "I made a difference for that one, didn't I?"

★ ★ ★

On my walk to the courthouse, I thought about the enormity of the problems facing Africa. I thought back to our sobering tour of the Holocaust-era Anne Frank House during our eight-hour layover in Amsterdam on the way to Uganda and about the isolation and fear young Anne had faced in her own prison. I thought about the imprisoned kids we were preparing to meet. And I thought about "The Starfish Story."

For most of my life, I'd been the man in that story, overwhelmed by the sheer magnitude of starfish on the shore. But now I saw myself as the boy. I asked God to grant me the opportunity to throw a starfish or two this week.

CHAPTER 9
YOU ARE WELCOME

AS I WANDERED AROUND the cluster of white and green concrete buildings comprising the Masindi courthouse, I stood out like an ivory chess piece on an ebony checkerboard. A slight breeze carried the scent of cattle grazing nearby. Several elderly women in traditional African dresses and head scarfs crowded on uncomfortable wooden benches in the shade along the side wall of the courthouse. They babbled quietly in a local language and eyed me suspiciously until the others arrived.

Inside, Napier handed a secretary his business card. "Good morning. I'm John Napier. I work at the High Court in Kampala and these are attorneys from the United States. I believe the judge is expecting us."

She inspected Napier's card, shot us a bewildered look, and disappeared through the heavy wooden door behind her.

I held my breath. It all came down to this. If the judge wasn't in, if he didn't know who we were, or if he hadn't been told we were coming, we'd be dead in the water.

"I think it'll be okay," Napier said. He'd said that once before—just before we bought our plane tickets.

★　★　★

Three weeks earlier, we'd faced a dilemma: we needed to decide if "Uganda 2010" was a go. Time was running out, and so was my courage.

I'd been quite proud of myself for finally jumping in, for doing something I was convinced eighteen months earlier I'd never do: a mission trip. But now my feet weren't just cold, they were frostbitten.

During the six weeks following my "moment" at the conference, Jay and I had exchanged numerous e-mails and phone calls with Bob regarding what we eventually dubbed "The Masindi Project." We would depart on Wednesday, January 6, 2010, and after landing in Kampala on Friday, head north to begin work on Monday at the Ihungu Remand Home. Our task was to prepare the prisoners' cases for trial.

Bob and a few others had done something similar at the Naguru Remand Home in Kampala the year before, and he made it sound manageable to prepare all twenty cases in a week. As had been the case in Kampala, Bob's organization would cover all necessary costs associated with a juvenile court session in Masindi. But I had more questions than anyone had answers. What documents existed? Who and where were the witnesses? Would they talk to us? What access would we have to the court and police files? What exactly would we prepare, in what format, and to whom would we deliver our work product?

Having worked on large and complex civil cases while at Kirkland, I struggled to comprehend how *one* case could be prepared for trial in a week, let alone *twenty*.

In late November, I called Bob; I didn't want Jay to know I was having serious reservations about proceeding with the trip. I knew Bob would shoot straight with me.

"As you know, Bob, I teach Torts, not Criminal Law. What use will I be to these kids? I've never represented a criminal defendant or even counseled someone charged with a crime."

"Me neither, dude. I don't even know what a criminal court looks like inside," he half laughed, half shouted. "Other than in Uganda, that is," he added, still laughing. "I got to see one when we did the session for the kids at the Naguru Remand Home. That was my first time."

His lightheartedness was equal parts reassuring and unnerving. "So how did you know what to do? How will *I* know what to do?" I asked.

"Look, you were a big-firm lawyer, right?"

"Right."

"You took lots of depositions and interviewed lots of clients, right?"

"Right."

"You wrote lots of briefs summarizing stuff and making arguments, right?"

"Right."

"Well, just do lots of that and you'll be great, Jim. The most important thing is that you'll be there and these kids will have someone on their side. That means so much to them. You'll figure out how to help them; I know you will."

Bob can deliver a pep talk with the best of them, and he was making some real progress with me. "Okay, so what will the end product look like? What's the briefing format the court will expect?"

Bob laughed again, but this time he choked back some of his gusto. "When you get there, you'll see things are quite different in Uganda. Think Wild West. The judges are great people and really smart, but their system is less efficient and functional than what you're used to. Whatever briefs you write will be better than anything they ever see in their courtrooms.

"When we wrote up the cases in Kampala," he continued, "they were a few paragraphs long and summarized what we could find out. Some of the guys helping weren't even lawyers. The important thing is to put something in writing to get the process started."

Though I struggled to wrap my head around how this would be helpful, I trusted Bob. By the end of the call, my nerves had calmed enough that I was confident we were going. I just needed to let go of my desperate need for control and trust it would all work out.

By early December, however, fear was neck and neck with trust, and fear was inching into the lead.

I kept telling myself legitimate concerns accounted for my reluctance to fully commit. Deep down, however, I knew otherwise. My innate desire for predictability and manageability was pummeling my courage, and courage was leaning heavily on the ropes. But in my defense, there were still real logistical challenges to overcome.

During the trip planning, it became increasingly clear that in addition to David, Ray, Jay, and me, we needed one or two Uganda-based team members to handle the in-country logistics and advance work. We needed someone familiar with Ugandan society to help us navigate the cultural barriers we would encounter. Fortunately, we knew precisely where to start.

John Napier first introduced himself to me during new-student orientation in August of 2006. He'd been admitted late in the admissions cycle, but said he knew all along he'd get in because he firmly believed coming to Pepperdine was part of God's plan for his life. I liked him instantly.

Over the course of his three years at Pepperdine, Napier emerged as a leader who knew how to get things done. He took extra classes at every opportunity so he'd graduate with not only a law degree but also with a master's in dispute resolution through Pepperdine's top-ranked Straus Institute. He'd also gone on a global justice trip to Uganda.

While Napier was a student, Herbert and Elinor Nootbaar generously endowed the Nootbaar Institute for Law, Religion, and Ethics, which hosts national conferences, brings in speakers from around the world like Baroness Cox, and serves as the home for our Global Justice Program. As a student, Napier actively participated in all aspects of the Nootbaar Institute. This, coupled with his master's degree, rendered him the perfect inaugural Nootbaar Fellow upon his graduation in 2009. Dean Starr launched the fellowship program to provide alumni the opportunity to use their talents and training to serve those in greatest need around the world for the year following their graduation.

Napier's fellowship landed him in Uganda, where he became the country's first ever court-appointed mediator for the Commercial Court, working directly for Justice Geoffrey Kiryabwire, a rising star in Uganda's legal profession who also serves as the liaison between Pepperdine and the Ugandan judiciary. When Jay and I invited Napier to participate in the Masindi Project, he immediately accepted.

For most of November and into December, Napier had worked behind the scenes to secure the necessary letter from the Ugandan judiciary authorizing us to spend a week with the children in the remand home. Though he'd been assured it wouldn't be a problem, he still didn't have the letter by mid-December. Furthermore, we had no guarantee we'd be given access to the police files for each of the cases. Napier had placed numerous calls to the Masindi courthouse registrar but had yet to speak with her.

"Guys, I think it'll probably be okay if you just come," he said. "Things are very different here. It's difficult to get anything done without being there in person. Still, I can't guarantee anything, and I don't want to be blamed if things fall apart," he added, half joking.

I knew where he was coming from. I didn't want to be the fall guy with David and Ray, who'd be leaving their families and jobs for two weeks. They had certain expectations I wanted to make sure we met.

Jay, whose easygoing demeanor and casual appearance resemble a stereotypical surfer, seemed unconcerned and eager for the adventure. But Jay and I are cut from different cloth. We had to pull the plug or pull the trigger, so we called Bob one last time.

"There are just too many uncertainties," I said. "We still don't have permission to go to the remand home."

"Wait, you need permission?" Bob laughed. Then, sensing I was looking for a way out, Bob offered, "Look, guys, I understand if this trip has too many question marks right now. We can reschedule it for the spring and I can go over with you then. How does March look for you?"

From the beginning, I'd wanted to go with Bob because I knew he'd ensure things ran smoothly, so I was relieved at his suggestion. After we hung up, I said, "Which of us should call David and Ray to tell them the trip has been postponed?"

But Jay wasn't ready to give up yet. "Let's wait a few days to see if Napier has any luck securing the letter."

Because the holidays were fast approaching, I figured the chances of everything coming together were slim to none, so I agreed. Three days later, Napier contacted us. "It's all set—we're a go," he said. "I met with the head of the High Court's Criminal Division and the Masindi registrar. They're ready for us."

"Did you get the letter?" I asked.

"I met with the Principal Judge today. He's the head of the entire High Court system. He's delighted you're coming and promised to send the letter immediately, granting us access to Ihungu, the court files, and the police files. He also wants to meet you when you're here."

Adrenaline surged through my veins as a mixture of excitement and fear hit me like a blitzing linebacker. When we hung up with Napier, Jay raised his eyebrows and flashed a grin. "Well, dawg, is it a go?"

"Call the travel agent. Uganda 2010 is a go," I heard myself say. I was out of excuses. There was no turning back now.

We'd be gone for seventeen days. And then my life would go back to normal.

* * *

"You are welcome," the court clerk said to Napier as she closed the wooden door behind her. "The High Court justice is in Kampala at the annual judicial conference, but the magistrate is here, and he is expecting you . . . but not until Wednesday."

Relief and concern jockeyed for position as I drew in a deep breath. On the one hand, they knew who we were and presumably why we'd come. On the other hand, if we weren't expected until Wednesday, would we be allowed to get started today?

Napier, ever the diplomat, pressed on. "That is unfortunate. We can return on Wednesday, of course, but it would be an honor to meet His Worship today. Is he around?"

"Yes, he is around," she said tentatively. "Let me see if he will receive you." Again she disappeared behind into the office behind her, this time leaving the door ajar.

"Sorry, guys," Napier whispered. "I specifically told the judges in Kampala we were coming today."

"'His Worship'? What's that about?" Jay whispered back with a smirk.

"Actually, in Uganda, High Court justices are 'My Lord,' and magistrates and registrars are 'Your Worship.' You'll get used to it."

As we quietly waited to learn the fate of the Masindi Project, I read the numerous Bible verses and uplifting messages that were taped to the wall behind the secretary's desk. *Not at all what one sees in American courthouses*, I thought. On another wall was a cartoon poster depicting a court official taking a bribe and a stern rebuke of the evils of corruption. On a nearby desk sat a precarious pile of pink folders with faded handwritten pages jutting out.

"You are most welcome," a deep and warm voice from the office doorway broke the tension in the room. "Please come in. I am Francis Ojikhan, Magistrate Grade II."

He looked to be in his early forties and had a friendly demeanor. "How is America?" he asked playfully.

We all nodded and mumbled something positive as we sat. Napier took the seat closest to the desk and explained that both he and Niemeyer lived in Uganda. "These lawyers have traveled a long way to come and help the children at Ihungu. We would like to meet with them and begin our work today, Your Worship. Would that be possible?"

"I understand, only there is a problem. I received a letter last Friday from the Principal Judge. He instructed me to gather the court and police files for you when you arrived on Wednesday and to assist you however I can. Today is Monday, and we are not ready for you. We have to send for many of the files from the other courthouses and police stations in the district." He raised his palms in a gesture of regret.

Sensing our skepticism, he slid the letter across the desk.

"I see. We can wait until Wednesday to review the files, but we'd like to go see the children today. Can we?" Napier said while nodding slightly.

The magistrate pondered this for a moment. "If the probation officer is around, we can go."

Napier pressed his luck. "Great. Do you have *any* of the court or police files here?"

"We definitely have a few. My secretary can get them for you this afternoon. I also have a cause list for the juvenile session Justice Ochan, the Masindi High Court judge, will conduct." He handed Napier two copies of the two-page document.

We all gathered around to examine the list, which contained the names of the children and the charges against them. It also provided the case numbers, the first four of which corresponded to the year the juvenile had been arrested. Several began with "2008." Someone named Tumusiime Henry appeared twice on the list with two different case numbers—one in 2008 and one in 2009. Both charges were for murder.

"Why is one juvenile listed twice?" I inquired.

"He was first arrested in 2008 for murder, and then he was charged with a second murder of a boy at Ihungu last month," Magistrate Ojikhan grimly replied. We glanced at each other nervously, wondering if this kid was dangerous.

We'd intended to spend the morning reviewing court files to prepare for our interviews, which we hoped would begin that afternoon. But it was now clear the only information we'd have about the cases before meeting with the children was their names, their alleged crimes, and the years of their arrests. That is, if we were allowed to meet with them before Wednesday at all. Not exactly a lawyer's dream scenario, particularly because we needed to finish by noon on Thursday so we could get back to Kampala for a dinner meeting Napier had arranged.

"Let me call the probation officer. If he is around, I can take you to Ihungu," Magistrate Ojikhan said as he stepped out of the room.

A cursory review of the list revealed twenty-one children and twenty-two cases—six murders, one abduction, three thefts, one weapons possession, nine aggravated defilements, and two simple defilements. I'd learned from reading the Uganda Penal Code on the plane that *defilement* is Uganda's term for unlawful sex with a minor.

"The probation officer is coming now. Shall we go?" Magistrate Ojikhan said as he stepped back into the room.

We all proceeded outside to the parking lot, and a slight man on a small motorcycle pulled up next to us. "This is William," the magistrate said. "He is a probation officer and the warden of Ihungu." William seemed genuinely happy to see us and kept saying, "You are welcome."

I'd been in Uganda just a few days and had been told "You are welcome" several times in situations where I didn't realize I should have said "Thank you." I was apparently offending virtually everyone I met.

Napier hopped into Magistrate Ojikhan's car, William mounted his motorcycle, and the rest of us piled into Niemeyer's Toyota Land Cruiser. The next ten minutes felt like a rickety carnival roller coaster as Niemeyer four-wheeled his way out to Ihungu.

I had no idea what to expect.

When we'd arrived at the Kampala Sheraton our first night in Uganda, scores of soldiers carrying AK-47 rifles were stationed outside the hotel gate. Jay had assured me guards with loaded weapons were everywhere in Uganda and that I'd get used to it. So as we turned off what masqueraded as a road and drove up the narrow driveway to Ihungu, I looked for gun-toting guards preventing the children from escaping. There were none. There was no fence either. Instead, I saw about ten young teenagers milling around in front of what looked like a cross between a barn and a warehouse. They gaped at us as if we were from another planet.

A boy in a yellow T-shirt climbed the stairs, removed a golden padlock from the large wooden door to the barn-house, and disappeared inside.

That night I e-mailed Joline and described my impressions as we first entered the custody:

What we saw was disturbing. The remand home was a one-room concrete rectangular warehouse about 5 feet by 20 feet. The ceiling was about 12 feet high, and there were open-air slits near the ceiling that let in air but very little light. Inside, there were 12 foam pads (for 18 boys) covered with tattered blankets. There were no chairs, and virtually nothing else but a few jugs of water and a chalkboard.

This isn't okay with me, was all I could think.

CHAPTER 10
RETURN OF THE MZUNGUS

JANUARY 11, 2010

This day began like the others after Innocent died, but I will always remember it. We did not have to work anymore because Rose had been arrested, so I stayed inside the custody after breakfast.

I was reading my Bible when Joseph came in and said there were six mzungus with Mr. William and another Ugandan man. I said a quick prayer that today was the day someone would help us.

When the mzungus entered the custody, I recognized one of them from before. I knew then God had been listening.

The boys sat quietly on their mats. Most avoided eye contact with us, instead fixing their gaze on their hands folded in front of them. It was pin-drop quiet when Magistrate Ojikhan spoke, first in English, then in Swahili: "These lawyers came from America to help you. They have questions to ask you. Tell them the truth. Do you have any questions?"

No one did.

"Who speaks English?"

Two boys sitting together on the mat closest to the doorway slowly raised their hands. None of the others reacted at all. A sinking feeling enveloped me as I realized how much a language barrier would complicate an already difficult process.

"You will be the translators for the others," Magistrate Ojikhan informed the pair. They simply nodded.

William turned to us. "Henry and Joseph are brothers. They are very smart and speak English very well." After he said something to them in another language, they both scurried out of the custody.

"Thank you for coming to Uganda to help these children. I am so happy you are here," William said. "Please tell me how I can help."

Outside, Henry and Joseph were setting up chairs in a circle in an open area next to what I had been told was called "the custody." We mzungus convened briefly and decided to pair up. But because we had only two translators, we decided four of us would remain at Ihungu to conduct the interviews. Napier and Niemeyer went back to town to see if they could get their hands on any files.

This division of labor made sense for two reasons. First, Napier and Niemeyer lived in Uganda and knew how to navigate the culture. And second, Napier had just graduated from law school six months earlier and Niemeyer wasn't a lawyer, so we decided that the more experienced lawyers would conduct the deposition-like interviews.

William decided to stick around, seemingly compelled by curiosity and concern for the children. A lump formed in my throat when he introduced us to the three girls—Nakunda, Scovia, and Katwe were just kids. None of them looked older than my fourteen-year-old daughter, Jessica. The youngest, Katwe, would giggle whenever we looked at her.

We walked over to Henry and Joseph and introduced ourselves. When we did, I noticed something tentative in their handshakes. As we released, there was an awkwardness, like we were missing something. I'd also noticed this when I had shaken William's hand earlier.

"I am called Henry," the shorter of the two boys said. He stood about five foot four and looked to weigh about 120 pounds—the same size as my twelve-year-old son, Joshua. "And I am called Joseph," said the slightly taller and heavier brother.

Both wore sweatpants, flip-flops, and T-shirts—Henry in blue and Joseph in yellow. Though heavily accented by a mixture of British and I-don't-know-what, their speech was sufficiently clear and confident.

Not ideal to have fellow prisoners translating, I thought, *but I think this will work.*

"We'll need two circles of four, rather than one circle of eight," I said to Henry, who was standing closer to me at the time.

David and I followed Henry as he took four of the plastic lawn chairs and moved them into the shade of a large mango tree. Without discussing it, David and I selected Henry as our interpreter. I'm now convinced something much bigger than coincidence ensured this young man and I would be grouped together. As I removed my computer from my backpack and turned it on, Henry watched intently. He told me later it was the first time he'd ever laid eyes on a laptop.

"Which case is yours?" I asked Henry after I showed him how my laptop worked.

He pointed to a murder charge near the top of the list. "This one." He turned the page. "And this one," pointing to the most recent case. Realization hit me like a lightning bolt—*This is the boy Magistrate Ojikhan mentioned in his office, the one accused of killing another prisoner*. I resolved to avoid making him angry.

A short while later, David and I sat facing Henry and the empty chair to his left. We gave him our business cards and again told him our first and last names. We explained we'd be asking the children questions about their cases and that it was very important they were honest with us.

"I understand," he said.

I turned my computer around and showed him the interview template I'd created and walked through the types of questions we'd be asking.

Henry again said, "I understand," and we believed him.

"Should I bring the first prisoner?" Henry asked, obviously eager to get started.

David and I decided to start with the capital cases. "Which crimes are capital offenses again?" David asked.

I searched my memory banks. "I'm pretty sure the murders, the abduction, the aggravated defilements, and the weapons possession cases are all capital cases."

"That sounds right. I still can't believe all these crimes would be eligible for the death penalty if committed by adults. Good thing the maximum penalty for these kids is three years."

"Let's hold off on the murders until we get comfortable with what we're doing," I suggested.

"Good idea. How about we start with . . . Wabura? Can you get him, Henry?"

Henry returned from the custody with a tall, slender boy. David and I stood, smiled, and extended our hands while loudly enunciating our names and pointing to ourselves.

It happened again. I was *definitely* missing something with the handshake. As I pulled my hand away, Wabura seemed to be moving his in a way I didn't understand.

David pulled out his camera. "Henry, will you ask him if I can take his picture?"

Henry said something in Swahili, and Wabura sheepishly nodded.

"Smile!" David said.

Wabura stared blankly back, not understanding the meaning of this strange mzungu word. David took his picture anyway, then turned the camera around and pointed to the screen. "This is you."

Huge, toothy smiles burst onto the faces of Wabura and Henry as they chatted in Swahili and pointed at the screen. After a few back-and-forth exchanges, Henry said, "Okay, he says he is the real one."

Huh?

"One more with *that* smile," David said while exaggerating a smile himself. This time the camera captured Wabura's beaming face. He and Henry laughed heartily at the picture.

Once again, Wabura emphasized something to Henry in Swahili. "He says this is a picture of him, but he is the real one." Henry proceeded to explain that many people in the villages are superstitious about pictures and feel compelled to clarify they are the real person and not the image. Several other prisoners later made similar comments.

During the interview, we learned Wabura could neither read nor write because he'd never attended school. He was born in 1995, but didn't know which month, making him either fourteen or fifteen. He'd lived his entire life in a small village nearby until one year earlier, when his parents hired him out to work as a herdsman for a family in another village. As was customary, Wabura lived with the family for whom he worked. That family had a daughter. Wabura confessed he and the girl had "played sex" three times. We initially chalked up the odd description to difficulties in translation, but later learned this was common terminology in Uganda.

Wabura assured us the sex was consensual and that the girl was fourteen years old. While Uganda's age of consent is eighteen, fourteen represents the dividing line between aggravated defilement, a capital offense, and simple defilement, a noncapital offense. Wabura said the police arrested him seven months earlier, and his parents didn't know where he was. He knew of no way to contact them because they didn't have a phone, and addresses don't exist in the villages. In fact, when we asked about an address, Henry initially didn't understand what we meant.

With no police report or other information, we had no way of verifying anything Wabura said. We concluded the interview by telling him we'd be preparing a report to assist in his defense. We told him we'd try our best to help him get released and that we'd be praying for him. Wabura sounded out a "thank you" in the best English he could manage as he bowed toward us with his hands together in a praying pose. This type of subordination made us uncomfortable, so we stood and extended our hands. Another awkward handshake.

As he left, I said to Henry, "How do Ugandans shake hands?"

David immediately chimed in, saying, "Yeah, I feel like I'm missing something."

Henry was confused at first but eventually understood what we were asking. "With strangers, we shake like this." He demonstrated by shaking my hand in the customary way. "But friends greet each other differently, like this." He took my hand in his and moved them both from a normal handshake to an arm-wrestling grip, then back to a normal handshake.

All at once, it clicked. Wabura had wanted to shake our hands as friends, but we'd responded as strangers. I felt more than a twinge of sadness as Wabura walked away. We'd missed a chance to convey to him—and to the others with whom we'd already shaken hands—that we wanted to be their friends rather than remaining strangers. We vowed not to repeat our mistake.

Our interview of Wabura had taken an hour. Niemeyer wouldn't return for another hour, so we showed Henry the list and asked him to select someone who'd been charged with a capital offense. He chose Bo, our first murder case.

While somewhat tentative, Bo was more confident than Wabura because he and the others had been studying us from a distance as we interviewed Wabura. Through Henry, Bo told us he and his younger brother, Derrick, had been arrested in January of 2008, *two years earlier*, and charged with killing their father. Bo said his father had come home drunk one night and that he and Derrick found him dead in bed the next morning. He steadfastly denied having anything to do with his father's death. Without the police report or medical records, we couldn't think of any more questions to ask.

Before we left for lunch, Henry and I smiled broadly as we shook hands in the way that signified we were friends.

Over lunch, David and I learned Jay and Ray had completed four interviews in the time it took us to finish two.

"How'd you guys do?" David asked Niemeyer and Napier.

"Great. We managed to get access to several police files," Niemeyer said.

"Why don't Jay and I stay here to review the files and call potential witnesses we identified in our interviews this morning?" Ray suggested.

"Sounds good," I said. "David and I will continue with the interviews."

As we turned the corner from the main road and started up the path to Ihungu, the kids ran over to our car with relieved smiles plastered on their faces. They had endured so many broken promises from others about returning to help, but we'd come back like we said we would. A surge of adrenaline flooded my veins as I turned a corner in my own mind. The *What am I doing here?* questions were becoming distant memories. I no longer wondered whether we could be helpful to these children. I yearned not only to hear more of their stories but to help them tell these stories to the court. Most of all, though, I felt an unquenchable desire to help secure their freedom, to restore their childhood.

When David and I made our way through the crowd and sat down under the mango tree with Henry, the others gathered around us, hoping to be chosen next. Rather than choosing among them, we decided to start that afternoon with Henry's first case in which he, Joseph, and their father were charged with the murder of the herdsman. Because the other prisoners were anxious to tell their stories, we decided to address Henry's second murder charge the following day.

David and I interviewed three more juveniles before Niemeyer drove us back to the hotel. On the return, David asked him how he ended up in Uganda.

Niemeyer laughed. "You know Bob Goff, right?"

"I haven't actually met him yet," David answered.

"Well, three years ago I took a business class he taught at Point Loma Nazarene. Bob challenged us to live a life of service. After graduation, a volunteer position with Restore became available, and I jumped at the chance to work with Bob. A month after I arrived here, the

Country Director position opened up and I was hired. I've been here two years now."

"Any plans to return home?"

"Not anytime soon. I love it here."

Niemeyer also told us he, Napier, Ray, and Jay had made substantial progress in gathering and reviewing police and court files and in locating and interviewing witnesses. During each of our interviews that afternoon, Henry had instructed those whose parents had mobile phones to write the numbers in the dirt with a stick. We relayed those to Niemeyer between interviews using Jay's Ugandan phone so he and a courthouse interpreter could call the families. The interpreter informed the family members we'd pay for their round-trip transportation to Masindi if they'd come and meet with us at the hotel. Most of them showed up a few hours later on the backs of boda bodas.

One of the first calls, which had been placed before Niemeyer had secured an interpreter, was to Bo and Derrick's uncle. He either didn't understand or didn't believe we'd pay for his transportation because he showed up at our hotel in the early evening after having walked *seven hours* to get there. Like we did for the others, we fed him at the hotel restaurant, interviewed him, and then paid for his transportation home. Each of the family members expressed profound gratitude to us for helping their loved ones.

That evening we had dinner with one of the lawyers who'd be representing the kids in court. She was pleased to learn of our progress but seemed rather skeptical we'd have twenty-two cases fully briefed by Thursday. Truth be told, I shared her skepticism.

After dinner, David and I converted our interview notes into summaries, as did Jay for the four interviews he and Ray had conducted. The others reviewed the police and court files we'd secured and tried to piece together the individual cases we'd begun that day. Before turning in, we discussed the case against Henry and Joseph.

Jay and Ray had interviewed Joseph during the morning session so we could compare notes. We soon discovered their descriptions perfectly matched each other's, and all four of us fully believed them. Niemeyer added, "Bob said if we found any kids we thought would be a good fit for the Restore Leadership Academy, he'd be willing to admit them after they are released." We resolved then and there to strive to get Henry and Joseph out of prison and into Restore.

Since the hotel's Internet was down, I jogged three-quarters of a mile to an Internet café at 10:00 p.m. and sent Joline a quick note:

Things went even better than we had expected or hoped today. We really feel like we are going to be able to make a huge difference in the lives of twenty-one children. And they are blessing us more than we are blessing them. I can't wait to give you all the details. We are going to be working late into the night and early in the morning for the next few days, but we wouldn't rather be anywhere else doing anything else.

I fell asleep that night wondering if Henry and Joseph were going to be my starfish.

JANUARY 11, 2010

When Jim and David left with the others for lunch, some of the boys asked me if they were coming back. They had not been chosen to talk about their cases yet and were afraid they would not have their chance. I told them I was very sure they would return. Jim and David were my friends now, and I believed them when they said they would come back. And they did.

After they left in the evening, I called my mom and told her the mzungus from America had returned and were going to help us get released. She cried because she was so happy. She said she had been praying very hard and knew God was hearing her prayers. She also asked me if I thought the lawyers could help my father get released as well. I promised I would ask.

We sang and praised God that night like we had never done before at Ihungu. It was like being in a church again. I thanked God for answering our prayers. I also prayed for forgiveness for doubting Him.

CHAPTER 11
ROUND TWO

I WAS WIDE AWAKE AT 4:00 a.m., so I resumed working on the interview summaries. By sunrise, the entire team had joined me in the hotel's courtyard, our adrenaline pumping at full tilt.

After breakfast, we resumed our work from the previous afternoon. Joseph was eager to play his part in this liberation effort, so he had helped Henry assemble the chairs into two groups of four, hoping both groups would return. David and I briefly contemplated splitting up, but the system we'd devised the day before had worked—I asked the initial questions on each subject and took notes on my computer, while David followed up and took notes on a legal pad. So we decided to stick together and stick with Henry as our interpreter.

One of the girls watched us closely but always turned away whenever we looked at her, as if she were allergic to eye contact. We decided to start with her. Her name was Nakunda, and she was charged with murder.

When we were introduced, she made no effort to give us the "friend" handshake; her grip was limp and lifeless. It took David several attempts to even secure a faint smile for her picture, her countenance was so hollow. During the interview, she spoke softly and haltingly. Henry had to ask her to repeat herself several times because she just mumbled vacantly.

Her story still haunts me.

Nakunda was born on Christmas Day of 1993. Shortly after her tenth birthday, her parents both died of AIDS. Then she bounced from place to place and ended up working for a man selling "herbal medicine" door to door. In December of 2008, while living with a distant uncle, she became pregnant. Shortly thereafter, her boyfriend was deployed out of the country by the Ugandan Army. She continued working until her pregnancy prevented her from walking long distances.

Because she could no longer contribute to her upkeep, her uncle kicked her out. After spending some time on the streets, her alcoholic grandmother grudgingly took her in. Nakunda was all alone the night the baby came. She named her new baby girl Kirabo, which Henry, who was quite emotionally affected himself, somberly told us meant "gift" in Swahili. The beginnings of a smile flickered across her face when she said how much she loved her baby, but her smile vanished as quickly as it appeared.

Over the next two weeks, Kirabo vomited quite a bit and seemed sick to Nakunda. When she asked her grandmother for money for a doctor, the woman refused and assured the new mother that Kirabo was fine. One evening, the baby was especially in distress. Nakunda pled for help, but her grandmother again refused and left to go drinking. A few hours later, Kirabo died in Nakunda's arms. She held the baby for two hours as she wept.

Her grandmother ordered Nakunda to leave the next day. She also threatened to call the police and tell them Nakunda had killed the baby if she didn't dispose of the body. Because her grandmother feared the curse of evil spirits if her granddaughter buried Kirabo on her land, Nakunda wrapped her child in a blanket and took her out into the bush and left her there. The following day a local villager found a dog eating Kirabo's remains and called the police. Nakunda was arrested and charged with murder based solely on her grandmother's sworn declaration that Kirabo had died while she was out, so Nakunda must have killed her.

We cried as Nakunda finished her story. We wanted to hug her—and should have. Instead, we told her we were very sorry for her loss and we'd do whatever we could to help.

When we later reviewed the police report, it confirmed her account. The murder charge rested solely on her grandmother's unsupported statement.

Our final interview of the morning was with Abdul, who'd been arrested for aggravated defilement, or so our list indicated. When we interviewed him, however, he wasn't sure why he'd been arrested, but he *knew* he hadn't "played sex" with anyone, let alone an underage girl. Abdul was illiterate and didn't know his birthdate, only that he'd been born in 1993. We found this to be all too common among the children—they remembered only their birth year and thus considered themselves a year older with each new calendar year.

After we assured him that we'd pray for him and work hard to free him, he said through Henry, "Even if you can't help us get free, I want to thank you for coming all the way from America to visit us." Later, David and I discussed how Matthew 25:35–40 immediately rushed to mind for both of us.

"'For I was hungry and you gave me something to eat, I was thirsty and you gave me something to drink, I was a stranger and you invited me in, I needed clothes and you clothed me, I was sick and you looked after me, I was in prison and you came to visit me.'

"Then the righteous will answer him, 'Lord, when did we see you hungry and feed you, or thirsty and give you something to drink? When did we see you a stranger and invite you in, or needing clothes and clothe you? When did we see you sick or in prison and go to visit you?'

"The King will reply, 'Truly I tell you, whatever you did for one of the least of these brothers and sisters of mine, you did for me.'"

It felt good to be fulfilling a biblical charge to visit those in prison, but we agreed it would feel even better to help set the captives free.

The following day we received Abdul's police report, which accused him of being involved in a mob killing, not defilement. Our subsequent interview revealed nothing but surprise from him and denials of even knowing who'd been killed.

Just as we finished with Abdul, Niemeyer called to tell us he'd pick us up in fifteen minutes. So rather than starting another interview, I pulled out my iPod and showed Henry how it worked. I put the headphones on him and clicked Play. He grinned from ear to ear and yelled, "Who is singing this song and what is it called?"

"Bon Jovi, and the song is called 'Living on a Prayer,'" I yelled back.

"Oh, okay, a Christian song!"

Not exactly.

At the end of the song, I placed my computer in his lap and showed him how to operate a touchpad mouse. He laughed heartily as I called up pictures of my family and my dog. "Can I put my name on your computer?"

"Of course."

When I looked up, I noticed many of the other children watching Henry from a distance. They were laughing and wiggling their fingers like they were typing. I then showed Henry my cell phone. After inspecting it, he declared, "This one is better than mine." He reached into his pocket and pulled out a mobile phone of his own.

I was stunned.

"Mr. William lets me have it so I can call him if there is an emergency. Please do not tell him you know about it because he could get in trouble for letting me keep it."

He handed me back my phone and pulled from his pocket the business card I'd given him the day before. "Is the number for that phone on this card?"

"Actually, no. That number rings to a phone in my office at work."

He pointed at my cell phone. "What is the number for that one?"

His simple question caught me completely off guard. My answer to this question depended upon my answer to a *totally different* question. Was I just a do-gooder tourist checking my mission-trip box, or was

I willing to personally invest in the sixteen-year-old Ugandan prisoner into whose eyes I was looking? I'm embarrassed to say I paused much longer than I should have. Eventually I smiled and recited my number as he programmed it into his phone and then typed his number onto my computer screen next to his name.

Just then Niemeyer pulled up, and he and an attractive woman in her late thirties got out. She wore a patterned skirt, a striped sweater, and an elegant head scarf. Henry's face lit up, "Ah, that is my mother! Come and greet her."

She bear-hugged Henry and Joseph and smiled broadly as Henry introduced David and me. Her round face beamed as we complimented her boys and told her how much they were helping the other prisoners.

Occasionally, she would rattle off something to Henry and Joseph in Runyoro, and they would all laugh. "She speaks English well, but it is hard for her to understand what mzungus are saying. She says you talk funny." We all laughed.

"Did you know she was coming?" I asked Henry.

"No, I am very surprised to see her."

"We called her this morning," Niemeyer said. "We offered to pay for her trip if she'd come. And here she is. We just finished interviewing her, so I figured I'd bring her out to see her boys."

Watching Henry's mother interact so lovingly with her boys brought our work into sharper focus than anything else could have. It was one thing to sit and talk with the prisoners about why they had been arrested, what evidence may exist in favor or against them, and what they hoped to do once they were released. But actually seeing them with their loved ones, observing firsthand the intimacy shared between a parent and child that imprisonment so cruelly denied them on a daily basis, propelled to new heights my yearning to help these kids reclaim their childhood. I had to go for a brief walk alone when I imagined myself in her position—visiting my wrongfully accused children in prison. It wasn't yet time for these kids to see me cry.

Before we left for lunch, David took a picture of Henry and Joseph with their mother. She clapped with delight when she saw the image on David's screen, and she insisted we take one with David and me in the picture.

"Does she need to be dropped somewhere on our way?" Niemeyer asked Henry.

"Thank you, but she will stay and visit for a while," Henry said.

During lunch, I went to my room, removed the color printer from my suitcase, and lugged it to the hotel restaurant. Napier figured out how to print an 8 x 10 of the photo of David, me, Henry, Joseph, and their mother on the photo paper I'd brought.

On the way back to Ihungu, David and I lamented the fact that their soccer ball had gone flat a few weeks earlier.

"Let's get them a new one right now," Niemeyer suggested. *Great idea.* The local merchant also had a pump and filled the ball for us. I concealed it in my backpack and decided to wait for the right time to pull it out.

When we arrived, Henry and Joseph were sitting alone. "Where's your mother?" I asked.

"She left about ten minutes ago. She wanted to say good-bye to you, but she had to go so she didn't miss the matatu," Henry explained.

I pulled the 8 x 10 photo out of a manila envelope and showed it to Henry. He smiled widely and then summoned Jamil. Henry said something in Swahili and handed him the envelope. Barefoot, Jamil darted away in a full sprint.

"It is a long walk to where my mother will find transport. I think maybe Jamil will get there before she leaves," Henry remarked. Sure enough, Jamil returned fifteen minutes later and triumphantly reported to Henry that he'd caught her just as she was boarding the matatu. Jamil looked at us and said in halting English, "She . . . much . . . happy."

Under our mango tree, I unzipped my backpack just enough for Henry to see the ball. I wish I had a picture of his face when he saw it.

Before I could tell him we wanted to surprise the others at the end of the day, he'd yanked it out and flashed it to Joseph, who broke into a broad smile and ran back to the custody. Soon, the other boys came around the corner sporting Christmas-morning faces. We promised we'd play the next day after we finished all the interviews.

Joseph translated. They cheered.

David and I powered through several more interviews, including that of sixteen-year-old Okello, who'd been charged with aggravated defilement for "playing sex" with a fourteen-year-old girl. He'd been at Ihungu for twenty-two months without any contact with his family because they didn't know where he was. The following day we tracked down his father and facilitated the tearful reunion. I think I cried more than either of them did, though I again did so away from the others.

During this second day of interviews, David and I noticed Henry wasn't simply translating our words—he actively directed the questioning as well. He often turned to the prisoner after we asked a question in English, carried on a short conversation in Swahili, then gave us answers not only to the question we'd asked but also to the next few on our template. In fact, a few times when the inmate responded, Henry shook his head, asked the question differently, then gave us the answer. "He was confused and didn't remember the date correctly," Henry said.

It was our turn to be confused. "How did you know he was mistaken about the date of his own arrest?" David asked.

"There is a copy of each juvenile's indictment in the store," Henry sheepishly admitted. "Whenever a new prisoner arrives, I read the papers so I can get to know them more quickly and help them if I can."

This provided us a glimpse into just how much Henry cared about the other children.

David and I left Ihungu that evening with just four interviews remaining. We'd spent much of the afternoon talking to Henry about his second case and the day Innocent died. Our self-imposed deadline of noon Thursday weighed heavily on us, so we worked late into Tuesday night on the interview summaries, integrating the information Jay and Ray had gleaned from the police files and witness interviews. Realizing I'd remember little of what I was experiencing unless I wrote it down, I spent an hour each night documenting the day's events. The hotel's Internet connection had finally been restored, so I Skyped with my family for the first time since arriving in Africa.

The wheel. Air travel. Skype. These constitute mankind's three greatest achievements, though not necessarily in that order. The first picture that pops up when one searches Google Images for "irony" should be me in the heart of Africa having a live video chat with my wife and kids in California. Joline had been reading the kids my daily journal entries, and I'd talked to them briefly a few times using Jay's cell phone, so they were mostly up to speed on our progress. I'm incapable of articulating how gratifying it was to see them face-to-face, though. I walked around the hotel to show them what it looked like, and they caught me up on what was happening at home.

After a few minutes, Joline took her laptop upstairs so we could talk privately. She reassured me the kids were great, and she was holding up well. She also expressed how proud she was of what we were doing. This caused the dam that had been holding back my emotions during the phone call to spring a leak. As anyone who knows me can attest, I'm a crier. I don't cry when I'm physically hurt or angry; I cry when I'm overcome with emotion, which happens far more often than I'd like.

I felt trapped inside a very sad movie, and the characters had become my friends. It was good to get a little of it out, but there was still so much to do that I shut down my emotions before they got out of hand. Had I known how things would unfold in the coming days and weeks, I would've directed some more water over the dam that night to make room for the torrent rushing downstream.

CHAPTER 12
HAT TRICK

AT 5:30 A.M. ON WEDNESDAY MORNING, I awoke to a vaguely Arabic voice emanating from what sounded like a cheap bullhorn. A full minute passed before I could deduce the source—a Muslim religious leader calling the faithful to morning prayers from a local mosque. I took the opportunity to send up a few prayers of my own, albeit through a different Mediator.

While David and I returned to Ihungu for the last four interviews, the rest of the team stayed behind to finish interviewing the family members and witnesses and to review the files we'd been promised would arrive that day from neighboring towns.

After finishing our last interview right before lunch, the two of us pulled Henry aside and updated him on our progress in preparing the briefs. "We have lots of work ahead of us today and tomorrow. We have to leave at midday tomorrow to get back to Kampala," I explained.

"I understand, but the prisoners would be so happy if you played soccer with them. They have been talking about it constantly since you brought the new ball."

I did some quick calculations before responding. My internal economist considered how much time it would cost us to be away from our work and how much we still had left to do to bring the end product up to our standards. My internal social worker couldn't bear the thought of pouring more disappointment into the already overflowing cups from which these kids daily drank. In the end, my internal lawyer won out, concluding that the spirit behind Jesus' directive to visit those in prison was to replace their sorrow with joy, if only temporarily. And from what Henry told us, only liberation would bring them more joy than a good soccer match. While their release might have to wait, soccer would not.

"We'll be back at three for the Ihungu Cup," I declared.

Over lunch, our team briefed each other on the morning's activities and mapped out the next twenty-four hours. We needed to transform our notes and summaries into a format helpful to the lawyers, the probation officer, and the court.

"Over the past several months, I've developed a good sense of the format the courts are used to seeing," Napier offered. "Why don't I design a template for the briefs?" He added, "We need to get the A4 paper and folders Ugandans use in court filings," knowing that the standard 8 ½ x 11 paper I had brought differed from the British A4 standard, which Uganda had adopted while under British control.

"I know the folders you're talking about," Niemeyer said. "And I have a fair amount of experience bargaining with Ugandan shopkeepers, so I can pick up the supplies we need." Niemeyer also volunteered to be the logistics guy, running the printer and assembling and collating the briefs as we completed them.

Just before we left for the soccer match, David had an idea. "I had no clue whether food in Uganda would be any good, so I brought a bunch of protein bars, and I'm sure some of you did the same. I suspect that if we pooled all of ours together, we'd have enough for each kid." He was right. Together we had twenty-five, more than enough.

The site for the epic match spanned about half the size of a normal soccer field. A noticeable slope cut across its width, and its shape more closely resembled an oval than a rectangle. To call the terrain "uneven" would be charitable—the playing surface was mostly weedy, patchy grass littered with gravel and small rocks. Makeshift goals stood at either end, and a thirty-foot tree next to a dilapidated concrete toilet facility was situated inside the field of play.

In advance of our arrival, Henry had created lineup cards, making sure each team had its share of mzungus. The team captained by Henry was to include Ray, Napier, and me. Jay, David, and Niemeyer were put on the team captained by Joseph. At the last minute, Napier decided to stay behind to finish the template so we wouldn't be delayed that evening.

Because the field was small, only nine—rather than the standard eleven—played on each side at a time. The substitutes climbed up into the tree, which doubled as box seats. We divided into shirts and skins. Unfortunately for everyone in attendance, I was a skin. My pasty complexion nearly blinded them, though they kindly refrained from laughing and pointing. Well, everyone except Jay.

Only the mzungus wore shoes. About thirty seconds into the game, the ball went beyond the concrete toilet structure on the downhill slope of the field so Ray picked it up. "*Handuh, handuh,*" came the cry as Ray prepared to throw the ball in. We learned then that (1) *handuh* was Swahili for "Hey, stupid mzungu, you can't pick up the ball in this game"; and (2) the tree and toilet are actually in bounds.

After a few minutes, Jay substituted out so he could preserve portions of the epic match on film.

The game was competitive, and the kids raced around as if they were playing on a perfectly manicured field while wearing state-of-the-art footwear. We soon realized that whenever the ball got near a goal, the boys would attempt to pass it to one of us to score. I guess that was their way of thanking us for helping them.

Though I had played soccer from ages six through sixteen, I wasn't nearly one of the best out there. Henry just kept setting me up, so I ended up scoring a "hat trick." After I headed in one of my three goals set up by a perfect cross from Henry, I celebrated like I'd just scored the winning goal in the World Cup. I found a patch of grass and slid on my knees like the professionals do and then, to the delight of the group, topped off the celebration with a cartwheel—my childhood gymnastics training finally paying off. Jay captured the latter on film.

After all the substitutes had the opportunity to play in our forty-minute match, we called it quits. My team won 4–2. It was true that we had to stop so we could finish their briefs, but a couple of us were also courting a coronary.

We gathered everyone together in an open area north of the boys' custody, including the three girls. (They'd remained in their sleeping quarters while we played.) I asked Henry to arrange everyone into a circle with him directly opposite me, and as he translated, I announced, "Tomorrow we'll bring each of you a picture of yourself to keep."

They smiled and excitedly whispered to each other. "We also have a protein bar for each of you."

"I beg your pardon?" Henry said.

Apparently there's no Swahili equivalent for "protein bar." "Um. We have a candy bar for each of you," I clarified.

Close enough.

They clapped and bowed as Jay, Ray, and David handed each kid a Clif Bar or PowerBar.

"Joseph, will you translate this next p-portion?" My voice hitched as emotion gripped my throat. *Here we go again.*

I took a deep breath, cleared my throat, and soldiered on with Joseph translating. "I would like to say a few words about your leader. Over the past three days, we have come to know and love Henry very much. He cares greatly about each and every one of you. You are blessed to have such a great Katikkiro."

Tears streaked my cheeks and my voice quivered with each phrase, but I was determined not to let this moment pass without expressing my true feelings. "Today we want to honor Henry with the captain's jersey. He is the captain of Team Ihungu."

Jay handed me the new Pepperdine Law shirt we'd brought for such a time as this. "Henry, please step forward." Everyone roared with applause as I hugged him and presented him with his jersey.

Henry quieted the crowd and gave his own speech while Joseph translated. "For all of us at Ihungu, I want to thank you for coming to Uganda. Thank you for helping us with our cases. Thank you for loving us. Thank you for being our friends." More applause from the kids. More tears from me.

I took the hands of those on either side of me and asked the others to do the same as I led a final prayer. The pause between each sentence as Henry translated barely allowed me the time to maintain my composure as I prayed for freedom and justice for these children. After the prayer, the mzungus walked around the inside of the circle and gave either a hug or a friendship handshake to each of the boys and girls. I opted for the hug.

We promised to return the next day at noon to say our final good-byes and to deliver the photographs.

Back at the hotel, we arranged what lawyers call a "war room" out in the restaurant's courtyard. We had five laptops, our color printer, piles of photographs, stacks of briefs in varying stages of completion, and the folders we'd ultimately give the lawyers, probation officer, and court.

We worked late into the night integrating our notes into Napier's well-designed briefing template. Flash drives migrated between computers as we conveyed the briefs down a makeshift assembly line. Whenever there was a lull in the printing action, Napier and Niemeyer printed out color cover sheets containing each child's picture, name, and case number and affixed them to the outside of the folder we created for each child.

We still had plenty left to do, but we went to bed at 3:00 a.m., confident we could finish in the morning in time to say our final good-byes at Ihungu by noon. That ended up being overly optimistic.

JANUARY 13, 2010

We had another great night of praise and worship in the custody. We were tired from the soccer match, but we were also very happy because we thought we would be going home to our families very soon. I was a little sad because I knew the American lawyers would be leaving the next day.

Before my mother went home the day before, she told me she had sold the last cow. We had no more animals and no more money. I didn't know how my family could afford school fees for me and Joseph. We had been out of school for twenty months. I didn't know if we would even be allowed back at school. But God had answered our prayers and brought the American lawyers, so I prayed very hard that God would find a way for us to go back to school.

CHAPTER 13
DEPARTURE

ADRENALINE ADEQUATELY ATONED for our sleep deficit, at least in the short term. Whenever I reminded myself how I would feel if these were my kids in prison, I felt a surge of energy and determination. At the risk of sounding self-congratulatory, we fully understood the kids needed our help more than we needed sleep.

We reassembled the war room inside the hotel's restaurant before breakfast and resumed our feverish pace at 7:00 a.m. Because Napier needed to mediate a case in Kampala that afternoon, his driver picked him up at 10:30. We promised to join him for a dinner meeting he had scheduled for that evening. Niemeyer also had to get back to Restore in Gulu to prepare for the beginning of the next term. He had impressed us with his intellect and initiative over the previous four days, so I asked him before he left if he'd ever thought about going to law school.

He laughed. "Bob keeps telling me I should, but I don't know. I love it here and want to finish some ongoing projects before I even think about leaving."

"Understood, but rest assured there's a place for you at Pepperdine if you decide to become a lawyer," I said.

We finally finished at 3:00 p.m., having printed out four sets of briefs—one for the court, one for the children's lawyers, one for the prosecution, and one for us. After some reflection, we decided that because the prosecutor's office had been less than helpful, we would keep its copy for ourselves.

En route to Ihungu, we dropped off the copies for the court and the lawyers and stopped in town to buy the children some supplies. We split up, determined to purchase whatever any of us thought they could use.

The town was little more than a patchwork of small store fronts along the main road and three or four side streets. There was a bookstore with a few hundred offerings, a handful of clothing stores selling both new and used items, a mobile phone shop that not only sold phones but also charged phone batteries for a small fee, two fuel stations, a few restaurants, and a smattering of variously sized convenience stores. Some were no larger than a counter, while others were the size of a small 7-Eleven. They all sold the same items—water, bread, rice, locally grown fruits and vegetables, an assortment of canned goods, prepackaged snack foods, soap, toilet paper, school supplies, and mobile phone airtime.

Twenty minutes later, we reconvened with our arms full of loot. We had colored pencils, paper pads, a new calendar to replace the 2005 edition hanging in the custody, four children's books, a world atlas, various kinds of food, masking tape for posting their pictures on the wall, and a few other odds and ends. I also bought some airtime for Henry's phone. As in most of Europe, mobile phones in Africa don't have monthly calling plans. Instead, the user keys into the phone a series of numbers from scratch-off cards to add minutes.

When we finally pulled in at 4:00 p.m.—four hours later than we had planned—the prisoners and Mr. William were outside waiting for us. They watched wide-eyed as we laid out the parting gifts. Henry stood with us and translated.

Ray led off, showing them an example of the briefs we'd prepared on their behalf. He explained what the brief contained, who would receive copies, and that we hoped the briefs would help them get released. They clapped excitedly when Henry translated "released."

I went next, presenting them with the food and supplies from town. The colored pencils and paper registered the most excitement. We'd also emptied our backpacks of anything we didn't need on our return journey. I left a Ugandan guidebook containing a comprehensive history of the country and some colorful Post-its. They'd never seen Post-its before and had fun sticking them on each other.

Then came the moment for which they'd been anxiously waiting. David called them up one by one to present them with their photographs. Each child received two pictures—one of just them and one of the entire group. As each came forward, the others raucously cheered as if they were receiving diplomas. They laughed, pointed, and strained to see the pictures as the recipient sat down. Jay captured it all on film.

As we readied to leave, Henry asked the children to sing us a song. The simplicity of the tune and the poignancy of its lyrics penetrated us to the marrow. The first verse was in Swahili; the next two were in English:

Let the Spirit of the Lord come down
Let the Spirit of the Lord come down
Let the Spirit of the Lord, from heaven come down
Let the Spirit of the Lord come down

Let the Angels of the Lord come down
Let the Angels of the Lord come down
Let the Angels of the Lord, from heaven come down
Let the Angels of the Lord come down

Their swaying and clapping matched the rhythm of the song. Their mouths may not have known the meaning of their words, but their souls certainly did.

So did ours.

As the others readied to leave, I pulled Henry aside to say good-bye and to pose a burning question.

JANUARY 14, 2010

Before the American lawyers left, Jim asked me to take a walk with him. He gave me airtime cards and said he was proud of me for taking care of the others. He said John Niemeyer worked in Gulu at a very good Christian school. He asked if Joseph and I would want to go to that school after we were released. I was so happy I could hardly speak. I could not believe I might have the chance to go to school again.

I told Jim we definitely wanted to attend. Jim stopped walking and looked at me. He said, "I promise you, Henry, I will do whatever I can to get you and Joseph out of here and into school. I cannot promise it will happen in time for you start in February when the new term begins, but I will try."

I was very happy and believed what he told me.

After the lawyers left, the others were all very happy because they thought they would be going home very soon. We taped our pictures to the wall above where we slept, and I put a group picture above the custody's entrance. After a few days, the walls were covered with drawings we had made with the colored pencils and paper.

As we pulled onto the main road to Kampala, no one said a word. We'd been in Africa less than a week, had more than a month's worth of experiences, and would have a lifetime to reflect on them. I doubted that would be long enough. The mood remained somber for most of the way. After about two hours, a few stray words turned into small talk, which gradually morphed into a hearty conversation as we began processing all that had happened.

Over dinner, Napier introduced us to Mike Chibita, who was then the president of the Uganda Christian Lawyers Fraternity. Mike described UCLF, and we summarized our efforts in Masindi. This dinner conversation planted a seed that would eventually grow into a substantial tree.

That night I slept like a hibernating bear.

✱   ✱   ✱

Uganda's annual judicial conference is timed to coincide with the Law Day celebration marking the beginning of each new judicial year. This celebration takes place on the lawn attached to the main courthouse and involves numerous speeches, police and military parades, and traditional music and dancing. After this kickoff event the next day, we were invited to a reception for the judges. We stood out like sore thumbs, and not only because we were the only mzungus; we were the only attendees not draped in the traditional colorful robes or wearing British wigs.

On the off chance we'd run into Masindi High Court justice Ralph Ochan, we carried with us the copies of the twenty-two briefs we'd originally earmarked for the prosecution. Justice Kiryabwire, with whom we'd met before traveling to Masindi, spotted us immediately. "How was the trip, guys? Were you able to do what you intended?"

"It went great," Napier responded as he handed over the folder. "We finished up the briefs for each of the children."

Justice K's eyes widened as he leafed through them. "These will be *very* helpful to Justice Ochan."

Scanning the room of about fifty, he fixed on a short, wise-looking man with glasses. "Ah, there he is. Let me introduce you."

As Justice K approached him, he said, "Justice Ochan, my friend, please greet some of our friends from Pepperdine."

"I am delighted to meet you," Justice Ochan said as he adjusted his glasses and extended his hand.

We exchanged hearty Ugandan friendship handshakes.

He noticed our attempts to embrace this aspect of Ugandan culture. "I see you are finding Uganda agreeable. How was your time in Masindi? I hope you were able to meet with the children."

Justice K responded, "They were, and they have prepared briefs for each of the prisoners. Here, take a look."

"These are beautiful!" he exclaimed.

"We left a complete set of them for you with your assistant," Ray said, "but you can keep these also if you'd like."

"Splendid. I will read them on my way back to Masindi." He looked directly at each of us and said with obvious sincerity, "Thank you for coming to Uganda to help our children. I regret our system was not able to process them more quickly, but I am grateful to you for showing us the way."

During the reception, which thankfully took place indoors, the skies opened up like I'd never seen before. Had it rained that hard on Noah, forty days would have been thirty-nine more than necessary.

That afternoon, Justice K escorted us to the chambers of the Chief Justice of the Ugandan Supreme Court. We had met and briefly chatted with Chief Justice Odoki at the reception, and he'd invited us to stop by that afternoon to tell him more about our time in Masindi. He listened with keen interest as we briefed him about our work.

"Your dean came to visit me here last year," he said. "I want to pay my friend the same courtesy. When should I come to Pepperdine? I want to meet your faculty and talk to more of your students. Geoffrey has been to Pepperdine, and he will come with me," he said, gesturing toward Justice K. Within a few minutes, we'd settled on September of 2010.

We also stopped by to thank the Principal Judge for his assistance in making the Masindi Project possible—the letter he wrote had cleared the way for our visit and had narrowly averted a trip cancellation.

Our final stop was at the chambers of Justice Lugayizi, who served as the head of the High Court's Criminal Division, reporting directly to the Principal Judge. He greeted us warmly and expressed his love for Pepperdine.

"I have had two wonderful sets of Pepperdine interns. They are like family to me now. In fact, earlier this week, I presented a report at the

Jim and his children, Jennifer, Joshua, and Jessica, on Europa Point in 2008.

The boys' custody at the Ihungu Remand Home.

PHOTO BY JAY MILBRANDT

Jim with Henry and his brother Joseph just after meeting them in January 2010.

Henry translating for Jim while interviewing one of the boys at Ihungu.

PHOTO BY JAY MILBRANDT

Jim and David meet Henry and Joseph's mother at Ihungu.

PHOTO BY JAY MILBRANDT

Working late at night preparing summary briefs in the hotel war room.

PHOTO BY JAY MILBRANDT

Jim celebrating a goal during the soccer match at the remand home.

PHOTO BY JAY MILBRANDT

Preparing summary briefs in the hotel war room.

PHOTO BY JAY MILBRANDT

With the work complete at the remand home, the lawyers say goodbye before heading to Kampala for their flight home.

PHOTO BY JAY MILBRANDT

Inside the boys' custody at Ihungu.

PHOTO BY JAY MILBRANDT

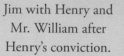

Jim with Henry and Mr. William after Henry's conviction.

Celebrating Henry's graduation from Restore Leadership Academy with his family.

Surprising Henry's family with the cattle delivery.

Unloading cows that were purchased for Henry's family.

Jim with the cow named after him: Big Jim.

The Gashes and
their "twin family,"
the Gregstons.

Jessica beginning
her medical career
after overcoming her
crippling fear of needles.

Joshua and Jennifer
registering patients and
dispensing medications.

Jim and his wife, Joline, on Henry's first day of school at Martyrs.

Henry returns to Ihungu in 2012 to encourage the prisoners there.

Bob Goff presents Jim with one of the Ihungu Remand Home doors (with Jay Milbrandt and John Niemeyer); the other door is in Bob's office.

At the court of appeals for Henry's hearing in March 2013, with Ugandan lawyer Edward Sekabanja, who assisted Jim.

Ugandan judges with U.S. District Judge Beverly Reid O'Connell (4th from right) during a 2013 plea bargaining study tour in the United States.

Launching plea bargaining at Luzira Maximum Security Prison in 2014.

Judicial Conference about bringing plea bargaining to Uganda. The report your interns wrote last year started this process moving. The Chief Justice is reviewing the report, and I hope he will approve it so we can begin. It takes far too long for those arrested to get to court. Plea bargaining can be very helpful."

At dinner that night, the waitress asked us if we were all brothers. We roared with laughter, thinking she was joking. But with a perfectly straight face, she declared, "I have a hard time telling you apart; mzungus all look the same to me." We laughed some more but gained a new perspective on what it's like to be a "minority" in a community.

The next morning, Jay and I took a one-hour flight to Rwanda for the final leg of our African adventure while David and Ray flew home. Never one to shy away from making new friends, Jay had simply written to the top leaders of Rwanda and requested a meeting with them.

Over the next several days, Jay and I met with the Deputy Chief Justice of the Supreme Court, the Minister of Justice, and President Paul Kagame to discuss possible future collaboration.

When we finally landed in Los Angeles, I switched on my cell phone for the first time in more than two weeks. I had several voice mails, the last of which caught me completely off guard.

"Hello, this is Henry. I hope you had a safe journey. Thank you for coming. Good-bye."

Henry's voice mail brought a tear to my eyes and a yearning to my heart.

The next day, Henry and I opened the next chapter of our relationship—the weekly international phone calls.

PART
THREE

CHAPTER 14
WAITING FOR JUSTICE

"HELLO. WHO IS CALLING, PLEASE?"

"Hello, Henry, this is Jim. From America."

"Oh, hello! Are you home now? How was your journey? Hello?"

It took a few minutes, but eventually we got used to the one-second delay between the speaking and the hearing on our international call.

"How is everyone?" I asked.

"Not very okay. I am in the hospital now."

"Are you hurt?" My mind raced. *Did the villagers come to Ihungu and attack Henry? How badly is he injured?*

"I am fine. It is Joseph. He has malaria. They gave him some tablets, and I think he will be okay soon. Please pray for him."

While I was relieved Henry wasn't hurt, I knew tens of thousands of Ugandans die from malaria every year, though mostly children and the elderly. "How are the others?"

"They are very okay. We play soccer every day, and they are drawing many pictures with the pencils and paper you gave us. The custody walls are almost full. They are very happy."

I was thrilled, hoping this meant the young people there no longer felt anonymous and forgotten.

After a pause, Henry tentatively asked, "When are you coming back?"

I reminded him that while I would not be coming back for the court hearings, Niemeyer would be checking in regularly to ensure things proceeded according to plan. I promised I would call him every week until he gained his freedom.

After I hung up, I leaned back in my chair and wished I could be there at Ihungu to see what the kids had drawn, how they were expressing what had welled up inside of them over the long and lonely months they'd spent in prison. Once again, I realized how much I took for granted the opportunity I had to see my children's art projects through the years and resolved to give them each an extra-long hug that evening. I also pondered the real answer to Henry's direct question at the end of the call: *When am I going back to Africa?*

I'd surrendered control and taken a step in faith beyond my comfort zone—and nothing had gone terribly wrong. But I wanted to settle back into my comfortable life again for a while before I thought about any return trips. I'd decided Henry and Joseph were my starfish, and two were plenty for now.

Yet I couldn't deny that, deep down, I felt something stirring that I couldn't fully explain and wasn't ready to acknowledge.

JANUARY 20, 2010

When I came to Ihungu, I wanted to continue studying, but there was no school for us. After I became Katikkiro, Joseph and I tried to start a school for the prisoners with some workbooks Mr. William and a boy who lives near Ihungu gave us. But because we had to work so much for Rose, it never got started.

After the Americans went home, we started the school. We divided the prisoners into three groups. I taught nursery school to the ones who did not know how to read and write. I wrote in English on one side of the board and in Swahili on the other side. They all learned to write their names, and they were so happy to be in school.

Joseph taught the children who had completed P1 to P5. He

taught them how to read better and to write in English. Many of Joseph's students tried to read the storybooks the Americans gave us, and some were able to read them a little.

I also taught those who had completed P6 to S1. I taught them math, English, and science from nine in the morning until midday. After lunch, Joseph taught until it was time to play soccer at five. We told the children they should try to speak only in English at Ihungu until they were released. Some tried, but most continued speaking in Swahili.

We made report cards for them so they would know they were making progress in their studies. The children liked their report cards very much.

✷ ✷ ✷

"I have some good news for you," I said, barely able to contain my excitement the following Friday.

"For me? What news?" Henry asked.

"I talked to Niemeyer, and everything is set for you to attend the Restore Leadership Academy when you are released. You are now officially a student at Restore!"

"That is fantastic! I am praising God," he said jubilantly. After a beat, he added, "And maybe Joseph too?"

"Of course Joseph too. You will be in Senior Three, and Joseph will be in Senior One. The school term begins next week, but Niemeyer said you can join once you get released, whenever that happens."

Henry was so excited and grateful. He also explained to me that Mr. William had told him the court hearings would begin the following Friday. He expressed confidence that many of the children would be released soon after going to court. "I think maybe I will be among them and can start school at Restore in two weeks, maybe three."

I didn't want to dampen his enthusiasm, but I felt I needed to help him manage his expectations. I told him it would likely be several weeks before his case was actually heard.

A couple days later, Bob told me Niemeyer would be in Masindi the next week when the hearings began. Everything seemed to be coming together as planned.

✳ ✳ ✳

"Bad news," Niemeyer said the next week. "I met with Justice Ochan and the registrar yesterday, and things are on hold. Justice Ochan's schedule doesn't permit him to begin hearing the capital cases until March 1 at the earliest. His docket is full until then."

"Does Henry know about this one-month delay?" I asked.

Niemeyer didn't think so, but he assured me he would hold spots for Henry and Joseph at Restore.

"At some point, though," he cautioned, "they will have missed too much school to start this term."

He was right, of course, but because they were arrested during the second term two years ago, it wouldn't be so bad if they had to start at the beginning of the second term rather than picking up in the middle of the first.

"I have some good news to report," Niemeyer continued. "William has located relatives willing to take in several of the children who told us they had nowhere to go once they were released. There are only two left to place, and I have some leads I'm pursuing for them."

✳ ✳ ✳

The phone rang six or seven times the next day before Henry finally answered. He was panting. "We were playing soccer when you called. Bo heard my phone ringing and brought it to me. He sends his greetings to you."

"That's nice. Please greet him for me, Henry."

"He is here, listening to me talk to you. They are all here. They gather around me whenever you call. They send their greetings."

William hadn't yet informed Henry of the delay, so I caught him up on my call with Niemeyer. While clearly disappointed, he took it in stride and remained in good spirits. I wondered, though, whether he was merely putting on a brave face for the others. He was their leader and knew they took their cues from him. He told me they would "pray hard" that many would be released on Monday when those with noncapital cases went to the Magistrate Court.

And that's precisely what happened. The prison gates opened, and several captives were set free.

Over the course of the week, five boys accused of petty offenses were released and went home to their families. Some were found innocent, while others pled guilty and were sentenced to the time they'd already served.

FEBRUARY 8, 2010

Everyone was happy when five boys went home on Saturday; the others were sure they would be going home soon also. We had finished eating our lunch outside on Sunday when two men arrived on a motorcycle. I recognized one of them. He was the father of Innocent. He had come to Ihungu to talk to Rose two days after Innocent died. He was very angry then.

Mr. William was not around, and no adults had replaced Rose at Ihungu after she was arrested. I tried to call Mr. William, but he did not answer his phone.

The two men asked a boy where the Katikkiro was, and the boy pointed to me. Innocent's father said he and the other man needed to talk to me alone. He was very angry, and I was afraid. They grabbed my arms and took me behind the custody. Innocent's father said I needed to sign the document he was holding. He told me it said Rose and I had beaten Innocent to death. I said this was not true, and I refused to sign. This made him angrier, and he said he would make me sign.

I tried to get away, but the two men were bigger and stronger than me. So I asked if they had a pen I could use. When one of them let go to get the pen, I twisted away from the other and ran as fast as I could away from the main road into the trees behind Ihungu. I ran for several minutes before checking if they followed me. I did not see them. I stayed hidden for five hours. When it got dark, I came back to the custody. The others told me the men had tried to follow me but gave up and left.

That night I called Mr. William and told him what had happened. He said he would talk to the police and try to make sure they did not come to Ihungu when he was not around. He said to run away again if they came back.

A few days later, while Henry was telling me about the incident with Innocent's father, he paused mid-sentence. I could hear yelling in the background and then his heavy breathing . . . like Henry was running.

"Are you okay?" I shouted.

After an agonizing delay, he whispered, "This is not good."

"*What* is not good?" I frantically asked.

"Innocent's father is here again. I must go."

The line went dead.

My heart galloped as I weighed my options. I couldn't call him back because I didn't want his phone to ring if he was hiding. I could call Niemeyer, but he was several hours away in Gulu. I knew Henry would call Mr. William when it was safe to do so. There was nothing to do but pray even more frequently and fervently than I had before. I also e-mailed the rest of the team, with a copy to my wife, Joline, and urged them to double their prayers because of the increasing risk Innocent's father would take the law into his own hands.

I called Henry every day for several days. Each time that my call went unanswered, my fear barometer rose.

I breathed a huge sigh of relief when Henry finally answered four days later. The battery on his phone had died, and he hadn't been able to get it recharged until that day. He recounted that shortly after Innocent's father had arrived at Ihungu, so had Mr. William, who convinced the man to leave without incident. Henry had run away and watched from a distance. Innocent's father hadn't been back since.

The High Court session remained on schedule to begin the following Monday, March 1. But Henry was due in court the prior Friday in conjunction with the second case.

"I think maybe they will not proceed against me," he said. "I heard on the radio last night that the police had completed their investigation of Innocent's death and concluded Rose was responsible. I was not mentioned." I hoped he was right.

But on Friday, Henry was officially charged with murder. The consolidated case against both Rose and Henry was then added to the coming Monday's High Court session. While I'd prayed for an outright dismissal, I hadn't allowed myself to expect it, and was glad the case would move forward without delay, rather than being scheduled for the next adult court session, whenever that might be.

What Henry told me next, however, plunged me into a state of grave concern. "Mr. William told me my lawyer said I should plead guilty."

"Wait, why would your lawyer suggest that?" I asked in disbelief.

"Mr. William said that if I plead guilty, I will probably be released like the other juveniles."

I was shocked at the terrible advice these men were giving him. "Henry, it is important you understand what I'm about to tell you. The juveniles who have been released were charged with *noncapital* offenses. Under Ugandan law, the longest sentence they can receive is one year.

Many of them have already spent a year at Ihungu. You're charged with a *capital* offense. The longest sentence you can receive as a juvenile is three years. Do you understand?"

"Yes, I understand."

"If you plead guilty to murdering Innocent, you will most certainly *not* be released that day and you'll be a sitting duck for anyone who wants revenge, including Innocent's father."

"I will be a what?"

Apparently ducks don't sit in Uganda. We talked for a few more minutes about how a murder conviction would affect his future and how important it was to be completely honest with the court. He said he understood, and I trusted he did. He said he never intended to plead guilty but wanted me to know what his lawyer said.

On Sunday, February 28, the day before the hearing, I called Henry and reminded him not to plead guilty and told him I'd be praying for him. That night, when Joline and I tucked in our three kids for bed, each of them prayed for Henry.

MARCH 1, 2010

On Monday, Joseph and I were brought to court and taken to a room with adult prisoners. We were surprised and very happy to see my father there. We had not seen him for almost two years. He was smiling very big and was very happy to see us. He told us he was proud of us for being strong. I told him lawyers from America had come to Ihungu to help us and that I talked to one of them every week.

I told my lawyer before going into court I was not guilty and would not plead guilty. He said he understood and did not try to change my mind. When the judge called the case against Rose and me, I found out my lawyer was also Rose's lawyer. He told the judge we were both pleading "not guilty." The judge told us the trial would start three days later, on Thursday.

When the judge called the case against Joseph and my father and me, I found out my father had a different lawyer than we did. The lawyers told the judge we were pleading not guilty. The judge said the trial would begin the next week.

On one hand, I was relieved to learn nothing had gone wrong in court. I was also gratified that Ugandan criminal procedure required consolidation of cases when adults and juveniles are charged together in capital cases. This allowed Henry's father to be tried alongside his sons. Absent consolidation, their father would've most likely languished for another three to five years in jail before his trial.

On the other hand, when I learned that Henry and Rose shared a lawyer, it set off alarm bells in my head. Rose would very likely blame Henry for the events preceding Innocent's death. For his part, Henry would want the truth to come out—that the punishment Innocent received had been directly ordered by Rose. This divergence, of course, created a serious conflict of interest for the attorney, who would be unable to fully represent the interests of both clients.

"Have any of the juveniles at Ihungu been asked to testify?" I queried.

"I don't think so. No lawyers have come to Ihungu to meet with them. They would all tell the truth, though. I am not afraid of them testifying."

As we hung up, an urge to catch the next plane to Uganda rose up in me like a sudden fever. I solicited the thoughts of the team at the end of my customary e-mail summary that I sent after every phone call with Henry. My wise and supportive wife responded right away:

Part of me feels that if you are going to return to Uganda, now is the time to go. I don't know what the rest of the [Pepperdine] dean's suite thinks, but if they are in favor of you going, then you should. On the other hand, if the Uganda Johns

[Niemeyer and Napier] can help Henry and his family with his hearings, then perhaps you do not need to go right now. I will help you do whatever God is leading you to do. I am praying about it.

Ray responded next:

Hey Jim, . . . I would like to be there as well, and if I were in a different place with my personal life, I would. The process is not complete so it is hard to have faith in it—perhaps the best we can do is have hope. The things that hold you back from going were also impediments in January, but you were guided to make the journey all the same. You are so right, God hears our prayers, but He also guides us in our actions. . . . Look . . . to your heart and to your prayers and God will guide you to where you can do the most good in His name, next week and beyond.

Niemeyer soon also chimed in, expressing confidence that things were under control. Justice Ochan had opened the court session by declaring he wanted both justice to be served and righteousness to be restored in each child. Niemeyer also relayed that the headmaster would be available to testify that Henry and Joseph had been in school when the mob killing happened. Finally, Niemeyer passed along that the prosecutor was considering reducing the charges against Henry and Rose to manslaughter because the postmortem failed to attribute Innocent's death to the strokes on his buttocks. In closing, he offered:

Jim, I'm trusting the system will ensure justice is restored. But that isn't to deter you from jumping on a plane! I agree with Ray. I'll keep you in prayer, as well as all the juveniles waiting for their trial.

Niemeyer's e-mail helped convince me to stay home, at least for the moment. I copied the rest of the team on my response to him:

Receiving your e-mail has lifted me so much and is a rather quick answer to prayer. I can see (through your eyes on the ground) that Justice Ochan is proactively making sure that these kids will be treated justly and fairly. I can also see that the kids have real lawyers who are reading what we have prepared and are thinking through the proper arguments and defenses. It is so hard to let go and let God work through those in Uganda to ensure that justice is done. It is time for me to trust.

✳ ✳ ✳

The advice from others and the leading from God not to return to Uganda were powerfully confirmed. Had I gone, I couldn't have stayed long enough for the events to unfold, and I couldn't have changed what was about to happen.

I'm not sure how well I would have weathered the coming storm had I been there in person.

CHAPTER 15
TRIALS

"COME WITH ME," Henry's father whispered insistently as he ushered his son away from the dozen other prisoners in the Masindi courthouse holding cell and into a private corner. Henry had just arrived for the start of the trial against him and Rose.

After confirming that others weren't listening, he said gravely, "There is a problem, son. One hour ago, a man came in here to talk to one of the prisoners. I was lying down nearby and heard what they said. They thought I was asleep and didn't know I was your father."

He paused and glanced over Henry's shoulder, making sure their conversation remained private. Deep concern creased his face. "The visitor told the prisoner he was Rose's son."

Henry's eyes widened. *Why would Rose's son come here, and who was he talking to?*

"He told the prisoner he would pay him 100,000 shillings if he would testify Rose did not hit the boy who died and did not tell anyone to beat him. He said, 'You must say it was the Katikkiro who beat him and that Rose tried to stop him.'"

Henry stared in disbelief. *Who could it possibly be?* He narrowed his eyes and nodded to his father to continue.

"The prisoner agreed to say that in court if he was given the money. And then I saw him receive the money *right here in the cell.*"

"But none of that is true!" Henry whispered. "Who is the one who took the bribe?"

"Do not turn around now, but he is the younger one with the shaved head closest to the door. Do you know him?"

A few moments later, Henry turned and scanned the room. It was Simeon, the boy who had arrived at Ihungu with Innocent. He was also one of the four Rose had ordered to give Innocent ten strokes right before he died. Simeon had left Ihungu a few days later with Mr. William and hadn't returned. Henry had assumed he'd been released. But Simeon's yellow prison uniform, the same as Henry's father, meant that Simeon had been transferred to the adult prison instead.

This first day of trial was off to a rough start.

✸ ✸ ✸

Everyone stood as Justice Ochan entered the courtroom. In front of him sat a stack of blank paper that would soon become the official trial record.[3] His bodyguard slid the judge's chair in for him as he gestured for the courtroom to be seated.

He picked up a pen resting on the indictment. "The first matter for today, Thursday, the fourth day of March, 2010, is *Uganda v. Mpairwe Rose and Tumusiime Henry*. We have in place two assessors to advise me during this trial. Is the prosecution prepared to proceed?"

The robed lawyer sitting opposite Henry, Rose, and their lawyer stood. "Yes, My Lord."

The trial officially commenced with the prosecution's introduction into evidence of two Police Form 24s—one for Rose and one for Henry.

✸ ✸ ✸

The scarcity of birth records in Uganda, particularly outside Kampala, compels the Ugandan legal system to rely upon other means of age identification. On occasion, the outcome of a case is dependent upon this detail, as different punishments apply depending upon the age of the accused or the victim.

Adults are punished much more severely than juveniles. For example, if an adult is convicted of murder, the maximum penalty is death. But if the accused is under eighteen, the maximum penalty is three years. Consequently, Ugandan police doctors routinely examine those they arrest to ascertain their age and general fitness level. These exams include a variety of measurements, but they pay particular attention to the teeth. Apparently some change in the back teeth at around age eighteen enables a doctor to determine with some level of confidence whether the accused is a juvenile or adult in the eyes of the law. After the examination, the doctor completes and submits a document to the court called a "Police Form 24."

✷　✷　✷

Rose's PF 24 declared her to be "approximately 40" years old, while Henry's, dated December 9, 2009, declared him to be "about 17." In fact, Henry was to turn seventeen three months later.

"Our first witness is Okot Simeon," the prosecutor announced.

Henry's heart sank like a heavy stone in a deep well. He wanted to object. He wanted to tell the judge about the bribe. He wanted to tell the judge that just before Simeon left Ihungu, he stole from under Henry's mat 80,000 shillings Henry had earned by selling the pig Rose allowed him to raise. He took comfort in knowing he would later have his own chance to tell what really happened.

Simeon testified he was eighteen years old and in jail on theft charges. Prior to his arrest, he'd lived in the same village as his friend Innocent. Simeon further stated that on the day before he died, Innocent had been partially buried by another boy, not Henry, because he was working too slowly. A little while later, Rose permitted Innocent, who was crying, to be uncovered so he could resume work.

So far, so good, Henry thought.

The next day, Simeon said, the prisoners were taken back to the same farm. When Innocent tried to escape, Rose sent Henry and another boy to bring him back. Then, according to Simeon, Henry and the other boy gave Innocent multiple strokes with sticks as Rose tried to stop them. Henry wanted to protest, but he remained quiet.

After the punishment, testified Simeon, Innocent rested under the shade of a mango tree until another boy found him near death.

On cross-examination, Simeon admitted he was moved to the adult prison when it was revealed he'd lied about being under eighteen. Henry's lawyer did not, however, confront Simeon about his involvement in Innocent's punishment, even though Henry had told him what had really happened.

Next, a sixteen-year-old girl testified that she lived near the farm where Innocent died. She said she heard Rose order Henry to punish those who were falling behind, and when Innocent refused to continue working, she told Henry to beat the "dog." She also said she saw Rose beat Innocent herself and order another boy to dig a trench and place him in it. Finally, she testified that Rose told Henry to remove Innocent from the trench. The girl also clarified that she hadn't been present the day Innocent died.

MARCH 4, 2010

I had never seen a real trial happen before, so I didn't know what to expect. Before we went into court, my lawyer told me not to say any-thing out loud unless he or the judge asked me a question. I thought I was going to be sitting with my lawyer, but when I was taken into court, I was told to stand on the side of the courtroom away from my lawyer in a place the guard called "the dock."

Rose was already standing in this area that was surrounded on three sides by wooden walls as high as my shoulders. I tried to make eye contact with Rose, but she wouldn't even look at me. I wanted to ask her why her son was paying Simeon to lie, but my lawyer told me to keep quiet, so I did.

When Simeon came in to court to testify, he didn't look at me either from where he stood on the opposite side of the courtroom. I wondered whether I would be standing next to Rose when it was my turn to testify, or whether I would be standing where Simeon was standing. When Simeon said that Rose tried to stop Innocent from being punished, Rose smiled and nodded. I kept saying, That is not true, that is not true *in my mind, but I remembered that my lawyer had told me not to say anything. It was very difficult to remain quiet, but I did.*

When there was a break, I tried to get alone with my lawyer, but Rose was always there also, so I didn't have a chance to tell him Simeon was bribed by Rose's son on this day.

Once the trial started, Henry and I talked daily. After the first day, he was quite frustrated and disappointed. I was livid when he told me about the bribe.

"Did your lawyer ask Simeon any questions?"

"Not many."

"Did your lawyer call any witnesses of his own?"

"No. He said the prosecution has not completed its case yet. He said he will decide if he will call witnesses when the prosecution is finished."

"*If* he will call witnesses? He *needs* to call Joseph, Jamil, and several others."

"Okay, he told me he cannot call the other juveniles who were there because that would be bad for Rose." A mixture of confusion and frustration coated Henry's voice.

That is precisely why the lawyer's conflict of interest is beyond intolerable, I thought. I was enraged, but didn't want to alarm Henry.

"My lawyer is sure the charges will be dismissed when the prosecution is finished. He does not think he will have to call witnesses."

"What makes him so sure?"

"He says the postmortem does not show Innocent died from the strokes he received."

I was familiar with this Grand Canyon–sized gap in the prosecution's case and was somewhat heartened to hear Henry's lawyer was reading the summary brief I'd prepared on Henry's behalf, featuring this point front and center.

"Does the trial resume tomorrow?"

"No, it will continue next Friday."

"Wait, I thought the case against you, Joseph, and your father starts next Thursday."

"Yes, that is true. The case against Bo and his brother Derrick is fixed for next Thursday as well. Nakunda is not pleading guilty to killing her baby, so her trial is fixed for the Tuesday after that."

This sort of docket management initially baffled me, but I later learned that cases were overlapped to minimize downtime when witnesses fail to appear, which happens quite frequently.

The next Thursday, the case against Henry, Joseph, and their father was postponed another week. The murder trial of Bo and Derrick for allegedly poisoning their father, however, did get underway that day, as did the case against Abdul.

When the trial resumed against Rose and Henry, the prosecution's next witness added little. He was a local villager who said he saw Rose hit Innocent with her umbrella after he was uncovered, and she then ordered him back to work. Like the girl who testified previously, he wasn't present the day Innocent died. Because the prosecution's two remaining witnesses weren't available that day, the trial was set to resume the following Friday.

After court, Henry's lawyer told him he didn't think it would be necessary for him to call any witnesses. While this was encouraging, this roller coaster of a trial was draining me emotionally and spiritually. I found myself losing patience with God, something I rarely allow myself to do.

An e-mail from David later that day, however, injected me with a potent dose of much-needed perspective:

Sixty-one days ago, we had never met these children, and they had never met us. Today, sixteen of twenty-one have had a trial. By my last count, eight have been released, maybe more. Of the remaining children that have had their trial, they are all sched-uled for sentencing next week. Some or all may be released at that time. Others may have more time to serve, but if so . . . the clock will be ticking toward a release date at a point that can't be too far in the future. The other five are all actively in trial with a judge that we know will be fair. Henry and Joseph have a place at Restore. . . . The ongoing process certainly is not without issues. . . . But, friends, what has happened during the last sixty days in Masindi, and what is continuing to happen, is nothing short of miraculous.

The following Tuesday, Magistrate Ojikhan released all five of the juveniles who appeared before him. The next day two more gained their freedom. The justice train was rolling in our direction and gathering speed. Henry's spirits were soaring, and mine were finally gaining some altitude.

When trial resumed on Friday, the prosecution called its final two witnesses—the doctor who performed the postmortem and the police officer who investigated Innocent's death.

The doctor testified he'd conducted the exam on Innocent's body the day after Innocent died. The body was in "fair nutrition" but appeared somewhat dehydrated and showed surface skin peelings on both buttocks indicative of caning. He also noted softness in the right rib cage but found no internal bleeding. He declared that the external injuries from caning couldn't explain the boy's death.

When pressed, he speculated that the softness in the victim's rib cage *might* have caused an injury to his liver, which *might* have led to internal bleeding, which in turn *might* have caused his death *if* accompanied by prolonged denial of food and water. The doctor conceded he hadn't opened the body to check for internal injuries because he lacked the equipment and expertise to do so. He also admitted he hadn't investigated whether any sickness or other condition could have caused or contributed to Innocent's death.

Finally, the investigating police officer testified that Rose told him Innocent had died from an asthma attack. He also said the villagers who lived near the farm had told him Rose ordered Henry to cane Innocent the day before he died.

After confirming that this concluded the prosecution's case, Justice Ochan asked Rose and Henry's lawyer if he had a motion he wanted to bring. Excitement filled Henry's chest as the man stood and addressed the courtroom. "My Lord, the prosecution has not satisfied the ingredients of murder. The witnesses called and the evidence offered falls short of the level required for the defense to have to present a case. I ask that the case be dismissed immediately and that the accused persons be released."

Is today the day? Henry wondered as he studied Justice Ochan's face. *Will the case be dismissed?*

Two minutes passed as Justice Ochan scribbled on the paper in front of him. Finally, he set down his pen and peered over his glasses at the defense lawyer. Henry held his breath and closed his eyes. "I will consider your motion and make my decision next Tuesday," said the judge. "We are adjourned for the day."

Ugandan phone network difficulties had prevented me from connecting with Henry the day before to see if the trial against him, Joseph, and their father had begun, so I was especially eager to speak with him Friday, after the trial against him and Rose resumed.

He answered on the first ring. I'd learned to detect Henry's mood within the first moments of a call.

"Hello, Mr. Jim. How are you, and how is your family?"

Excellent. It is good news.

"My family is okay, and I am fine," I said quickly. "How did it go today in court?"

"My lawyer said today went very well."

"Great, but how do *you* think it went?"

"Very okay. The doctor had problems answering the questions my lawyer asked. He did not know exactly how or why Innocent died."

"How did Justice Ochan react?"

"I could not tell, but he seems like he is seriously considering our request to dismiss the case. He said he will decide on Tuesday."

"That's great news. Did your other trial start yesterday?"

"No, it did not. After my father was brought to court with me and Joseph, the prosecution said he could not find any witnesses against us." The vindication and hope in his voice wrapped around me like a warm blanket on a frigid night.

A moment later, a rush of exhilaration overcame me as I realized what this meant: The nearly two-year nightmare might finally be over. Henry's mother and father could finally be reunited, and Joseph could resume school. And while I knew the dismissal of this first case wouldn't mean immediate freedom for Henry, it would constitute a giant step in that direction.

Caught up in the news, I momentarily forgot about the phone delay, and we talked over each other until I finally took a deep breath and said slowly, "Henry, was the case against you, Joseph, and your father dismissed?" My anticipation swelled like a water balloon hooked to a fire hydrant.

"No, it was not," he said.

Instant deflation.

"Justice Ochan was very angry with the prosecutor. He said we had been in prison for almost two years, and it was not fair to keep us there much longer. He threatened to dismiss the charges very soon if the prosecutor could not find any witnesses. I am praying very hard, and I know God will release us." Henry's patience and trust dwarfed mine.

"How are the others doing?" I ventured.

"They are all okay, but they were disappointed we didn't get to play soccer today."

"Why not?" I asked, fearing the ball had finally succumbed to the rocky playing surface.

He laughed. "Too many juveniles have been released. We didn't have enough to play a game."

How gratifying it was to know that before we came, the inmates had to substitute in and out because there were too many of them. Now there weren't enough even for a game. This was progress.

✽ ✽ ✽

Justice Ochan opened court Tuesday by reading his ruling on the motion to dismiss the case against Henry and Rose. Henry didn't understand or absorb what Justice Ochan said after his hopes were shattered by the word *denied.*

The judge had ruled the prosecution had produced sufficient evidence against both Rose and Henry for the murder trial to proceed. The clear implication, of course, was that they now needed to call witnesses in their defense or they'd likely be found guilty.

Justice Ochan then explained to the defendants their three options about testifying. First, they could choose to remain silent. Second, they could testify without taking an oath to tell the truth, without being cross-examined by anyone, and without being subject to perjury if they lied. Such unsworn testimony, however, would naturally not carry much weight with the assessors or the judge. And third, they could testify under oath, under penalty of perjury, but they would then be subject to cross-examination.

The flawed nature of this third option either went unnoticed or was simply ignored. If either Rose or Henry testified against the other, then the same lawyer eliciting the damning testimony from one client would be duty-bound to attack this testimony through cross-examination on behalf of the other client!

Justice Ochan adjourned the case for two days so Rose and Henry could discuss with their lawyer how they wished to proceed. But before doing so, Justice Ochan issued an additional, and wholly unexpected, order—one that sent shockwaves through the courtroom.

✶　✶　✶

"The judge said we have a case to answer," Henry said dejectedly once we got on the phone. Having read through Ugandan criminal procedure law, I knew this meant the case would proceed.

I chided myself for letting my guard down. Dismissing a case before the defense even put on evidence would be a slap to the prosecution and to the police. The judge's approach was prudent, and I should've expected it. *The charges could be dropped after the defense case*, I reasoned.

"Did you talk to your lawyer about who he'll be calling as witnesses?" I asked, trying to sound encouraging.

"A little. I told him I wanted to testify, but he said we would talk about it tomorrow."

"Okay, but what about Joseph or Jamil?"

"He hasn't even talked to them at all."

"Make sure you tell him they are available and want to testify."

"Okay." After a pause and a sigh, he added, "There is something else disturbing me. After Justice Ochan said we had to present a case, he made another order. He said I have to be examined again by a different doctor."

"Why? What's wrong?"

"I am okay. The doctor is supposed to examine me to determine if I am eighteen years old."

That bombshell caught me totally off guard and sent me into panic mode. *I need to get on a plane tonight!* was the first thought that raced into my mind, but I tried to remain calm and asked, "Did he say why?"

"He said something about what had been written in a police report in Hoima. He told the prosecution to bring him the new doctor's report before next Wednesday."

After a few confused moments, the full weight of reality trampled me. *What if the next doctor looks at his teeth and concludes he is eighteen? How accurate are these tests anyway? Would the local doctor be pressured, or even bribed, by Innocent's family to say Henry is eighteen? Would Henry be moved from Ihungu to the adult jail and have his phone confiscated? Would the trial be vacated and then start over at some much later date with Henry being charged as an adult?*

These questions and fears pinballed inside my head as we spoke. I couldn't shake the fear that Henry could be wrongly declared eighteen, convicted, and then sentenced to death. He didn't yet seem to grasp the seriousness of the situation, so I opted not to alarm him.

"I am not eighteen," he said with confidence. "I believe this doctor will say that in his report."

I prayed he was right.

★　★　★

Ugandan cell phone network outages again thwarted my repeated attempts to reach Henry later that week. I finally got ahold of him early Friday morning, March 26. It was evening his time, and two court days had passed since we last talked. I was a nervous wreck, and this was the wrong day for that.

Pepperdine's annual Admitted Students Open House was taking place that day at the law school. Two hundred prospective students were descending upon the campus for an entire day of immersion into the Pepperdine culture. They would meet the deans, tour the law school, attend a class, learn about student organizations, listen to panels of current students and faculty, and generally get a feel for what it's like at Pepperdine. As associate dean for Student Life, this was my show; I'd be on center stage the entire day. I needed to be on, and I needed to be focused.

But my call with Henry that morning liquefied me. There was no way this day would go according to plan. What Henry told me obliterated my ability to concentrate.

Ten minutes earlier, Henry was positively giddy when he answered, speaking like an over-caffeinated auctioneer. The voice delay, the accent, and the poor reception combined to render him totally unintelligible. I could tell, however, that whatever he was saying was good.

"Henry . . . Henry," I interrupted. "Start over. Did you meet with the doctor?"

"Yes, on Wednesday. He asked me questions and looked at my teeth with a machine."

"So his report is due next week, right?"

"No, he already decided. The prosecutor gave the report to the judge yesterday."

I sat up straight in my office chair and crammed the receiver so hard to my ear that it hurt. "What . . . did . . . it . . . say?"

"He said I am seventeen."

Praise God!

While this was indeed good news, it came as no surprise to Henry, who had celebrated his seventeenth birthday just over a week earlier. *So why is he so happy?*

"What else happened in court yesterday? Did you testify?"

"Me? No. But Rose did."

"What? Why did she testify but not you?"

"The day before yesterday my lawyer said I would not testify because Rose could be sentenced to death if she was found guilty. He said if I testified, I would be helping the prosecution convict her because I would say she beat Innocent and told others to do so also. He said if I was convicted, I would probably only have to remain one year in prison because he would ask the judge to remove the two years I had been at Ihungu."

This was so wrong on so many levels that I didn't even know where to start. First of all, Henry's lawyer owed a duty of loyalty to both Rose *and* Henry, and he was clearly throwing Henry under the matatu. Second, while the Children Act mandates the amount of time spent on remand "shall be taken into account" when a sentence is issued, it's not entirely clear whether the juvenile is entitled to a day-for-day credit. And third, Henry had only been in custody on *this* charge for three months. The time he spent on remand for the other charge would almost certainly *not* be considered.

I bit my tongue for the moment and asked whether Joseph and Jamil had testified.

"No. The lawyer said they would also help the prosecution against Rose, so he did not allow them."

My blood boiled, but this was not the appropriate time for me to vent. "Okay," I said as calmly as I could. "What did Rose say?"

"She said that on the day before Innocent died, he told her he could not work because of his asthma. She said she told him to sit and rest. She said villagers later told her some juveniles and I were burying Innocent and that she rescued him." I seethed, but neither erupted nor interrupted.

"She said the next day Innocent tried to escape and that Jamil and I caught him and beat him. But this was not true; I did *not* do what she said. She said that the farmer came and took him back to Ihungu on his motorcycle and that he later died."

"Did your lawyer cross-examine her?" I asked.

"Did he what?"

"Did he ask her questions? Did he ask if she ordered Innocent buried? Did he ask her if she hit him with an umbrella?"

"Oh, okay. No, he did not ask her any questions. The prosecutor did not ask her any questions either because her testimony was unsworn."

Having Rose testify unsworn prevented Henry's lawyer from acting on Henry's behalf by cross-examining her. This had to be intentional. So in a very real sense, Henry's own lawyer called a witness to the stand to testify against him, and he did so in a way that prevented the lawyer from protecting Henry's interests.

Outrageous.

I chastised myself for not insisting that Henry tell the judge he wanted his own lawyer and offering to pay for that lawyer myself. I had foolishly relied too heavily on Henry's reports that his lawyer was convinced he wouldn't be convicted.

"So what happened after Rose testified?" I asked.

"When Rose finished, my lawyer said he had no more witnesses."

The case was over. Justice Ochan ordered the lawyers to submit written summations the following Thursday.

As angry as I was about Henry being denied the opportunity to testify in his own defense, I was mystified by Henry's unmistakably buoyant mood. So I asked him, "Why are you so happy?"

MARCH 26, 2010

After Rose testified in court, my lawyer said he did not have any more witnesses. The judge said he would take a short break and then the case against me, Joseph, and my father would begin. Twenty minutes later, guards brought Joseph and my father into court and the judge came back. The lawyer for the prosecution stood up and told the judge that the prosecution would not continue with the case against us because there were no witnesses who said we were involved in killing the herdsman. Justice Ochan then said he was dismissing the case. We asked our lawyers what this meant, and they told us we were found not guilty and would be released the next day. We hugged each other hard, and we were very happy. We were so thankful to God for delivering us.

I knew I was not going to be released because of the other case, but I was so happy Joseph and my father could finally go home to be with my family.

That was it. Twenty-one months after being arrested, the initial charges were dropped.

Henry was barely able to contain his excitement as he told me, "Just before you called me, I talked to my mother. She said Joseph and my father have arrived home. The neighbors have organized a big party and they are celebrating right now. I am praising God for their release!"

Absent from Henry's voice was even a hint of resentment or despondency. His whole heart rejoiced that his brother and father had been reunited with his family, even while he still languished at Ihungu.

When he told me this news, I lost my breath and found myself unable to speak for quite some time. The emotions were so raw, tears streamed down my face. I rejoiced as I pictured Joseph and their father coming home after nearly two years of unjust confinement. But I also despaired as I pictured Henry now sitting at Ihungu, alone—without his brother and best friend by his side for the first time since June of 2008. Really for the first time in his life.

I marveled at Henry's undaunted courage as he trusted that God would also deliver him from his present condition. I had so much to learn from this boy.

The following Tuesday I called Henry to check in. He was again in excellent spirits and told me he'd spoken with his family the day before. Everyone was well.

"Joseph talked to John Niemeyer, and they decided it was too late to start at Restore this term. He will start there in the second term in May when I can go with him."

I loved his optimism and envied his confidence. "What about the others? Has anyone else been to court?"

"Yes, Nakunda has been to court. And she has accepted the charges against her."

I was dumbstruck. There was no way this girl killed her baby. *No way.* "How could this happen?" I finally managed.

"I think they changed the charges to illegal burial of a body or something," he said. That made much more sense, but I was still irritated they hadn't dropped the charges outright.

I then did something I'd steadfastly resisted doing up until that point—I allowed myself to dream with Henry. Previously, I'd hesitated to put any ideas into his head about what life could be like after Ihungu. But the emotional roller coaster we'd been riding together had weakened my resolve, so I told him everything I knew about the Restore Leadership Academy. We talked about what Kampala was like—he'd only visited once when he was in primary school—and we talked about my family, his family, and Bob Goff, the man whose vision and charisma had set our lives on a collision course.

We also dreamed about Henry coming to the United States. He laughed out loud when I told him about the modern world—computers, the Internet, electricity, television, microwave ovens, indoor plumbing, highways. He was particularly impressed I had a television that was bigger than he was, and he couldn't quite envision a movie theater.

As our conversation came to a close, he asked me to pass along his greetings and gratitude to all who'd helped free his brother and father. Then, before we hung up, he asked me the question that had been rising within me like boiling lava: "When are you coming back to Uganda?"

"That's a good question, Henry. I really don't know. I promise you someday I'll come back and see you. I'd love to meet your father. He's done an excellent job raising his sons."

Throughout the rest of the day, Henry's question periodically bubbled to the surface. When was I returning to Uganda?

Sooner than I expected. Much sooner.

CHAPTER 16
THE VERDICT

THREE SHARP RAPS on solid wood brought those in the courtroom to their feet. Justice Ochan's bodyguard scanned the room while he escorted the judge to the bench. To his right sat the lone remaining assessor; the other had been excused the prior week on account of illness.

When everyone was seated, Justice Ochan announced he would read his summary of the case for the assessor and then seek his guidance. Henry watched the assessor closely as Justice Ochan rehashed the testimony of each witness and explained the necessary elements of Uganda's murder law. The assessor's countenance and body language remained unchanged.

"I will take your advice into account, but it is my responsibility to make a final determination of guilt or innocence," the justice told the assessor. "What is your view? Should I find the accused persons innocent or guilty?"

Henry drew in a sharp breath and fixed a hopeful gaze on the assessor. Justice Ochan remained stoic as the assessor declared his opinion and underlying reasoning to everyone in the courtroom. He then thanked the assessor for his service and recommendation, turned to the prisoners, and asked them to stand.

Joline and I were enjoying a weeklong vacation for her fortieth birthday on the Caribbean island of St. Martin while our three kids spent spring break with their grandparents. Because Henry only had a cell phone, and because my cell phone didn't work where we were, I had to call Henry via Skype's voice call feature. I nervously typed Henry's phone number into my computer and clicked the Call Phone icon. My wife held my hand as we huddled next to my laptop. We'd just finished praying that this—the day before Joline's April 10 birthday—would be the day that Henry's nightmare would finally end.

I'd managed to connect with Henry two days earlier and had told him there were literally thousands of people praying for him that week. David, Jay, Ray, and I had friends and relatives around the country following the events as they unfolded, and because many of us had told our churches about the young prisoners in Uganda, an army was interceding on Henry's behalf. He'd been exceedingly grateful and had predicted he'd be released today. But when he answered, I could tell something was wrong.

"How did things go in court today?" I nervously asked. Joline squeezed my hand.

"Not good. Not good at all."

"What happened? Please start at the beginning," I said as I bowed my head, half in disappointment and half to get closer to my computer's speaker.

"The assessor said we are both guilty of murder."

This revelation knocked the wind out of me. I knew full well that assessors aren't like jurors in the United States—they don't have the power to convict, only to advise. Justice Ochan was free to disregard the recommendation. I also knew, however, that as the community's voice, the assessor's opinion was highly persuasive.

"What about Justice Ochan?" I pressed. "What was *his* verdict?"

But Henry had already begun speaking again, and my delayed

question stepped on his response, which caused him to stop speaking. "What?" he asked.

"Go ahead, go ahead, go ahead," I said, trying to assure him I wouldn't interrupt him again.

"Okay, okay," he finally said as my words reached him. "After the assessor spoke, Justice Ochan told us to stand. He said we had been found guilty by the assessor, but he was the one who had to decide if we were guilty of murder."

"So what did he decide?" I blurted without thinking.

"Justice Ochan said he would give us his decision two weeks from yesterday, on Thursday, April twenty-second."

Are you kidding me? We have to wait two more weeks? As torturous as the waiting was for me, I couldn't even imagine how this prolonged uncertainty was brutalizing Henry.

Though I had so many thoughts racing around in my head, I let Henry talk. "If the assessor thinks I am guilty, won't Justice Ochan agree? What is going to happen?"

This was the first time Henry expressed genuine fear about how it would all end. I considered reminding him how many people were praying for him, but I didn't want to give him a reason to question whether God was listening. Our prayers, after all, had been that Henry would be found innocent and immediately released. Instead, I focused on the legal aspects of the case. I reminded him Justice Ochan didn't have to agree with the assessor. "He's a lawyer and understands the legal rules. Assessors don't. He'll decide the case himself and won't be pressured into finding you guilty."

"That is what my lawyer said. But I am still afraid . . ." His voice trailed off, and it sounded like he had started to cry.

I'm afraid too, I thought, but I gave him my best pep talk and ultimately did remind him many people were praying for him.

After we hung up, I felt such grief. I walked out to the balcony of our third-floor vacation condo, not knowing how to release the pent-up emotions trying to force their way out. After giving me a few minutes alone, Joline silently joined me on the balcony. The contrast between my life and Henry's couldn't have been starker at that moment. I stood at the rail overlooking a pristine island bay with my wife. Henry sat in a windowless concrete prison alone.

Eventually, Joline took my hand.

"I don't know what to do," I said quietly as I slowly shook my head. "I should have been there today. I should have been with Henry when he received this news. Now what do I do?"

"If you need to go, you shouldn't hesitate. But this may be the time to be patient and trust that God is in control. I know it doesn't *feel* like He is, but you know that He is faithful. No matter what happens, He *is* faithful. God has sustained Henry for the past two years, and He will continue to do so."

I nodded slightly. She was right, of course. She always is. Her trust has always outpaced mine, but I had hoped I was catching up.

"Bob's going to Uganda next week, so he'll be there for the final verdict," she said. "Things are always crazy when Bob's around, but nothing seems to go wrong, right?" she added, half joking, half serious.

This made me grin, which cut through the tension. It was time to trust again.

My summary e-mail to the team ended with the following lamentation: "Even though this is not even remotely about me, I feel like God is teaching me patience and trust in an awfully painful way."

✷ ✷ ✷

Joline and I decided to send new Bibles for Henry and Joseph with Bob. I'd heard other prisoners at Ihungu call Henry "Hillary," and he'd typed "Hillary" on my computer when he'd given me his cell phone number. I wanted to make sure their names were inscribed on the front of their Bibles exactly how they would want them.

On our next call, Henry explained he actually has two names—Tumusiime Henry and Tumwesige Hillary. There'd been some disagreement between Henry's mother and father about his name, and so he'd used both over the years, which is not at all uncommon in Uganda.

When I asked him what he'd like me to call him, he responded, "I prefer Hillary, sir." From that point forward, I've called him Hillary, but for ease of understanding in this book, he will remain Henry here.

What he told me next spiked my blood pressure once again.

"Yesterday two men came to Ihungu and tried to make me sign a document. They said it was called a civil judgment. They said it would give Innocent's family money if Rose and I were found guilty."

"You didn't sign anything, did you?"

"No, I did not."

"Good. Did they try to hurt you?"

"No. They just wanted me to sign."

"Do you feel safe at Ihungu? Should I call Mr. William?"

"I am okay. Mr. William comes to Ihungu every day, and I told him about the visitors. He said they wanted him to sign papers also, but he refused too. I think I am okay here."

While less than convinced, I took comfort in knowing Bob would be there soon.

"My friend Bob is coming to Uganda next week. He started the Restore school you and Joseph will attend once you are released. He will be there when Justice Ochan issues his ruling."

The next day I delivered the inscribed Bibles to Bob to take with him to Uganda. But Bob only made it as far as Chicago; a volcanic eruption in Iceland halted intercontinental air travel because of the threat floating ash posed to jet engines.

After two days of waiting, Bob had no choice but to return home. The following Monday I told Henry that Bob wouldn't be coming. He'd heard about the volcano on the radio, but hadn't realized it affected air travel.

He told me Bo and Derrick—the other pair of brothers who'd been jointly charged with murder—had been to court that day and been instructed to return on Thursday, the day Justice Ochan was scheduled to announce Henry's verdict. Everything was coming to a head on that day, and while Bob wouldn't be there, Niemeyer promised he would.

APRIL 22, 2010

I was so nervous when Justice Ochan entered the courtroom. He began by describing the evidence presented against Rose and me during the trial. He also summarized the arguments from the documents submitted by the lawyers after the trial. After a short pause, he cleared his throat, removed his glasses, and asked Rose and me to stand.

When Justice Ochan looked down at me from where he was sitting, his eyes told me what he had decided before he said it out loud.

"I find in the final analysis that the State has proved to this Court, beyond a reasonable doubt, all four ingredients of the offence of murder against the two accused, Rose Mpairwe and Henry Tumusiime. I find both guilty as charged and accordingly convict them."

Henry wobbled as the verdict crashed into him and closed his eyes as his future slipped away. *How has this happened? Why has this happened? Why is God turning away from me?* The wave of despondency that overwhelmed him prevented him from hearing or understanding an additional order Justice Ochan appended to the devastating verdict. That second order placed Henry's very life in jeopardy.

Within fourteen days, Justice Ochan declared, Henry would be reexamined by a *third* doctor to determine whether he was eighteen. This order, however, carried with it an additional twist that tilted the scales heavily against Henry: this reexamination would be conducted in Henry's hometown of Hoima—by a doctor employed by the Hoima Police.

The order provided that if Henry was deemed to be seventeen or younger, his case would be remanded to Magistrate Ojikhan for sentencing. But if the doctor found Henry to be eighteen, Justice Ochan would issue the sentence. And since Henry was convicted of murder, he faced a possible death sentence.

Mr. William was somber as he drove the still-reeling Henry back to Ihungu. His words of encouragement fell on deaf ears, and Henry tumbled into a depression far deeper than ever before.

✷ ✷ ✷

My conversation with Henry that evening was sobering, to put it mildly. He spoke softly and haltingly as he described what had transpired. He was still in shock, and his confidence that everything would be all right had been pulverized. Before we hung up, he told me Bo had pled guilty so his younger brother, Derrick, could be released.

This left only four of the original twenty-one—Abdul, Bo, Nakunda, and Henry.

After we hung up, I sat in stunned silence for several minutes—thinking, praying, questioning, and praying some more. I was adrift, no longer moored to my naïve notion that justice would ultimately prevail. *Why?* I asked God. *Why is this boy's future being taken from him?*

The more I thought about it, the more another question emerged: *Why do I care so much?* I'd never cared enough to do anything about the injustice extending to all four corners of the globe before. *Why now? Why do I feel so invested in* this *instance, in* this *boy's plight?*

My mind drifted back to "The Starfish Story." I couldn't escape the vision that Henry was stranded on the shore with the sun beating down on him. And I couldn't—and didn't want to—escape the conviction that Henry was *my* starfish, and that *I* needed to throw him back into the safety of the ocean. *But how? What could I do from Malibu? For that matter, what could I do from Masindi?*

I spent the next twenty-four hours soliciting the advice and prayers of those I trusted most. I also spoke extensively with Brett LoVellette, one of my former students then serving alongside Napier as a Nootbaar Fellow in Uganda. Providentially, Brett worked for the Deputy Chief Justice—the head of the Ugandan Court of Appeals. Brett walked me through the entire appellate process, familiarizing me with what needed to happen next. He warned me, however, that it could take several years before an appeal was actually heard.

I couldn't wait that long.

The next morning I learned from Henry that his medical examination in Hoima would take place the following week. It was time to be brutally honest. I swallowed hard and said, "Henry, I need you to understand what's going to happen next and what the consequences could be."

"Okay."

"If the police doctor decides you are eighteen, you'll be sentenced by Justice Ochan and not by Magistrate Ojikhan."

"Yes, I understand."

"If Magistrate Ojikhan sentences you, the longest sentence he can give you is three years."

"But I have already been here almost two years. Would that be one more year or three more years?"

"Three more years. Since the conviction was in the case that arose four months ago, your sentence would probably only be reduced by that amount of time. And understand that Magistrate Ojikhan will feel pressured by the community to impose a harsh sentence. I think it would be at least two more years."

"Wow," he said after a long pause. "That is not good."

"But, Henry, if you are found to be eighteen, Justice Ochan might sentence you to ten years, twenty years, or . . ." I paused, trying to choose my words carefully.

"I understand," he said softly. "Mr. William told me Justice Ochan could even impose the death penalty."

"I think it's very unlikely to happen, but he has that authority."

The melancholy tone in his voice caused me to steer the conversation toward the appellate process. "I've been doing some research, and I've talked to some friends in Uganda. We can file an appeal as soon as you are sentenced. I will try to move your case forward as quickly as possible."

"How long will an appeal take?"

"I hope we can get it heard in a year . . . or less," I fudged.

Brett told me the odds of getting him released on bail pending appeal were slim, so I opted not to tell him I was exploring that possibility.

"Thank you for continuing to help me. I know you will try your best to get me released."

After we hung up, I prayed for Henry's safety and asked God to sustain him during this intense time of trial. I prayed for patience and for greater trust in Him for both of us. I also prayed God would reveal to me my next steps.

Shortly after I finished praying, I received an answer. I walked into the office of my trusted colleague Tim Perrin. By the time we finished talking, I knew the answer to the question Henry had been asking me for three months—"When are you coming back to Uganda?"

Now.

I still had many more questions than answers; I had no idea if my going would make any difference in the outcome of his case. But I did know one thing for sure: my dear friend was scared and alone in an African prison. At the very least, I could alleviate some of his loneliness, if only for a few days. Though I didn't want to face it, I also knew I might not be allowed to visit him after he was sentenced and transferred to another facility.

That afternoon I e-mailed the team my plans: I would leave the next morning for Kampala, stay with Napier on Sunday night, then head to

Masindi on Monday morning. With Napier's and Niemeyer's help, I would focus on helping prepare for the sentencing hearing and appeal during the week, fly out of Kampala on Friday evening, and be back in Los Angeles, God willing, on Saturday afternoon.

As usual, David was wise and encouraging in his reply:

I have been silent, because I have not known what to say. Frankly, I have been struggling. It occurred to me for the first time in my life that, in the parable of the Good Samaritan, we aren't told what happens to the man who was helped by the Good Samaritan. Did the innkeeper continue to care for him? Did he survive his wounds? I always assumed a happy ending, but we don't know, because Jesus doesn't make that part of the story. I don't know why. Maybe it's because loving our neighbor is for us, and results and meaning are for God. . . . I also remembered a quote from C. S. Lewis: "If Satan's arsenal of weapons were restricted to a single one—it would be discouragement." So true. Yet we all know that what appears to be a moment of ultimate defeat can be a moment of ultimate victory. So Jim, God bless you. DO NOT BE DISCOURAGED! BE ENCOURAGED! This trip is an act of love for a neighbor. That is all God asks of us. Results and meaning are for Him, and He is good. I will pray for you without stopping while you are there.

Thank you, Pepperdine folks and Restore folks, for supporting Jim on this trip—also an act of love for your neighbor.

As I drove to the airport, I had no idea how dramatically my life, and that of my entire family, would change as a result of this return trip. I often wonder if I would have had the courage to proceed had I known where it would lead. Deep down, I fear I might have turned back.

CHAPTER 17
BACK INTO THE BUSH

APRIL 25, 2010

After the ruling, I became very sad. I told my mom I might be in prison for fifty years, so it would be okay if she stopped visiting and tried to forget about me.

I kept asking God why this was happening, but I tried to trust Him and kept praying. I talked to Jim almost every day, and he tried to explain to me the procedures, but I did not understand all of what he said. I was very surprised and thankful when he told me he was coming back to Uganda to help me.

THOUGHTS OF, *What am I doing here? I should be with my wife and kids. How can I possibly help at this point?* crowded out all others as I left Kampala Monday morning with Tango.

In Uganda, biblical names such as Moses, Amos, Samuel, and Abraham proliferate. This is precisely why Solomon—the driver Napier arranged for me—had adopted the distinctive pseudonym "Tango." If his American and European clients could easily remember it, he'd be far more likely to have enough repeat business to support his wife and young child.

On my first car ride from Kampala to Masindi just three months earlier, we'd traveled before sunrise, so I hadn't seen much of the countryside. On the way back, our vision had been clouded by the fog of our intense experience at Ihungu. This time I got to take in the landscape—but except for several small villages and one little monkey by the side of the road, there was nothing other than bushy plains as far as the eye could see. Thankfully, Tango sports a permanent smile and likes to talk.

During our three-hour conversation, I learned more about daily life in Uganda than I had on my entire prior trip. I also learned all about Tango. He grew up in a village near Hoima but didn't know Henry and Joseph. Tango is a Seventh-Day Adventist; his wife is Muslim. When I asked if being married to someone from a different religion was difficult, he screwed up his face as if it were a silly question. "We worship the same God, just differently and on different days."

Interesting perspective, I thought, nodding as though it made perfect sense.

We stopped only once, when Tango said he needed to make a "short call." During our trip, he'd initiated and received several brief cell phone calls, so I was puzzled—until we paid a man a few hundred shillings for the privilege of urinating on the side of a wall. That was a "short call." I must be a genius, because I guessed the meaning of a "long call" on my first try.

After I checked into the Masindi Hotel and said good-bye to Tango, I walked over to the probation office next to the courthouse to meet up with William. He caught me up on Abdul, Bo, and Nakunda, and informed me that Henry's sentencing before Magistrate Ojikhan had been scheduled for May 7—ten days later. This, of course, presumed the Hoima police doctor agreed with the two previous doctors that Henry was under eighteen.

"Will you take me out to Ihungu after I speak with the registrar?" I asked.

"Yes, but Margaret is not around yet. If you want to go back to the hotel, I will call you when she arrives."

Masindi's High Court registrar, Margaret, handled all the logistics for the courthouse, and I needed to meet with her for two reasons. First, I couldn't review Henry's court file without her permission. Second, William couldn't take Henry for his medical examination until she signed the court order authorizing it, and I wanted to talk to her before that happened.

As I waited back at the hotel, I started drafting various aspects of the Pre-Sentence Report that needed to be prepared on Henry's behalf before he could be sentenced. I finally gave up on Margaret at 3:00 p.m. and asked William to take me to Ihungu. He swung by the hotel, and I hopped onto the back of his motorcycle. The ride would have been bad enough on a good road, but the road to Ihungu is decidedly *not* a good road.

As we pulled in, Henry, Abdul, Bo, and Nakunda eagerly greeted us, along with two others I didn't recognize. Henry introduced the teenage boy as a friend who lived nearby. "He is the one who charges my phone when the battery runs out."

The other stranger was a female in her early forties who'd recently been hired to serve as the matron, finally replacing Rose after the children had gone a lengthy period with no adult supervision. During this interim, Henry had overseen everyone's care and feeding.

Henry's eyes conveyed his feelings. He was thankful I was there, but quiet resignation had replaced his bubbly enthusiasm. "Thank you for coming back, Mr. Jim. I knew you would."

In an instant, I knew I'd made the right decision. I vowed to make sure I never left Henry alone in a time of need.

Eager to get to work, I grabbed two plastic chairs, and we parked ourselves under the mango tree where we'd spent so much time together in January. I walked him through the applicable Ugandan legal provisions and explained what I hoped to accomplish on this trip. I also showed him my outline of the topics we needed to cover so I could write his Pre-Sentence Report.

When I opened my laptop, the others swarmed to us like moths to a light bulb. Soon we were all crowded together under the tree. I reminded myself that part of the reason I returned was to visit those in prison and to be a friend to all the kids, not just to Henry but also to Abdul, Bo, and Nakunda. So I decided Henry and I would hold off and start fresh in the morning. I reached into my backpack and pulled out the latest edition of *Pepperdine Magazine*. Henry flipped through it until he came to the story about our trip to Ihungu earlier that year. "Wow. This is us!" He beamed as he showed the others.

One of the main pictures featured Abdul peering through the hole in the door to the boys' custody. He couldn't stop giggling as he struggled to comprehend how or why his picture was in a glossy American magazine.

During one of our previous calls, Henry had asked me to describe my house. I'd given it my best shot but didn't feel like he'd fully understood. So I took this chance to show him. Using a video camera, I'd filmed a five-minute walkthrough of my home in Southern California the night before I left and had uploaded it to my computer. I showed the group the camera and explained that what the camera filmed could be played on a computer. Henry's translation elicited blank stares from the others, as if he'd just translated my words into Chinese. So I pressed Play.

The inmates watched with rapt attention, periodically pointing to the screen, laughing and chattering away in Swahili as they met my family and toured my house. When the video ended, I handed Henry the camera and asked him to film his home for the past twenty-two months. He happily complied, and we spent the next thirty-five minutes walking the entire grounds of Ihungu with Henry narrating.

We started in the kitchen, where a dinner pot of beans slowly boiled over a makeshift fire. In the store, Henry showed me the cassava drying on the floor and the torn sack of corn flour used to make the posho the inmates daily ate for breakfast and lunch. As we walked through the soccer field, he proudly explained how he'd built the goalposts, and we laughed as we reflected on the epic match we'd played a few months earlier. At one point, Bo took over the filming duties as Henry acted as an on-camera tour guide.

When we entered the custody, I noticed two shirtless boys sitting on mats. *New arrivals.* Two of the group photos we'd taken in January were taped just inside the door. Dozens of colored pencil drawings adorned the walls. I welled up as I realized I'd be one of the blessed few to visit this unique art gallery—my own private Louvre. Among the masterpieces were a chicken, a flower, a cassava plant, a hand, a hut, a hunter killing an antelope with a spear, garden tools, a lion, and numerous depictions of the custody where the boys lived.

"These are a small few that are remaining. The boys who were released took with them the ones they drew. There used to be very, very many *covering* the walls," Henry said with obvious pride in his fellow inmates.

I pointed to an exceptionally good sketch of an ape. "Wow. Who drew this one?"

"I am the one!" Henry declared. He smiled as he retrieved the Ugandan travel guide I'd given him in January, pointing to the ape on the front cover. "It is this one." Using only an ordinary pencil, he'd captured the photograph's depth and texture by using several shading techniques.

Toward the back of the custody, a rectangle with a diagonal line bisecting it into two triangles was drawn on the chalkboard. Along the outer edges of the rectangle were numbers and equations. The familiar $A^2 + B^2 = C^2$ had been written below the rectangle, along with an algebraic equation solving the length of the diagonal line. "What's this? Who's doing algebra?" I queried.

"It is actually geometry," Henry chuckled. "This was done by one of my students," he said as he pressed his hand to his chest. "He is one of the new prisoners. I gave him a lesson in the morning, and then I gave him a test."

I stared at the equation like it was advanced calculus. It'd been way too long since I'd tried to solve for the area of a triangle. "How'd he do?"

"He was right! He is a *very* good student."

"It looks right to me," I fibbed. I didn't want Henry to lose confidence in the lawyer fighting for his freedom, so I didn't let on that I wouldn't have had a snowball's chance in Uganda of solving the equation. That, and he wouldn't have known what a snowball was anyway.

Before leaving home, I'd pondered what I could bring with me to provide Henry a glimpse of life outside of Uganda. The video of my house had been my first idea. I'm not particularly creative, so a bag of marshmallows had been my second.

After the tour, I tore open the bag and handed the first piece to Henry. He'd never seen a marshmallow and had no idea what to do with it. He studied it carefully and sniffed it. "What is it?"

"It's food. Try it."

The others stared transfixed as he took the smallest of nibbles, paused, then looked at me quizzically and said, "It is sweet."

I shoved an entire marshmallow into my mouth. He grinned and followed suit. The others exploded in laughter. Marshmallows all around.

Because our families had been a frequent topic of conversation for us, Henry wanted to see more pictures of mine and asked lots of questions about them. "I hope I can greet them someday," he said pensively. "And I hope they can greet my family as well."

"I would very much like that, Henry," I said, though I seriously doubted this would ever happen. I couldn't imagine a scenario where my family would come to Uganda or he'd travel to the United States—especially since he'd almost certainly be in prison for at least another two years, if not substantially longer.

As we were perusing vacation, birthday, and Christmas pictures on my computer, William arrived back at Ihungu. "Time for the death ride back to the hotel," he said. While those weren't his *exact* words, that's *exactly* what I heard.

I promised Henry I'd return in the morning for a full day of work on his Pre-Sentence Report. During the ride back, I asked William about Henry's trial. He'd attended parts of it and had been present when Rose pleaded with Justice Ochan for mercy before he sentenced her to a lengthy prison term.

At least she wasn't sentenced to death, I noted with relief.

"Why has Justice Ochan ordered another examination to determine Henry's age?" I asked.

"I don't know. Henry's mother brought a birth certificate showing he is seventeen, and two doctors from Masindi agreed he is seventeen."

Back at the hotel, I resumed work on the Pre-Sentence Report. That evening, just before Napier arrived from Kampala, Niemeyer called to tell me Restore's games at the national secondary school soccer tournament had been unexpectedly postponed a few days. "So does this mean you won't be coming?" I asked.

"Actually, just the opposite. I'm coming to Masindi tomorrow, but rather than staying until Thursday, I need to leave on Wednesday."

On the one hand, I was glad Napier's and Niemeyer's visits would overlap; I still felt like a fish out of water in Uganda, and having another mzungu around helped. On the other hand, this meant that if I didn't finish my work Wednesday, I'd be left to fend for myself on Thursday and arrange my own ride back to Kampala.

The next morning, Napier and I spent forty-five minutes with Margaret the registrar, a delightful woman who also pastors a church in Kampala. Her church duties occasionally detained her on Sundays, preventing her from making it to Masindi on Monday. This had been the case the day before.

I thanked her for shepherding the kids through the judicial process over the preceding three months. She was equally grateful to us for coming to help. When the conversation migrated toward Henry, Margaret expressed reservations about signing an order compelling him to undergo yet another age examination. She showed us the PF 24 prepared by the Masindi doctor the month before, as well as Henry's baptismal and birth certificates—all confirming he was seventeen. As we talked, her resistance to signing the order cemented. In fact, at one point, she impulsively called Henry's defense lawyer. We only heard her side of the conversation, but thankfully she spoke in English.

"You have seen the order requiring Henry to be tested again?"

"Why have you not filed an opposition? . . . Well, you need to file one right away."

Her tone was derisive, and she hung up without giving him a chance to respond to her last directive. *Why couldn't she have been Henry's lawyer?* I thought.

While I appreciated her passion, I feared an opposition motion would inject additional delay and thereby prolong Henry's incarceration. The lawyer probably wouldn't file the motion for several weeks, if ever. As far as he was concerned, the case was over.

Risking a chance of offending her, I gently reminded her that Justice Ochan had scheduled a hearing for the following Friday, and we hoped Henry would be sentenced shortly thereafter. She not-so-gently reminded me that this next doctor was a Hoima police officer, and if he found Henry to be an adult, the result could be a death sentence or at least twenty years in prison. I had to concede her point.

The critical question devolved to this: was it better to challenge the judge's order and face more delay, or comply with the order and move forward, knowing Henry's life potentially hung in the balance?

Ultimately, Margaret fashioned a Solomonic compromise. She rewrote the testing order and affixed to it photocopies of the two prior PF 24s. "The police doctor attended the same medical school as the Masindi doctor who most recently examined Henry," she explained. "When he sees that his colleague examined the boy last month and found him to be seventeen, he will know that a different determination will raise suspicions."

Perfect. One task down, one to go.

Napier personified diplomacy as he sought Margaret's permission for us to access Henry's trial record. We had no legal right to see it, but

Margaret seemed to be on our side. "I talked to several of the children at Ihungu after Innocent died," she told us. "They all said the same thing: the Katikkiro was not involved; the boy is innocent." She declared this without a hint of uncertainty.

She was equally certain we'd come to help Henry, so not only did she agree to allow us to read the court file, she also offered to have her assistant photocopy it for us, handwritten notes and all. "There is one problem," she lamented. "The power is off at the courthouse, so we cannot make copies."

We couldn't copy the documents at the courthouse because there was no power, and we couldn't copy them on the portable printer/photocopier I had at the hotel because the files couldn't leave the courthouse. *Stalemate*.

Not to be deterred, Margaret suggested that while we waited for the power to be restored, she'd have her assistant begin typing Justice Ochan's handwritten notes into her computer so we could have an electronic version of the record for the appeal.

I was perplexed. "Um, how can your assistant type the notes into her computer if there's no power?" I inquired.

"The generator is on, so she can use her computer," she stated as though no further explanation was necessary.

"Wait, there's a generator? So . . . why can't we use the generator to power the copy machine?" I said, trying my best not to offend her.

"The copy machine is not connected to the generator because it is not a core function of the court," she remarked as if it were again obvious.

Napier and I just looked at each other, befuddled by the curious designation of "core" versus "non-core" functions. Margaret promised to call Napier at the hotel when the power was restored.

On my way to Ihungu, William told me Henry's examination would be the next morning and that he'd take Henry to Hoima himself. This meant I'd need to gather all the information necessary for Henry's Pre-Sentence Report that day.

For the next two hours, Henry and I sat alone under our tree and powered through the outline I'd prepared. Eventually I asked Henry when he planned to eat lunch.

"I am not having lunch today," he said.

"Why not?"

"I am fasting and praying for an end to my imprisonment."

This completely caught me off guard. All I could muster in response was, "Well, then, I'm fasting too." So I called William and told him I'd be working through lunch.

An hour later, the battery light on my computer started blinking, so I shut down my laptop to swap out a fresh battery.

When I retrieved the backup battery from my backpack, I remembered I'd brought a bag of Tootsie Pops with me. I tore it open and handed one to Henry. He pulled off the wrapper and studied the curious blob on the end of a stick as though it were a science experiment. I grinned, shoved mine into my mouth, and invited him to do the same.

"I will eat it after my fast," he said politely and wrapped it back up.

Right, the fast. I couldn't even last an hour. Pitiful.

As we were concluding, Henry squinted over my shoulder at something behind me on the horizon. "It is going to rain," he said.

"What? When?" I gazed in the same direction and saw nothing that suggested rain to me.

"Five minutes. Maybe less. It is going to rain very hard. We must find shelter." He stood and grabbed his chair and my backpack.

"Are you a meteorologist too?" I mused.

"A what?"

"Never mind. Are you sure it's going to rain? How can you tell?"

"This is my home. I know. You will see," he said with a grin.

From the covered steps of the store, we watched the heavens open up five minutes later. The only other time I'd seen rain like that in my life was in January in Kampala.

✱ ✱ ✱

As William and I bounced and swerved along the rain-drenched road way, I reflected back on my seven-hour interview of Henry. Everything he told me was completely consistent with what he'd said before. My already great respect for his character and intellect quadrupled.

Before he returned to Kampala, Napier told me the power never came back on at the courthouse, so after dinner, I resumed drafting the Pre-Sentence Report. Because I'd already excerpted the pertinent provisions of the Children Act the day before, my task was to integrate the eleven pages of notes I'd taken that day with Ugandan law. Fortunately, law/fact analysis is what I did for a living when I practiced law, and it's precisely what I teach my students to do every day. My adrenaline kicked in as I worked until 1:00 a.m., finishing three-quarters of the draft before Niemeyer arrived. This intense and productive period of writing reminded me of the *good* part of the good ole days at Kirkland & Ellis.

Over a pineapple-laden breakfast the next morning, Niemeyer and I sketched out an action plan. Our goals were simple and twofold: photocopy the entire trial record and complete the Pre-Sentence Report. But when we arrived at the courthouse, there was *still* no power.

Are you kidding me?

Niemeyer took the lead, and for good reason. Restore International, under his supervision, had paid all court expenses associated with the juvenile session just completed. Consequently, Margaret had a soft spot in her heart for him.

After a brief discussion, Margaret authorized her assistant to accompany us back to the hotel, where we could photocopy the entire file with our own printer/copier. The day before, I had purchased from Margaret a signed copy of a book she'd written called *Biblical Principles of Love*. They were five dollars each. I bought four more copies after she said we could copy the record.

Just after 9:00 a.m., William and Henry swung by the hotel on their way to Hoima. As they sped off to see the doctor, I started praying. "It's in God's hands now," I said to Niemeyer.

"It's always been in God's hands," he shot back with a smile.

CHAPTER 18
CROSSROADS

AS I WORKED ON Henry's Pre-Sentence Report, I became hyper-concentrated and time slipped by unnoticed. So when my phone rang, it startled me. "Henry" flashed on the screen.

How much time has passed? I glanced at my watch. *10:05 a.m.—the examination couldn't be over yet.* Just over an hour had gone by since they left, and the trip was at least an hour by motorcycle. If he was calling so soon, something had to be wrong.

"Hello?" I swallowed hard. Niemeyer's eyes widened as he waited for any hint of what Henry was saying.

"Yes, hello. We arrived in Hoima safely. We are at the doctor's office now waiting."

I exhaled slowly and shook my head. "Thanks for telling me. John Niemeyer and I will be waiting for your call. Please let us know when you're finished."

"Okay, I will call you."

It all came down to this. We stood at a crossroads, with Henry's future hanging precariously in the balance. *Prayer time.*

I struggled in vain to reclaim my concentration as I anxiously awaited Henry's call. Every few minutes I checked to confirm the cell network was still functioning. As I waited, I reflected on our crazy ride together. I desperately wanted it to end. I prayed for stronger faith, for an undeniable and abiding conviction that God really was in control, not just of Henry's dilemma, but of my life as well. I had my doubts.

Ninety excruciating minutes later, my phone finally rang. My eyes locked on Niemeyer's and our pulses quickened. I punched the green Talk button and simply said, "Well?"

As Henry spoke, I felt the intensity of my emotions deep inside my core.

APRIL 25, 2010

Two doctors had examined me, and both had agreed what I already knew—I was seventeen. I was nervous because this third doctor was also a police officer, and I was afraid he would not be truthful. The police doctor asked me some questions and made some measurements. He looked at my teeth and used a machine to take a picture of them. I sat in the examination room alone for ten minutes, waiting. I prayed very hard.

When he returned, he sat down in front of me. He said the pictures of my teeth conclusively proved my age.

Niemeyer knew the answer by my expression. A smile exploded onto his face as if he'd just won the lottery, and he raised his hand for an exuberant high five. Like the two others, the police doctor determined Henry was seventeen.

Thank You, God.

I could tell Henry was eating, so I asked him where he was.

APRIL 25, 2010

When I left the doctor's examination room, I was so surprised and happy to see my mother there in the waiting room. She told Mr.

William she had been cooking my favorite foods all morning, hoping he would say it was okay for me to come home, just for a few minutes. She reminded him that I had not been home in almost two years, and I had not seen my sister and two brothers during that time. He told her he was not allowed to let me go home and that he could lose his job if he did. She took his hand and said "please" over and over again. Finally, he said if I could keep it a secret, I could stay for one hour. I promised I would go back with him then.

I was so happy to visit home. The first thing I noticed was how vacant and quiet our land was. My mom had sold all of our cows so our pasture was empty, and our chickens were also gone so there were no clucking sounds I was always used to hearing at home. My family was so surprised to see me because my mother had not told them I might be coming. We all hugged over and over again, and my sister cried a little. My mom had cooked for me rice, chicken, and Irish potatoes, which are my favorite. It felt so good to be home. I had almost forgotten what it would be like to live anywhere but Ihungu again. While I was eating, I called Jim to tell him the good news. When Mr. William returned after one hour, he said it was time to leave. I prayed with my family that I would be released soon and hugged them very hard. They did not want me to leave yet, but I knew Mr. William had done me a big favor, so I went with him when he said we had to go. Leaving was difficult, but God used this visit to give me confidence that I would again have some kind of life after Ihungu.

I completed the Pre-Sentence Report just as Niemeyer finished copying the court file. In the report, I traced the history of both of Henry's cases, highlighting not only the injustices he'd endured but all that he'd done for the other inmates. I concluded by boldly asking that Henry be set free immediately, even if it had to be on probation—he'd been imprisoned long enough and should be allowed to move forward with his life and education. I also attached a letter Niemeyer wrote at Bob's direction, stating that Henry had been granted a full scholarship to the Restore Leadership Academy and asking that he be released into Restore's custody.

On their way back from Hoima, Henry and William stopped by the hotel. I'd previously described Skype to Henry and really wanted to show him how it worked. Henry delivered the good news about the examination to my elated family and got to see them live for the first time. After the Skype call, I gave Henry and William each a copy of the report I'd written. As I did so, I flashed back to January, when I had seen Ray take off his tie and give it to William as we were leaving. William's face had glowed like the morning sun.

So I removed my tie and handed it to William. Same glowing face. Little did he know, the cumulative value of all my ties was unlikely to equal the value of the single tie Ray had given him.

I turned to Henry and said, "When I was here in January, I sent daily reports to my friends and family about you and the others at Ihungu. And after I came home, I continued sending reports about your case. Even this week I've been sending e-mails every night. I've received many responses from people who are concerned about you and praying for you. Two of these responses were addressed to you."

"They were sent to me? Really?"

"Yes, they're here on my computer. They were sent by my dear friends Jessie and Casey. This first one is from my student Jessie."

Wide-eyed, Henry turned my computer toward him and began to read.

Dean Gash,
Please tell Henry that his sister Jessie in Malibu is fasting today for him and with him that God will work a miracle in this situation and he will be exonerated. When I was 15, due to many

difficult things that happened in my family, I was moved to a group home facility where I, like Henry, celebrated an important birthday, my 16th. . . . I was scared, upset, lost, terrified, and did not know what my future held. I did not know if I would be able to return home or how my future would look. I identify and empathize with him, and although the facts aren't exactly the same, my heart breaks because I know what he is feeling. It has been a long road to recovery, but I have never given up hope, and that is our strength as believers. I was running on that beautiful track at Pepperdine today, just thinking of the freedom I wish Henry could feel right now.

God does not promise a verdict of innocent, and God does not promise that justice will always be done, although we are already free in the Lord and He is a God who loves justice. What He does promise is that He will work all things for good. My name, Jessie, means "God is gracious," and He, through all of my difficulty, has made good out of the biggest wounds of my life. He has been gracious and will be gracious with Henry. I just looked up "Henry," and it means "ruler of the house." God has great things in store for Henry.

Please tell him my story and let him know that God does have a plan for a hope and a future for him. God asks that we run with perseverance this race, and for you and Henry: keep running this race and under no circumstances give up.

Isaiah 40:29–31: "He gives strength to the weary and increases the power of the weak. Even youths grow tired and weary, and young men stumble and fall; but those who hope in the LORD will renew their strength. They will soar on wings like eagles; they will run and not grow weary, they will walk and not be faint."

In His Powerful Name,
Jessie

Henry read Jessie's message twice as he fought back tears. (I'd bawled when I first read it.) He asked for a pen and paper so he could write down the verse from Isaiah.

A dagger of regret stabbed me as I remembered that the volcano two weeks earlier had prevented Bob from delivering the Bible Joline and I had purchased for Henry. Because my decision to return to Uganda had been so quick, I didn't have time to retrieve the Bible before leaving. I'd seen the previous day, however, the unbound pile of tattered, well-worn pages of the Ihungu Bible, so I knew Henry had access to the scripture he jotted down.

Henry also read my colleague Casey's e-mail, which included a dozen encouraging scriptures about persevering and resting in the presence of God. I promised him I'd print out the e-mails and send them back with Niemeyer the following week.

"Please tell Jessie and Casey thank you for caring about me. Please tell them I love them."

Niemeyer and I promised to stop by Ihungu on the way out of town and hustled off to the courthouse to deliver the report.

The doctor's conclusion meant that Magistrate Ojikhan, rather than Justice Ochan, would be issuing Henry's sentence, so Niemeyer and I hoped to deliver the Pre-Sentence Report to the magistrate before leaving.

One might wonder how I could file a court document without being admitted to practice law in Uganda. The short answer is that I couldn't. We hadn't been authorized to prepare and deliver summary briefs for each of the children in January either. The longer answer, however, is that Pepperdine's relationship with the Ugandan judiciary has convinced them we're there to help, and they have gratefully accepted our assistance. Like the summary briefs, the Pre-Sentence Report wouldn't be part of the "official" court record.

When we arrived at 4:59 p.m., the registrar was just leaving. "Margaret!" I called out as I jogged across the parking lot. "The Hoima police doctor confirmed Henry is seventeen!"

"Praise God!" she said as she thumbed through the Pre-Sentence Report I handed her. "This is very nice. It will be helpful to Magistrate Ojikhan when he sentences Henry next week."

A few moments later, we met with the magistrate.

"Hello, Professor," he said as we exchanged friendship handshakes. "What can I do for you?"

"I wanted to give you a copy of a report I prepared on behalf of a boy you'll be sentencing next week. I've also delivered a copy to William, and he will file the official Pre-Sentence Report soon."

"Ah, yes, Tumusiime Henry. I know this case. Thank you very much. This will be helpful as I decide how long his sentence will be in this very serious matter." His grave tone and word choice reminded me that while the doctor's determination had produced a ray of light, ominous clouds still gathered on the horizon.

✳   ✳   ✳

Out at Ihungu, I announced to the remaining prisoners that tomorrow there'd be a feast. I'd previously asked William privately if I could buy them some better food. "Yes. You can buy them lots of meat, rice, and sodas," he suggested.

"Kill the fattened calf. How much will it set me back?"

"Twenty thousand shillings," he said sheepishly.

"Let's make it thirty thousand—throw in something else they like!"

In retrospect, I'm embarrassed to have contributed only what amounted to about fifteen dollars for this meal. We also presented the new matron and each prisoner with a photograph I'd taken of them the day before. As always, the pictures were a huge hit.

As we'd done the last time I departed Ihungu, Henry and I went for a walk. I told him we'd delivered the report and that he'd be sentenced next week. "I have read the report, and it is very good," he said. He stopped walking and turned to me. "Thank you for coming back. Thank you for helping me."

The sincerity in his eyes penetrated me. I simply nodded, as I knew I'd be overcome if I tried to speak. This moment alone made the trip worthwhile.

"Will you come back to Uganda again?"

I smiled as tears rimmed my eyes. The last time he asked me that question, I wasn't sure if I ever would. This time, however, I *knew* I'd be back and told him so.

"You should bring your family next time. I would like to greet them."

I laughed and nodded. "Maybe someday."

We hugged and said our good-byes, promising to talk early the next week . . . and every week thereafter.

The first half of the drive back to Kampala was uneventful. I enjoyed talking with Niemeyer about his life, what he did for Restore, and what the future held for him. I hoped we'd have the chance to get to know each other better in the future. A dreadful familiarity, however, enveloped the second half of the trip. Night fell, I grew sleepy, and the road got crowded with bicyclists and pedestrians.

Remembering our collision with the guy on the bike that first night, I inadvertently tensed my body so often that by the time we arrived back at Napier's apartment in Kampala, I felt like I'd been in a marathon Pilates class. Niemeyer had navigated the treacherous roads and darting obstacles like he'd been driving here his entire life. I swore that day I'd never drive in Uganda.

Napier's roommate, Brett, was on a safari, so I had a free place to crash. On a whim, I jumped online and was able to move my flight up a day, which would get me home in time for my daughter Jessica's last track meet of the season.

"By the way," Napier said before we went to bed, "I've arranged for you to meet tomorrow with Justice Lugayizi, the head of the High Court's Criminal Division. He heard you were in town and really wants to talk with you."

"Great. Any idea why?"

"He wants an update on Masindi and wants to talk about an idea he has. He didn't tell me what it was, though."

Little did I know that it was an idea that would one day bring my life, my family, and my career to a crossroads.

✳   ✳   ✳

"You should appeal. He cannot have this conviction on his record."

I nodded back at Justice Lugayizi, whose furrowed brow and insistent eyes added an exclamation point to his directive. Though in his early sixties, he didn't have a single gray hair in his medium-length afro. Within minutes, I could see why his Pepperdine interns adored him.

Earlier that morning, Napier had escorted me to Justice Lugayizi's chambers. He liberally expressed his gratitude for what we'd done in Masindi, but he also lamented that outside intervention had been necessary to address the injustices in his own country. My description of Henry's case had prompted his staunch recommendation to appeal.

Then, after pausing a beat, he shrugged, leaned back in his chair, and added wryly, "Though with the recordkeeping here, the boy's conviction may never be properly recorded." After yet another pause, he leaned forward again and declared, "But you really should appeal."

I shifted in my chair on the other side of his desk and said, "I'm glad you agree. I've spoken with Edward Sekabanja, and he's agreed to represent Henry in his appeal."

Approval instantly registered on the justice's face. "Sekabanja is a good lawyer and a good man. He will do well for the boy. Please keep me apprised as the case moves along." I promised to do so.

"Professor, there is something else I want to discuss with you," he added, narrowing his gaze. "I have been thinking about this for several months but was not sure how to proceed. When I learned you were here, the timing was perfect for me to move forward with this idea."

"Great. What is it?"

"As you know, two interns from Pepperdine, Micheline and Greer, prepared a report for us on plea bargaining last year. It was really quite good, and we have been discussing it among ourselves since then. We would like to take the next step and study the issue very closely. The Chief Justice has authorized funds for a few judges to come to America to learn more about it."

"Fantastic!" I was eager to encourage judicial reforms that would shorten the time prisoners spent awaiting trial. "Have you thought about how you'd go about this?"

"A little, but I was hoping you would have a recommendation."

I cocked my head and raised my eyebrows conspiratorially. "How about coming to Pepperdine?"

"Excellent!" he declared as he slapped his hand down on the table. "That is what I was hoping you would say! Justice Kiryabwire and the others at the Commercial Court still talk about their trips to Pepperdine. My colleagues and I would like to come and see your school for ourselves."

"It'd be an honor to host you," I said with unvarnished sincerity. "Who'd be in the delegation?"

"We would be five or six. The Principal Judge, my deputy head of the Criminal Division, and two or three other judges or registrars. Is that okay?"

"Absolutely." As we spoke, I mentally assembled a dream team of judges, lawyers, professors, and law enforcement personnel who would train our guests in plea bargaining. It would take a fair amount of planning and some lead time to pull it off, but the possibilities were exciting.

"So, when would you like to come?"

APRIL 26, 2010

When Jim left Ihungu with John Niemeyer, Mr. William also went home. But two hours later, he came back. I have never seen him so angry, and he had never been mad at me before. He took me away from the others.

"Why did you tell Jim about Rose ordering you and the others to work?" he yelled. "This report Jim wrote makes me look like a very bad man." He paused and looked at me with very sad eyes and said, "How could you do this to me, Henry?"

I was confused and didn't know what to say. Everything in the report was true. I was not trying to get Mr. William in trouble, and I told Jim that Mr. William did not know about Rose making us work. I had read the report, and I could not understand why Mr. William thought it made him look bad.

"I am sorry, Mr. William. I never wanted to hurt you. And Jim likes you very much. He would also never want to make you look bad."

He slowly shook his head and softly said, "I could lose my job, Henry. I have a family; I need this job."

"You have read the whole report?" I asked, still trying to understand why he was so upset.

"I started to read it, but when I saw the part about Rose making the prisoners work, I became so angry I came out here to talk to you."

"Okay, please read the entire report. It says you did not know about Rose making us work. Jim made that clear in the report. If you read all of it closely, you will see."

The next day Mr. William came back to Ihungu at midday and apologized. "I read the report very closely, and you are right. Please forgive me for what I said yesterday."

"It is okay. I understand why you were concerned. What is in the bags?" I asked.

"I went to the market this morning and spent the money Jim gave me for the feast. Help me carry it to the kitchen."

We piled our plates high with rice and more meat than we usually got for three months. I had two bottles of Mountain Dew, my favorite soda. We all ate until our stomachs hurt. We were not used to eating more than just enough food to keep us from being hungry all the time. We were not hungry again until dinner the next day.

Jim called later to tell me he was traveling home that evening.
He was glad to hear Mr. William had kept his promise to buy us
the food. I wished him a safe journey and told him my father made
me promise to bring him greetings and to say thank you for helping
him and his sons.

On my flight home, I finally had a chance to reflect on the week. I was so glad I'd come. More importantly, Henry was glad I'd come. In just over a week, Henry would finally receive the sentence for which we had waited so long. I prayed for leniency.

Back at home, my concentration was atrocious as I counted down the hours until Henry's sentencing on Friday. Thursday evening Bob e-mailed everyone, encouraging us to "bear down in prayer."

My hand trembled ever so slightly as I dialed Henry's number Friday morning. I told myself I'd be able to handle the decision, whatever it was. But God and I were still wrestling about how and why we were facing this verdict and potential sentence.

The phone rang several more times than usual before Henry answered, completely out of breath. "What happened in court today?" I blurted out.

"I beg your pardon?"

"What . . . happened . . . in . . . court . . . today?" *And why is he breathing hard?* The suspense was killing me.

"Oh, hello, Mr. Jim. How are you? How is the family?"

"We are all fine. Everything is good here. What happened today in court?"

"Actually, *nothing* happened. The magistrate was sick. We were told to come back next week. We are playing soccer now with some boys who live nearby."

Not again. The roller coaster of uncertainty was draining me emotionally and spiritually.

My e-mail to the team feebly offered: "While frustrating, we have to rest assured knowing that God's timing is better than our own."

Late that afternoon Joline and the kids brought dinner to my office. While I was hugging the kids, Joline tapped a few keys on my laptop, planted me in front of it, and then reached around me and clicked Play. Images of our January trip to Ihungu faded in and out, accompanied by Chris Tomlin's song "Everlasting God" and interspersed with scriptures. The poignant lyrics shredded me. As the song crescendoed, photos of my most recent trip flashed across the screen. Tears dripped from my chin. Once again, Joline had demonstrated just how much I married up.[4]

This long-overdue turn of my emotional release valve freed me to more clearly see God's hand in Henry's situation. While I didn't know how strength would rise as I waited upon the Lord, I drew comfort from knowing the everlasting God defends the weak and comforts those in need. I was also reminded that ceding control to God was a choice—one I still struggled to make every day.

Over the weekend, I prayed for strength to trust Him in ways I never had. But my call with Henry on Tuesday reversed much of my progress: now William was sick and couldn't bring Henry, Bo, or Abdul to court. My shoulders sagged as I absorbed the news, but I bolted upright and flushed with anger at what Henry said next. Concern dripped from his words as he spoke. "The new matron is leaving on Thursday for three weeks."

"Okay, so what does this mean?" I asked. "Who will take her place?"

"Mr. William said it is important for the two new prisoners to be supervised."

"I agree, but what are you trying to tell me?" I said, unmasking my impatience.

"Mr. William says there are only two options—him or me. He said he hopes I will still be here when the matron returns."

My jaw and fists challenged each other to a clenching contest. *Henry's sentencing is being delayed so he can take care of the inmates while the matron is gone?* Things were further complicated by Henry's insistence that neither William nor Magistrate Ojikhan find out Henry told me this. Because his fate rested in their hands, he knew he couldn't complain about his situation.

Before we hung up, Henry told me Niemeyer had delivered copies of the e-mails from Jessie and Casey. "I have read them many times and they are giving me courage." His positive attitude and trust in God once again put mine to shame.

After the call, I e-mailed the team, begging Niemeyer to call William and innocently offer to come to Masindi to drive Abdul, Bo, and Henry to court for their sentencing. As usual, Niemeyer was one step ahead. He'd spoken with William and Magistrate Ojikhan on both Monday and Tuesday and was closely monitoring the situation. He also confirmed that William was indeed rather sick. While relieved to hear that William's illness wasn't feigned, I was still concerned it would be used to keep Henry at Ihungu until the matron returned.

The next day, Magistrate Ojikhan called Henry directly and told him he was ready to sentence him and the others but that he had been unable to reach William. When Henry called William, he answered but said he was too sick to get out of bed. By early afternoon, however, the registrar was so fed up she sent a court clerk to William's house and ordered him to bring at least one of the boys to court.

God bless Margaret, I thought when Henry updated me.

MAY 12, 2010

When Mr. William arrived at Ihungu on Wednesday in the afternoon, he was very sick with malaria. He said he would bring us to court for sentencing, one at a time. I was disappointed we would not all be going because Magistrate Ojikhan said he was ready for all of us. I wanted to be the one to go, but I said he should take Bo first because he had been at Ihungu the longest.

When they drove away, I prayed Bo would be released. He had been here for more than two years, and I thought that if he was released, I might be released also.

I sat on the steps of the custody for two hours, waiting for them to return. When they came back, Bo was smiling. He was given one year of probation and was going home the next day. I was so happy. He made me promise to send his greetings and thanks to the American lawyers who helped him.

Mr. William said he would come back in the morning to bring me and Abdul to court. He told me the lawyer who represented me would be there so I could be sentenced.

Before we hung up on Wednesday, I promised to pray for Henry and to call him the next day. I cautioned him, however, not to get his hopes up—Bo was sentenced for a death that occurred more than two years earlier, while Henry would be sentenced in conjunction with a death only five months ago.

MAY 13, 2010

On Thursday, the matron left for three weeks. Abdul and I waited all day for Mr. William to come. Bo sat with us, hoping Mr. William would take him to a matatu so he could go home. Whenever we heard a motorcycle, we hoped it was him. But each time the motorcycle continued past Ihungu on the road. Mr. William did not answer my calls.

At 5:00 p.m., Mr. William arrived. It was too late to go to court, and I did not think Bo would leave this late, so I did not know why Mr. William had come.

He was feeling better, but he still looked somehow sick. He apologized for not coming earlier and said Bo would go home tomorrow.

He also said he would come tomorrow and bring me and Abdul to court.

Before he left, Mr. William took me away from the others. He said if I was released the next day, no one would be there to stay with the other prisoners. He asked if I would stay one more week even if I was released, which would give him time to find someone else. He had a family and did not want to stay at Ihungu himself.

I did not know what to say. Mr. William is my friend, and he had been kind to me for almost two years, but I really wanted to go home if I was released. I told him I would decide tomorrow after court. I knew Jim would call later and would help me decide what to do.

My blood pressure spiked into the danger zone as Henry explained what had transpired that day. Henry couldn't be sentenced without his Kampala-based attorney present, and Niemeyer had confirmed the lawyer would be in Masindi on Thursday. But we had no guarantee he'd still be around Friday.

Yet another opportunity for him to be sentenced had slipped away.

Henry was particularly worried for his own safety if he was released by the court but then kept at Ihungu. He feared Innocent's family might seek revenge. The fact that no adults would be at Ihungu greatly magnified this risk.

As his probation officer, William was required to recommend to the magistrate an appropriate sentence in his Pre-Sentence Report. I was more than a little encouraged when Henry told me William had apparently copied most of what I'd written.

As we hung up, Henry asked me to pray hard for his release. Since Henry was still insisting I not do anything to jeopardize this possibility, the only other thing I could think of was to call Niemeyer. He'd already called William and Margaret, who'd both assured him Henry's lawyer would be in court the next day. Niemeyer also said he'd sent William money to transport Bo home the next day.

"There's one potential hitch, though," he warned. "Henry's lawyer is also representing the accused in a different case this week in the High Court. That trial is scheduled for Friday. If this lawyer is tied up in the High Court all day, Henry can't be sentenced in the Magistrate Court—"

"And because this lawyer lives in Kampala, who knows when he'll be back to Masindi," I interrupted.

"Exactly."

We "prayed hard" to catch a break.

✱ ✱ ✱

This is finally it, Henry thought the next morning as he and Abdul watched Magistrate Ojikhan enter his courtroom at 9:00 a.m. "I have reached a decision on your sentences," he said, agitated. "Unfortunately, your lawyer is in the High Court, so we must wait." With that, he departed as abruptly as he'd entered.

Three hours later, a swell of voices and a stream of people spilled onto the parking lot from the High Court. Henry's heart skipped a beat as his lawyer strode into the Magistrate Court. *Now?* Henry wondered.

"The High Court has adjourned and will not resume today. Are we ready for sentencing? I need to leave for Kampala very soon," Henry's lawyer said to the magistrate's assistant.

"Sorry, His Worship has gone home for lunch. He will be back at two."

Henry held his breath as his lawyer checked his watch and sighed with exasperation. "Very well. I will return then."

Two excruciatingly long hours later, Henry stood to receive his sentence. His heart was pounding, his mind racing, and his spirit praying. He told himself he was strong enough to handle whatever sentence he received, even if it meant two more years in prison. But deep down, he had his doubts.

Magistrate Ojikhan began by praising Henry for the excellent job he'd done as Katikkiro for well over a year. "I am impressed, Henry, that you took the initiative to educate the other prisoners at Ihungu. It is clear to me that education is very important to you. There is a letter here from the Restore Leadership Academy that says you have a scholarship to that school. The letter says you can begin there once you are released."

So far, so good. Henry fidgeted on his feet and nodded slightly.

"It is also clear to me that Innocent's death at Ihungu was not your fault."

Again, Henry nodded.

"But I was not the judge in your trial, and you were convicted of murder. I am sorry, but I have no choice. I must give you an appropriate sentence—one which takes all circumstances into account."

The blood drained from Henry's face. Magistrate Ojikhan paused and looked intently at the boy. He cleared his throat and drew a breath.

Two. More. Years. I will be in prison two more years, Henry thought as the riptide dragged him under even before Magistrate Ojikhan began speaking.

✶　✶　✶

I looked at the calendar before I dialed. Only four months had passed since I'd met Henry. It seemed more like four years. *Will today be the day? Will Friday, May 14, 2010, be forever etched into my memory as Henry's Independence Day? Or will it be discarded on the scrap heap of disappointing delays?* I uttered a quick prayer as the phone rang once. Only once.

Henry immediately proclaimed, "I am rejoicing! I am a victorious man now . . . I will remember this day forever!"

So will I, Henry.

Henry recounted to me what the Magistrate Ojikhan had declared:

"This is my ruling, Henry. I sentence you to one full year . . . of proba-tion. The Restore Leadership Academy is hereby ordered to ensure you meet with a probation officer in Gulu every three months until your probation concludes. God bless you in your studies, Henry."

Henry told me he had wanted to scream with joy, but no words spilled from his mouth. Instead, *Thank You, God! Thank You, God!* over-flowed his soul.

Abdul also received one year of probation. Both were free to return home as soon as transportation could be arranged.

As Henry and I talked, I once again succumbed to emotion. Waves of relief and gratitude flooded in and poured out. I wanted so much to be there with him and his family for the homecoming celebration, but I took comfort in knowing I'd be coming back.

Here's how I closed my update to the team that day:

As Bob Goff often says, "Our God is a God of justice, and He's nuts about kids." This provides further evidence. Bob also recently told me that Jesus carries around a picture of Henry in his wallet. Henry is now smiling in that picture.

Fittingly, Niemeyer had been eating lunch with Napier in Kampala when William called him, giddy with delight. He really did love these kids. But he told Niemeyer the same thing he told Henry—Monday would be the earliest Henry and Abdul could go home, citing the lack of transport funds. "I'll deposit enough money into your bank account to transport both Henry and Abdul right away," Niemeyer told him.

As William stammered on about Monday, Niemeyer interrupted him. "Not Monday. They need to go home *by tomorrow*. They've waited long enough."

William promised to do his best. But when I talked to Niemeyer several hours later, he wasn't convinced William would follow through because of his weekly routine of traveling to Kampala on Friday and not returning home until Sunday.

There was nothing to do but wait.

★　★　★

When I called Henry the next morning from California, the sun was setting on another day at Ihungu. And Henry was still Katikkiro. William had indeed left for Kampala on Friday evening without making any arrangements to send Henry home.

"But he was just here," Henry said, brimming with confidence. "He came back a day early and promised me I will go home tomorrow."

"Do you believe him?"

"I do."

"Do you feel safe from Innocent's family for one more night?"

"I do."

That was good enough for me.

Before I left for church the next morning, I dialed Henry's number.

Three rings. Four rings. Five rings. Finally, the line connected. But I didn't hear his voice. Instead, I heard a screaming crowd.

"Hello, Henry? Are you there? What's happening? Are you okay?"

Excruciating seconds passed before I finally heard Henry's voice. He was yelling at the top of his lungs.

MAY 16, 2010

On Sunday afternoon, Mr. William arrived at Ihungu with money for my transport home. He said he would take Abdul home the next day. It was sad for us to say good-bye, but we promised to call each other often. He thanked me for being a good Katikkiro. As I walked down the path from the custody to the road, I made sure no one was waiting to hurt me.

When I stepped onto the road and started walking toward the matatu stop, I realized I was finally free. I stopped and looked back at Ihungu. It had been bad to be away from home and away from school, but I had made many friends and learned many lessons there. My struggles had taught me to trust in God more than I thought was possible. I finally understood what my mother said about always remembering God is in control. I was still not sure how God would use for good what happened to me and my family, but I believed God was good and would make this clear eventually.

As I turned away from Ihungu, I promised myself I would never go back there again. I wanted to remember, but I also wanted this part of my life to be over.

I called my mother when I boarded the matatu, and called her again when I got close to home. When I arrived, my family, friends, and neighbors were waiting to welcome me home. They all yelled and made celebration noises when they saw me. My brother Kegan and several others picked me up and carried me around outside and then into the house. While they were carrying me, Jim called.

There was so much food, and one of my neighbors had hired a DVD machine and a screen to show videos to celebrate. Because my family did not have electricity, our neighbor connected a very long cord to another neighbor's house, and we watched videos, ate food, and celebrated until very late. When I woke up in the morning, there were still people at our house from the night before. It was so good to be home, but I really wanted to start school again and knew Joseph and I would be leaving in less than a week for the Restore Leadership Academy.

"I just now arrived home!" Henry shouted. "They are carrying me around the house and neighborhood. They are so happy!"

He was effusive in his words of gratitude, and his family members started shouting into the phone when he told them who was calling—they all wanted to say thank you to the team who worked on his behalf to gain his release.

Our conversation was short and sweet; it was time for him to celebrate with his loved ones.

Two days later, Henry told me all about the night of celebration. I asked him whether his family was okay with him leaving the following weekend for Restore. He assured me they were.

The timing had been perfect—the second term was set to begin the next week, which is where Henry and Joseph had left off two years earlier. Joline and I had previously informed Bob Goff and John Niemeyer we'd pay for their education and accompanying expenses at Restore. We'd already mailed the initial check. Everything was set.

A week later, Henry, Joseph, and their father took a three-hour bus ride to Gulu. Niemeyer met them at the bus park and took them shopping for mattresses, school supplies, and other necessary items for their next three months at Restore.

On Saturday, May 22, 2010, Henry and Joseph began their new lives at the Restore Leadership Academy. That same day I picked up the entire Criminal Division of the Ugandan High Court at Los Angeles International Airport for a packed week of intense study and preparation to integrate plea bargaining into their criminal justice system.

What happened that week changed everything.

PART
FOUR

CHAPTER 19
THE PLEA

THE DAY BEFORE the Ugandan delegation arrived, my cell phone had rung. "Hey, Jay. What's up?"

"I'm at the airport with the Principal Judge. He came in a day before the others. Are you available to join us for lunch?"

In our meeting with Principal Judge James Ogoola in January, he'd been quite curious about our work in Masindi. Now, over lunch in Malibu, he peppered us with questions about what had transpired since then. Thanks to my frequent conversations with Henry, I was able to thoroughly update him, as well as extensively describe Henry's case.

"So the boy has been released on probation and will start school soon?" he asked.

"Yes. He starts Monday."

"That is good. Education is important. Are you going to appeal?"

"We are, and we have found a Ugandan attorney to represent Henry."

"Really? Who?"

"His name is Edward Sekabanja."

"Ah," he said, smiling, "I know Sekabanja. He is excellent." He paused and then leaned in as if telling me a secret, "Have you thought about representing him yourself?"

I told him I had looked into the attorney admission rules, but since I wasn't licensed by a British Commonwealth country, I would need to take a year-long course and an exam.

"What you missed in your research was the *exception* to the general rules," he said.

"Exception?" Now I leaned in.

"Yes. The Chief Justice can grant a special practicing certificate to any attorney authorized to practice in his or her home country."

My pulse quickened. "What would this certificate allow the attorney to do?"

"To appear in court on a specific case, as long as he or she was accompanied by a Ugandan lawyer."

My stomach somersaulted at the prospect of being Henry's lawyer. "Has this provision been used often?"

"Only once," he said, "for a Kenyan lawyer."

"Ah, I see," I said with obvious disappointment.

After another pause, he said, "Pepperdine has become a good friend of our Judiciary. Chief Justice Odoki appreciates what you have done for us. I suspect he would seriously consider your request if, of course, the boy wanted you to be his lawyer."

There was one way to find out.

MAY 25, 2010

Joseph and I loved the Restore Leadership Academy. We were so happy to be back in school, and the teachers were very good. Joseph started in Senior One, and I started in Senior Three.

The other students were nice and welcomed us. None of them knew we had been in prison. When they asked why we were starting at the beginning of the second term, we truthfully told them we had just been accepted to Restore and came as soon as we could.

At first, we did not know the local Acholi language most students spoke in the dormitory, but we learned it quickly, and the teachers all spoke English in the classrooms. A few weeks after we arrived at Restore, Mr. Bob gave us Bibles that had been sent by Jim and his family. Our names were printed on the front in the leather, and there was a note on the inside with a picture of Jim's family. The note said they hoped to meet us someday. About one month later, another student stole my Bible and some of my other possessions. He was removed from school a few days later, but I did not get my things back. The next time Jim came to Uganda, he brought me another Bible.

Restore's rules did not allow students to keep mobile phones, but John Niemeyer let me keep mine to talk to Jim. Jim called me for fifteen minutes every Tuesday at 6:00 p.m. During our call my second week at Restore, he told me a very good Ugandan lawyer had already agreed to represent me, but he asked whether I wanted him to try to get permission to be my lawyer himself. I knew he would do everything he could to help me, and I trusted him as much as anyone I knew. I said it would make me happy to have him as my lawyer and that I would pray very hard for this to happen.

I ushered Principal Judge Ogoola and his five colleagues into the conference room we'd secured at the Jonathan Club in downtown Los Angeles. One by one they filed in after their leader. The frenetic pace of the just-completed week had exhausted them, but they were determined that day to reach a consensus on the rough contours of a plea-bargaining framework for their criminal justice system.

Except for one of our visitors fracturing her big toe while exiting a minivan, the week's only scare had been losing a registrar named Alex for several hours during a shopping outing. When an observant security guard came to his rescue and asked what his friends looked like, he'd replied, "They are five Ugandan judges—they look like me!" Having previously noticed five black adults in suits at the food court, the security guard quickly facilitated the reunion.

The rest of the trip had exceeded expectations in every way. Over the course of six days, the court officials met with Pepperdine law professors, federal and state judges and prosecutors, public and private criminal defense lawyers, the Los Angeles Police Department, and the FBI. They also visited a federal courthouse, a state courthouse, a juvenile prison, and an adult prison. It wasn't all work and no play, however; Bob Goff had taken them to Disneyland for half a day. But in the conference room on this last night, the pressure was on to encapsulate what they'd learned into a summary report for the Chief Justice.

After making sure they were comfortable and had everything they needed to complete their task, I closed the door behind them and went to join the bittersweet festivities that were occurring at the Jonathan Club that evening—the farewell party for Dean Ken Starr, who'd been named president of Baylor University. While I was disappointed to lose my valued mentor and close friend, this move made sense, and I cherished the six years we'd worked together at Pepperdine.

The next morning, as I gave the judges a tour of Pepperdine's undergraduate campus before their flight home, Justice Lugayizi and I chatted about the future of Uganda's criminal justice system. "We have decided to implement plea bargaining, Jim. The backlog of prisoners waiting for trial is too long, and this will help tremendously."

I swelled with pride that a seed planted by Pepperdine law interns was sprouting in a way that would change the structure of criminal justice in Uganda. "Can we find somewhere to pray together before we leave for the airport?" he asked.

As we gathered around a circular table in the library, Justice Lugayizi asked me to lead the prayer. "I'd be honored to do so," I said and bowed my head.

"Before you pray," he interrupted as he took my hand, "I have one request."

"Sure, anything."

He looked directly at me with pleading eyes. "Please consider coming back to Uganda for an extended period of time to help us implement plea bargaining. We would very much appreciate your assistance in this important enterprise."

I was stunned. Relocating to Uganda was *not* on my radar. I didn't know what to say, so I said what I usually say in times of uncertainty: "I will pray about it."

And I did.

One week later, Bob invited Jay and me down to San Diego. Over omelets and orange juice, we planned our next trip to Uganda. Two days later, everything was set. I would go back in early July with Pepperdine Law's vice dean Tim Perrin and, along with the ten law students already in Kampala, we'd descend upon the Naguru Remand Home for another week of juvenile case preparation. I arranged to stay two additional days so I could visit Henry and Joseph in Gulu. I initially planned to surprise them by simply showing up at Restore, but I was too excited to keep it a secret.

I e-mailed Justices Ogoola and Lugayizi to tell them our plans. They promised to smooth the way.

Because the Naguru warden had been there when Bob and others had prepared cases at this remand home a year earlier, and because Pepperdine already had students working for the courts, the logistical details fell into place much easier this time around. Our two students interning for Justice Lugayizi—David Nary and Meghan Milloy—worked closely with the judicial officer who'd broken her toe during her visit to Pepperdine. Together, they identified the seventeen juveniles who'd been awaiting trial for more than a year.

John Napier and Brett LoVellette were still serving as Nootbaar Fellows and jumped at the chance to participate. This meant our team consisted of four lawyers and ten law students.

Over two days, we interviewed the juveniles and feverishly worked to complete the summary briefs before the start of the court session, which was set to begin the next day. On the second afternoon, I met with

Edward Sekabanja, the lawyer who'd agreed to represent Henry in his appeal. Napier had connected us after meeting Edward in Ethiopia at an Advocates International Conference—a gathering of Christian lawyers from around the world. When we turned our attention to the appeal, it was clear he'd already read the trial court record.

"Before we begin," he said, "Henry has been released and is now in school, right?"

"Yes. He's in school in Gulu. I recognize his conviction may never actually come up again or prevent him from getting a job or going to university, but it's important to Henry and me that his record be cleared of any wrongdoing."

He agreed.

"I hope it's okay that I've already prepared most of the appellate brief," I said sheepishly, handing him the file.

He was pleased.

Toward the end of our conversation, I raised the prospect of me potentially arguing the appeal, hoping he'd be supportive.

"Great! I am familiar with this provision, and my assistant can prepare the necessary paperwork. Have you talked with Henry about this?"

"I have, and he'd like me to argue the case, if possible."

"Then it is settled. If you can get permission from Chief Justice Odoki, then you will present the case in court and I will be the Ugandan cocounsel the law requires."

"What do you think are the odds the Chief Justice will grant my request?"

"How well do you know him?" he asked.

"I met him briefly in January during my first trip to Uganda, but he's coming to Pepperdine in two months, so I should get to know him better then."

"My advice is to wait until after he has enjoyed his trip to California and then ask him in person," he said with a devious grin.

I like the way this guy thinks, I said to myself.

Before I left, Edward confirmed what Brett had told me—it would likely be a year or more before the hearing was actually scheduled.

Over the next few days, nearly half of the cases from the Naguru Remand Home were summarily resolved as the judge, the prosecutors, and the defense lawyers all used the briefs we'd prepared. Many of those who didn't dispute the charges against them were sentenced to the time they'd already served; several others were also released when their cases were dismissed for lack of evidence.

The next morning, Tango drove Dean Perrin and me to Uganda Christian University for a meeting with Brian Dennison, an American lawyer who'd relocated with his family to help advance UCU's law school. On the way to UCU, we discussed how to leverage what we were doing. Though we were throwing starfish, we weren't training Ugandans to assist the juveniles themselves—we were treating the symptoms rather than fixing the problem.

Over lunch, Brian told us he was directing UCU's new clinical education initiative and seeking opportunities to connect his students with actual clients in real cases. He also told us about his relationship with the Uganda Christian Lawyers' Fraternity and encouraged us to get to know them better. This triggered my memory of meeting UCLF's president, Mike Chibita, the evening we returned to Kampala after our week at Ihungu. I resolved then and there to include UCLF lawyers and UCU students during my next visit to a juvenile prison.

To find myself planning my next trip to Uganda caught me off guard. But I couldn't help it; I was growing to love this country and its kids.

Before Tango and I ventured north to Gulu the next day, I updated Justice Lugayizi on the week's events. He was pleased and told me that he and his colleagues had submitted their plea-bargaining report to Chief Justice Odoki, who had given them the green light to proceed. Justice Lugayizi also reiterated his request that I temporarily relocate to Uganda to help them restructure their system. I prayed about it for much of the six-hour drive to Gulu.

Niemeyer had secured permission for Henry and Joseph to leave Restore for forty-eight hours so we could catch up. We talked, laughed, and ate. It was the first time they'd ever ordered food from a menu. At one point, I filmed them for about two hours talking about life before, at, and after Ihungu. I learned many of the stories recounted in this book that night. Henry also told me about joining the Restore soccer team for a few weeks, before being sidelined by a minor injury. He later decided to concentrate on his studies, which led to him being named the English Prefect for his class. A little while later, we spent an hour Skyping with my family, then twenty minutes Skyping with Colin and Amy Batchelor—dear friends from Texas who had taken quite an interest in Henry's plight. They had sent with me a backpack for Henry—his first—stuffed with school supplies.

During our second evening together, we watched the World Cup Finals between Spain and Holland, which was projected on a white bed sheet the hotel had tacked to the outer wall of the restaurant. Henry was a huge Spain supporter, having listened to numerous soccer matches with his fellow inmates on a small radio at Ihungu.

At 2:00 a.m., my alarm clock started beeping. Or so I thought. I was in such a deep slumber, it took me about twenty seconds to figure out that the sound wasn't coming from the clock; it was coming from my Ugandan cell phone. And it wasn't an alarm, but a call from Napier.

"Hey, what's up?" I mumbled groggily.

"We're all fine. Every student is accounted for and safe. Dean Perrin flew out before they closed the airport," he said reassuringly.

My cobwebs instantly cleared. "What are you talking about?"

"You haven't heard what happened in Kampala tonight?"

"No, but it sounds serious."

"It is. During the second half of the soccer game, two bombs exploded in Kampala. Dozens were killed and hundreds were badly injured. We're all fine though."

I was stunned. "You said Perrin got out okay, right?"

"Yes, his flight left just before the game. You should get to the airport early tomorrow. It should reopen by then, but security will be extra tight."

*　*　*

As we left the hotel the next morning, Henry pointed at a six-foot-tall wooden giraffe in the lobby. "What is this one called?"

"It's a giraffe. You've never seen one before?"

"I have not. Are they this big?"

I laughed. "Actually, they're *three times* that big."

It was his turn to laugh. "Really? Are they here in Uganda?"

"Yes, only about two hours from here."

"I hope to see one someday," he said, still smiling.

*　*　*

On my flight home, I thought about what I was doing in Uganda. I had morphed from a disengaged cheerleader into a reluctant participant in a one-time project, and then into someone actively considering ways to improve the system. I definitely did not identify with the man on the beach heckling the boy throwing starfish; I was the boy seeking out starfish to throw.

But why? I asked myself. Was I looking for an adventure? Was this my midlife crisis, as my oldest daughter had jokingly suggested? Or was this simply a glimpse of what it looked and felt like to surrender control of the future to God? I hoped it was the latter, but wasn't entirely sure.

I was sure, however, I'd be going back to Uganda and eagerly anticipated the trip, whenever it would be. I also knew an important part of Uganda—Chief Justice Odoki—was visiting me in two short months. And I had a very important question for him.

*　*　*

The Chief Justice and several others arrived in late September for a packed week of court visits, speeches, and dinners. In what was fast becoming a tradition, Bob Goff took the Ugandan visitors to Disneyland and got a great picture of the Chief Justice wearing Mickey Mouse ears, which now hangs in Odoki's office. Later in the week, a mesmerized crowd heard the Chief Justice reflect on life during tyrant Idi Amin's regime, his steady rise through the Ugandan judiciary, his lead drafting of the Ugandan Constitution in 1995, and the greatest challenges facing Africa. It appeared Justice Odoki was having a great week.

The next day I popped the question as we drove to the Ventura County Courthouse for a lunch with a group of judges. "As you know, I've been to Uganda three times this year," I began.

"Yes, you are becoming one of us," he said wryly.

"Well, that's what I'd like to do. I'd like to become a Ugandan lawyer, just for one case."

"Really? Which case?" he asked with bemusement.

"There's a boy I met during my first trip. He was convicted of murder but is now out on probation. He's attending Bob's school in Gulu." Everyone loves Bob, so I figured it couldn't hurt to drop the name of his Disneyland buddy. "This boy and I have become very close, and I'm working on his appeal with Edward Sekabanja."

"I have the authority to grant permission for a foreign lawyer to appear in court," he declared, anticipating where I was headed.

"Justice Ogoola actually told me that when he was here in May. He encouraged me to ask you to consider granting my request to argue this case in the Court of Appeals," I said and then held my breath.

"Oh, he did?" He chuckled. "We were classmates in law school. He is a good man."

He paused, seeming to search his memory banks. "I think I have granted permission only once." Another pause.

"Does the boy want you to be his advocate?" he asked.

"He does. I have also spoken with Edward about it, and he is willing to assist me."

Yet another long pause.

"Why not!" he exclaimed as he shot me a big smile and held out his hand to seal his promise. I would have hugged him if I wasn't driving.

I called Henry that night and told him the good news.

CHAPTER 20
GUIDEPOSTS

JUSTICE LUGAYIZI'S PLEA for me to relocate to Uganda gnawed at me. I'd been teaching at Pepperdine eleven years and had never applied for time off under Pepperdine's sabbatical policy.

When my older brother and I were growing up, we competed in track and field on a national scale—my brother twice finished second in the country in hurdles, and I was national champion in the pole vault at the age of thirteen. During this time, my dad periodically floated the idea of dropping out of life for a year to travel and be together as a family. The subtext had been his belief that the extra year of physical maturity would give us an advantage in our athletic pursuits in college. Ultimately, the idea never gained traction, largely because my parents were both public school teachers and we couldn't afford to go an entire year without an income. But this idea had always intrigued me, and now, almost forty years later, it resurfaced.

One evening in late September of 2010, shortly after Chief Justice Odoki left, I secretly set to work on a sabbatical application, seeking an entire year away to help the Ugandan judiciary restructure aspects of its criminal justice system. Because the application wasn't due for another month or two, I didn't worry about finishing it that night. I'd made a good start and decided to look for the right opportunity to broach this with my family.

Like me, Joline had never been on a mission trip of any sort growing up. But she had accompanied our oldest daughter, Jessica, to Honduras in June of 2010, and they'd loved their week of service. I naïvely figured this gave me a shot at convincing them to relocate to Africa for a year. I knew, however, that Joline and Jessica were still likely to mount the strongest resistance—Jessica because she'd just started at a new high school, and Joline because, well, the idea was a bit nuts.

About ten days after I started my sabbatical application, Joline and Jessica went on a weekend church women's retreat. During a jog that Saturday, I decided I'd raise the sabbatical idea with Joline when she returned.

"Welcome back," I said as I hugged them both on Sunday. "How was the retreat?"

"It was great," Joline said, "but I need a nap."

While she was sleeping, I did one of the dumbest things a husband can do: before talking to my wife, I gathered together all three children (then fourteen, twelve, and ten) and asked them what they would think about moving to Uganda for an entire year.

Joshua, who is always up for a new adventure, responded first. "Sounds good to me. When would we leave?"

"A little less than a year from now," I said. "We'd probably be gone from August of 2011 to August of 2012."

"Count me in," Joshua said without hesitation or reservation.

"Who would our friends be, and where would we go to school?" Jennifer, who is the social butterfly in the family, asked skeptically.

"You wouldn't go to school," I said. "You'd all take an entire year off and then join the class behind you."

Jessica, who, like Joline, prefers to plan things out and dislikes surprises, interjected, "You would work with kids in prisons, but what would we do?"

"We'd figure that out together between now and then," I said hopefully. "You could probably teach English in the Naguru Remand Home."

This suggestion failed to even budge her resistance needle, which was now bending against the force she was exerting on it.

The conversation flagged a bit, so I told them nothing had been decided and that we'd talk more after Mom's nap. I judged the current tally to be one strongly in favor (Joshua), one strongly opposed (Jessica), and one on the fence (Jennifer). I decided to go for another run while Joline was sleeping.

When I returned, Joline, Jessica, and Jennifer were all sitting at the kitchen table, crying. I instantly knew the idea was dead.

Joline and I excused ourselves to our bedroom so we could talk about this matter privately—something I should have done from the beginning. To her credit, Joline refrained from berating me for ignoring common courtesy and instead focused on the practical aspects of my proposal. How could we afford it? What would we do with our house? What would we do with our dog? Where would we live in Uganda? What would she and the kids do while I was at work?

I had few answers. My solution with our house was that we'd sell it and move into one of the campus condos at Pepperdine when we returned. This would also partially solve our financial challenges, because we wouldn't have a mortgage payment for an entire year. And since we'd already decided to move Joshua and Jennifer the following fall from their current public school to Oaks Christian, where Jessica had just started her sophomore year, their transition would be relatively seamless because they'd be making new friends anyway.

"But what about Jessica?" Joline pressed. "She's been at Oaks for just a month. She's worked hard to make friends and is finally adjusting. Is it fair to ask her to start all over again? And would the kids have any friends in Uganda? If they aren't in school, would they have anyone their age to hang out with?" Joline mercifully didn't even mention the two-year commitment she'd recently made to the one hundred women in the Community Bible Study she coordinated.

I hung my head. "I don't know, Joline. I feel like we're all going in different directions all the time. I thought this would be an opportunity for us to reconnect and serve together. I'm trying to let go of my need to control all aspects of my life, and I feel like God is leading me, leading *us*, to Uganda. Perhaps I'm wrong about that." She hugged me tight as we both cried together.

The next week passed without further discussion about Uganda. It wasn't going to happen, so there wasn't much point in stirring the emotional waters. But that didn't mean I wasn't still thinking about it.

In late October, I found myself wide awake at three in the morning. I rarely experience insomnia, so I was surprised I couldn't fall back asleep. By three thirty, I was downstairs finishing my sabbatical application. Because the application concerned the entire 2011–12 school year, I figured it couldn't hurt to keep all options open. I decided to suggest alternatives, proposing either a scholarly writing project or an extended stay in Uganda. Having considered my family's well-founded objections to spending an entire year in Uganda, I was contemplating a compromise—just six months, so the kids wouldn't fall behind a year in school and so our income wouldn't take a significant hit. This compromise would foist homeschool-teaching obligations on Joline, but she'd done it a few years earlier in London.

I finished the application just as the kids were getting ready for school. It was my turn to drive Jessica, so it was just the two of us when I gently raised the one-semester idea.

"Dad, I've been thinking about this nonstop since you brought it up. It has even invaded my dreams. Part of me really wants to go, but don't you remember high school? I really don't want to be away from my friends for an entire year. I want to graduate with them. If there's a way to go to Uganda and still do this, then I'm open to it. Let's pray about it as a family and see where God leads us."

We hugged before she got out of the car. "I love you, Daddy," she said. She always calls me "Daddy" when she wants to convey an extra measure of affection. As I drove away, I couldn't help but think the spiritual maturity Jessica displayed reminded me so much of Joline.

At lunch that day, I was looking for Professor Carol Chase, one of my fellow associate deans. "She's at a lunch meeting of the sabbatical selection committee," her secretary said.

"The selection meeting is *today*?" I asked in disbelief. Since the earlier apparent death of my sabbatical plan, I hadn't paid attention to the due dates. I incorrectly assumed I still had more time.

A few minutes later, Carol popped into my office. "I hear you were looking for me. What can I help you with?"

"I had a question about a student, but I figured it out. Thanks." As she turned to leave, I said, "So, the sabbatical selection meeting already happened?"

"Yes, I just got back. I thought you were applying," she said. A month or so earlier, I'd bounced the idea off of her and Dean Perrin, and both had encouraged me to go forward with it.

"I was, then I wasn't, then I was again. I actually finished the application this morning but didn't realize when it was due. I guess I blew it."

"Maybe not," she said cautiously. "We asked for clarification on one of the applications, so we postponed a final decision until tomorrow. We're going to vote via e-mail. Send me your application right away and I'll circulate it to the others. You certainly have my support. You've been an associate dean for five straight years—that in and of itself deserves a sabbatical."

That evening the Gash family discussed the idea of a six-month sabbatical, beginning in late January of 2012, *without any tears*. We agreed to pray for forty days and see which doors God opened and closed.

The next day, the professor who chaired the sabbatical selection committee stopped me in the hallway. "You know, Jim, I'm usually a stickler for compliance with deadlines. But my wife spent part of her childhood living in Uganda with her missionary parents, and I think the work you're doing there with the kids in prison is terrific. You have my support, and I'm pretty sure your application will be granted later today."

It was.

For the next forty days, my family prayed together for God's guidance. At some point during this time, Jessica wrote a paper for her sophomore Bible class.

WAKA WAKA

By Jessica Gash

This starts like any other story, but I promise it's one you haven't heard before. It was a Sunday afternoon, and I had just gotten back from my church women's retreat. I was tired and stressed and overloaded with estrogen. I don't really remember how my dad began, but the end effect was something like, "What would you think about moving to Africa for a year?"

The funny thing was, I wasn't really surprised. I mean, I did get that sickening feeling of dread at uprooting our family and going to a third world country, but not once did I think he was kidding, and not once did I feel surprised. You see, my family has been like this recently. We started off as this normal little American family, you know, self-absorbed and not really any big plans. But then Bob Goff came along.

Bob is this guy. And he's like obsessed with Uganda (a teeny little country in the middle of Africa). He got it into my dad's head that my dad should go to Uganda and rescue children from jail because he's a law professor and is actually allowed to do stuff like that. Since Bob brainwashed my dad, my dad has been three times and has rescued dozens of unjustly imprisoned Ugandan children.

So I'm sitting at my kitchen table doing chemistry homework half an hour later like nothing happened because really it wasn't a shock so why should I make a big deal out of it? And then my mom walked in and I started telling her my dad's brilliant idea. And started crying. The last thing I wanted to do was go to Africa. Sure, I'd gone to Honduras, but that was for like a week. I had just moved schools. I really didn't want to be uprooted after I had just gotten settled. Oh yeah, and there was the fact that I would have to graduate a year later. Survey 100 teenagers and 99 of them will tell you that that isn't exactly something they want to do.

The next couple weeks saw the death of my dad's idea. My mom and sister and I all ended up crying because that was how badly we didn't want to go. Every night, I prayed that God wouldn't make me go. I begged that he wouldn't make me leave my life, my friends, and my country. I told God that if he let me stay, I would try my hardest to serve him right where I was. Everyone started to forget about it.

Everyone but me. I had this nagging feeling that I should go. At my private Christian school, is it any wonder that we have to go to chapel? No, but it is surprising that this was like missions week or something. I was bombarded with speeches about mission trips changing lives and being worth any sacrifice. And it felt like everyone was speaking directly to me.

It turns out my dad hadn't forgotten about Africa. He proposed a compromise. We would go for a semester, not a year. That I could agree to. I don't think I had ever felt God's call like that before, and I didn't feel like I had a choice. There's this C. S. Lewis quote (I know, I know, I'm a dork) that says, "I don't pray to change God. I pray to change me." And after praying and praying, I stopped asking God to keep me where I was. I started begging and pleading for him to send me to Africa. Prayer changed me, and I knew even if my family didn't go to Africa this time, I would go at some point in my life.

I started thinking about Africa more and more. Africa

seemed to be everywhere. I saw it in my Spanish class in Shakira's "Waka Waka" song, and it leaked into my dreams. I met this little African girl in my dream one night. She reminded me of another quote (this one from *The Wedding Date*): "I'd miss you even if I'd never met you." I miss that little girl and I'm dying to meet her.

Then my family watched *Facing the Giants* and there's this verse in it from Revelation about not being able to open doors God closes and not being able to close doors that God opens. I felt like someone was screaming at us to hurry up and go to Africa. If God opened the doors for us, I would have bought my plane ticket that day. There's something of a rush in doing something crazy and stupid and doing it for God. If you've never experienced Christianity like that, you should try it sometime.

Then came door time. It's a lot less cool than hammer time or game time, believe me. Door time is when you have a bunch of doors in front of you and you wait to see which ones God slams in your face. If even one door was closed on our journey to Africa, then there's no way we could go. First there was my dad's job, then my school, then my brother and sister's school, then money, and so on. It's an entire hallway of doors and the silence is deafening while you wait for one of them to be shut.

I wish I could tell you what happened with the doors, but I'm still waiting. Patience has never been my thing, so sometimes the wait is agonizing, but I guess I can think of worse things. In the meantime, we just take one day at a time. Africa isn't going anywhere.

At the end of forty days, all five of us agreed we felt called to move forward with the planning. There were still many obstacles to surmount, but as each one fell away, it turned into a guidepost pointing the way to Africa.

In November of 2010, while we were looking at on-campus faculty condominiums, a Pepperdine-owned house twice as big as the house we'd be leaving opened up in the neighborhood immediately adjacent to campus. We pounced and agreed to buy the house the following June.

In January of 2011, Oaks Christian High School unexpectedly reversed its earlier decision to limit its online study program to freshmen and sophomores, and expanded it to include juniors for the first time. With this abrupt change, Jessica could now take the same classes as her peers.

In February, Uganda's highly contentious presidential elections occurred without the destabilizing unrest many had predicted.

In March, Joline's parents fell in love with our dog and offered to keep her while we were gone.

In May, our house inexplicably sold at above our asking price amidst the biggest real estate downturn in recent memory. This ensured we wouldn't have two mortgages to deal with while we were in Uganda.

God was opening doors all along the way.

✱ ✱ ✱

In June, I returned to Uganda with another team of American lawyers to work with another set of imprisoned juveniles at the Naguru Remand Home. I also used this opportunity to solidify our plans to relocate to Uganda. I had a wonderful meeting with the man who had replaced the now-retired Justice Ogoola as Principal Judge. In fact, during our meeting, we decided he and the newly appointed Deputy Chief Justice would visit Pepperdine three months later. Additionally, Justice Lugayizi's replacement as head of the Criminal Division eagerly renewed the earlier invitation for me to help them restructure a portion of the criminal justice system. And in the juvenile prison project this time around, we made sure not only to throw individual starfish but to work toward achieving a sustainable solution.

A few months earlier Mike Chibita, Uganda Christian Lawyers'

Fraternity president, had been appointed as a judge on the High Court. His UCLF successor was none other than Edward Sekabanja. With his assistance and that of Uganda Christian University's Brian Dennison, we put together four teams for the work at the Naguru Remand Home— each one consisting of one Pepperdine lawyer, one UCLF lawyer, two Pepperdine law students, and one UCU law student, who served as the interpreter for any prisoner who preferred to speak Luganda rather than English (which was most of them). Everything went smoothly, thus forging a lasting partnership between Pepperdine, UCLF, and UCU.

Because most of the Pepperdine team had never been to Africa, we scheduled a safari at the end of the trip so they could experience the local wildlife firsthand. Before we went to bed on the night I arrived in Gulu to see Henry and Joseph, I told them I had a surprise for them in the morning. When we woke up, I walked them into the hotel lobby and showed them the wooden giraffe. "How would you like to see a real one today?" I asked.

"Really? Where?" Henry asked, wide-eyed.

"We're leaving right now for a safari at Murchison Falls," I declared with a flourish.

Blank stares.

"What is a safari?" Henry finally asked.

"And where is Murchison Falls?" Joseph followed up.

Once I explained what we were doing, they were thrilled. The safari was amazing, and I won't soon forget the excitement in their eyes as they saw elephants, hippos, buffalos, crocodiles, and *real* giraffes for the first time.

The next day, I went apartment shopping back in the capital city. I eventually settled on a sizeable place at the Royal Suites in Bugolobi, a Kampala suburb. Joline and I had decided to heed the advice of several missionaries we'd consulted. They all encouraged us to find a safe, comfortable dwelling so our children could have a retreat from the culture shock. This apartment, with its three bedrooms, fit that bill.

By the time I returned home in the summer of 2011, everything was set for our 2012 Ugandan adventure, at least logistically. But mentally and emotionally, the seams were starting to fray. The novelty and excitement associated with new experiences had worn off, replaced by fear, uncertainty, and impending loneliness. The reality was that we were moving somewhere completely unknown to everyone but me. Joline and the kids would have no friends, no social network, and nothing familiar to fall back on. While they mostly put on a brave face, I could tell a sense of dread was setting in, which caused me no small amount of guilt.

Three months before we were set to leave, Joline again attended our church's annual women's retreat—one year after I had sprung the Uganda idea on her. During a quiet time of journaling, Joline wrote:

I have been trying to prepare for Uganda on my own strength. God is telling me—*I have called you, I will equip you. Why do you think you need to do this on your own? Ask me for help, and I will make your path smooth.* Help me, Lord! How many sleepless nights will I endure before I rely on you for peace? How much time will I waste chasing after unimportant things? What do you want me to do, Lord? Please give me strength. Please open my eyes to what is important to you. I need your peace. I need your vision. I can't do this alone. Thank you for your grace and mercy. Thank you for using imperfect people to accomplish your will. Thank you for loving me when I am unworthy. Thank you for carrying me. Thank you for your faithfulness, even when I am unfaithful. Thank you for your mercy. Thank you for your promise that you will be with me always, no matter where I go.

In the wake of these fears, we bore down in prayer, asking God to provide us a life preserver so we wouldn't drown in them and in our feelings of inadequacy.

✳ ✳ ✳

One of Pepperdine's public relations officers learned about my friendship with Henry and wanted to find a broader audience for the story. Ultimately, he zeroed in on *Guideposts*, a monthly Christian magazine similar in format to *Reader's Digest*. The publication's executive editor took an interest in the story and flew out to Pepperdine to talk with me about Henry, as well as my family's upcoming trip to Uganda.

A few months later, *Guideposts* published a story entitled "Saving Henry," though it could have just as easily been called "Saving Jim." In the aftermath, I received numerous calls, letters, and e-mails. One e-mail was from a man named Steve, an agricultural engineer in Oklahoma who kindly shared that the article had encouraged him to continue his ongoing work with a children's home in Uganda. Though neither of us knew it at the time, Steve had unwittingly become the vessel for God's answer to our family's fervent prayers.

My response was short but heartfelt. I thanked him for contacting me and for his work in Uganda. I also asked that we stay in touch and connect once our family arrived in late January. His courteous reply to my e-mail contained two sentences that entirely changed the course of my family's six months in Uganda: "Our group has an urgent care doctor, and his family is going to Uganda early in 2012 for 6 months. If you think it would be helpful to have a connection with them, please let me know."

I, of course, was eager to hear about another family also planning to relocate to Uganda in early 2012 for six months. I was floored when I read the first e-mail from Dr. Jay Gregston, the father of that other family. After some greetings, he wrote:

My family and I are planning on being in Uganda from Feb 1 to the end of July of next year. We are not sure where we will be based but possibly in Kampala or Jinja. We are feeling called to take health care to rural Uganda via mobile medical clinics, working in churches, schools, prisons, etc. We are talking with a couple of different NGOs and looking for the best fit. . . .

My wife, Jill, and I are 40; we have kids Jake (15), Jared (12), and Jayne (11). They are excited about serving on these mobile clinics with me.

We will have to meet up while we are there and get to know each other better. Perhaps we could do some medical care in some of the rural prisons that you work in.

God had dropped into our laps a "twin family"—they were also moving to Uganda for six months one week after we were. Their kids were fifteen, twelve, and eleven, while ours were sixteen, thirteen, and eleven. Their initials were all *JG*, just like ours. On a Skype call between the two families a few days later, we discovered that both Jill and Joline were retired schoolteachers, and both families had a Yorkshire terrier. Most importantly, both families were deeply committed Christians who felt called to serve the underserved in Uganda.

Within a couple days, the Gregstons had secured the only other available three-bedroom apartment at the Royal Suites and would be living directly beneath us for six months.

God had answered our prayers in a big way by providing us fellow travelers on our journey.

CHAPTER 21
SURPRISES

"WHEN DO YOU THINK they'll get here, Dad?" Jennifer asked.

"They're on the same flight from Amsterdam we were on last week," I said. "We pulled in at about 1:00 a.m., so they should be here any minute."

My entire family sat in the lobby of the Royal Suites, anxiously awaiting the arrival of our twin family. During our first week in Kampala, we'd explored the city and settled in to the apartment. We found a movie theater, a supermarket where we could find food we recognized, and a few good restaurants. Three hours earlier, we'd secured the key to the Gregstons' apartment so we could turn on their air conditioner and stock their fridge.

"That's them!" Jessica blurted as a van laden with suitcases and plastic trunks eased through the security gate. As they piled out of the van, we piled on the hugs as if they were our new best friends.

In fact, they were.

✷ ✷ ✷

Since our first Skype call in mid-October, the Gashes and Gregstons had been in almost constant contact. Jay and I exchanged e-mails regularly, and Joline and Jill spoke on the phone every few days. Eventually Jill hatched a plan to connect our two families before we went to Uganda.

"We're surprising our kids at Christmas with a one-week, mid-January trip to Cancun. Jay and I have been talking, and we'd love it if your family joined us. Would you be interested?" she had asked Joline. Since we weren't leaving for Uganda until late January, we thought a Mexican Riviera vacation would be a great way to start off 2012.

For five days our families "speed dated," and it was an excellent match. The four adults became fast friends, and the six kids bonded like siblings. So when the Gregstons arrived in Kampala that Friday morning in early February, we embraced like old friends.

Our Ugandan adventure was off to an excellent start. We had a comfortable place to live and fellow travelers on our journey. I'd already started working for the Judiciary, and Joline and the kids were eager to dive into the work I'd arranged for them. I also looked forward to fulfilling the promises I'd made in my heart to Henry's mother and father over dinner that November—and to Henry long before.

✶   ✶   ✶

At Restore Henry excelled, particularly in the sciences. By the time graduation day from O Level (Senior One through Senior Four) arrived in November, Henry had risen to number two in his class of forty-five.

Before I left Ihungu on my second trip after Henry's conviction, I had promised him I would come back for his graduation if we were able to get him released from prison and enrolled at Restore. Henry never directly reminded me of this promise, but it hung in the background of our conversations about the event. I wasn't going to miss it for the world, but I really wanted to surprise him. So I lied a little on our call the week before graduation.

NOVEMBER 2, 2011

At the beginning of November, Jim told me he could not come for my graduation from Restore because he had to work. I remembered him telling me at Ihungu that he would come back for my graduation, but I didn't want to make him feel guilty.

Joseph and I were surprised and very happy when he told me he gave John Niemeyer extra money this term to pay for my mom and dad to attend my graduation. My mom had never been to Restore and had told me many times she wanted to see where we went to school.

Jim said he was sorry he could not come, but promised that he and his family would visit me and the rest of my family in Hoima when they moved to Uganda a few months later.

I had landed in Kampala late Friday night that November and rode up to Gulu with Bob and a group of seven others who were traveling with him. When we reached Restore, a heated basketball game was underway on a dirt court. I scanned the crowd of kids who instantly mobbed Bob when he exited the vehicle. They all knew from past experience that crazy fun wasn't far behind when Bob arrived.

The last time he came to Restore, he'd shown up with a huge tarp and a skateboard—something the kids had never seen before. They'd all "tarp surfed" for the better part of the next day. Henry had emerged as the best "surfer" in the school. The time before that, Bob had brought a popular Christian recording artist with him for a concert. And not too long before that, Danny DeWalt—Bob's partner in both Restore and their law practice—had arrived with the two portable basketball hoops now in use.

As I hoped, Henry and Joseph were quite surprised to see me. "You said you weren't coming," Henry said, still in shock.

"I know. Sorry I wasn't truthful, but I wanted it to be a surprise."

"It is a surprise. A good surprise. I am glad you are here."

Just before the ceremony began the next day, Henry introduced me to his father and reintroduced me to his mother. We all teared up as we hugged.

The ceremony itself consisted of numerous impromptu speeches from teachers, local leaders, and Bob. And when the graduates' names were called, Bob whooped with delight and gave them each a massive bear hug. Toward the end of the ceremony, the head teacher announced several individual awards—for the valedictorian, the top debate student, and so on—and a few other specific awards voted by the faculty. I could not have been more proud when Henry received the one for "Most Outstanding Character."

Afterward, Joseph stayed behind with his friends as I took Henry and his parents to dinner. I very much enjoyed this time with them and was confident I was able to convey how special Henry was to my family and me. They invited our entire family to visit them in Hoima once we arrived in Uganda.

The next morning, Henry took the final portion of the Senior Four national exam. The results would dictate where he would be admitted to A Level (Senior Five and Six).

Henry and I had settled on Uganda Martyrs Namugongo as our dream school for A Level because Martyrs consistently had more students admitted into medical school than any secondary school in the country. We were also pleased that this elite boarding school happened to be only thirty minutes away from where my family would be living.

To be admitted to Martyrs, I knew Henry needed to score in the top 2 percent of all exam takers on the national exam. It seemed like a long shot, but we agreed to pray hard that it would happen. Though the scores wouldn't be released until late January, I was determined to make some progress on getting him admitted to Martyrs in the meantime. So I broke away from Bob's group and headed back to Kampala with Tango the day after graduation. The next morning, as I walked into the Court of Appeals Registry, Alex, one of the registrars who had come to California with the delegation, smiled broadly. "It is good to see you, my friend," he said.

"It is good to see you, too, Alex," I said as we embraced. "You haven't gotten lost again in any American malls, have you?"

He laughed heartily. "I'm never going to hear the end of that, will I?"

As we talked, he let me know he'd added Henry's case to a criminal session set for that February. We looked at a calendar and selected a date during the second week.

That afternoon I met up with three representatives of Sixty Feet. Jay Milbrandt had arranged for me to connect with this Atlanta-based Christian organization that had recently started working with Uganda's remand homes. Kelsey and Kirby—American women in their twenties— described the medical, spiritual, and material aid they were providing not only to the kids at several remand homes but also at Kampiringisa Rehabilitation Center, the prison where the convicted juveniles served out their sentences.

After our conversation, the lingering uncertainty surrounding how my wife and kids would spend their days melted away: they would work directly with Sixty Feet in the remand homes.

★　★　★

A couple days after the Gregstons arrived in Uganda in early February, I arranged for Joline to meet the Sixty Feet team at the Naguru Remand Home. Everything was set.

And then it wasn't.

Out of the blue, the newly appointed commissioner overseeing Uganda's remand homes decreed that only organizations with completed and approved paperwork would be allowed to continue working with the juveniles. And while Sixty Feet had been in the remand homes for nearly eighteen months, they were abruptly expelled because the commissioner's office had yet to finish processing their paperwork.

I felt like such an idiot. I'd convinced my family to drop everything and move to Uganda to serve, and now their service project was shut down. *What now, God?*

The answer came quickly and from nearby. "Why don't you guys work with us on mobile medical clinics?" Jay suggested to Joline during dinner that evening. "We're in the process of nailing down which schools, churches, and villages we'll be serving and what our schedule will be. We'd love to have you join us for as many clinics as you'd like."

"What would we do?" Joline asked. "None of us has any medical training."

"We have a Ugandan doctor and two Ugandan nurses who'll be working with us, so we have the medical side of things covered. Jill and our kids plan to help with registration, filling prescriptions, and spiritual counseling. You and your kids can certainly help out there as well."

"Joline is highly organized," I said, trying to encourage the discussion.

"I'll be homeschooling Joshua and Jennifer two or three days a week, but if you think we can be helpful, it sounds like a plan," Joline said. "We don't really have any other options at the moment."

Our kids were excited about the opportunity, so it was settled. I'm now certain God used the hiccup with Sixty Feet's paperwork to fulfill a larger plan.

✳   ✳   ✳

"This morning's edition of the *New Vision* says the national exam results will be released later this week," I told Henry a few days later.

"Oh really? That is good. I am eager to receive my scores."

"As soon as we have the scores, I'll meet with Father Kasasa again," I said.

The week prior, I'd met with Martyrs' headmaster about the possibility of Henry being admitted into the Senior Five class. I'm a huge fan of Luke 18's parable of the persistent widow, so by the time the scores arrived, the three front office workers—Ruth, Judith, and Justine—all knew me by name. So when I requested a meeting with Father Kasasa, they had squeezed me in.

"Excellent. We must pray hard they will admit me," Henry said. "My family is praying every day, and I believe I will be admitted."

"Speaking of your family," I said, "is it still okay for us to come visit you on Saturday?"

"It is very okay! My family is so happy you are coming to greet us. They have a surprise for you."

"Really? What kind of surprise?"

"You will see when you arrive, but make sure you are hungry."

We agreed to meet at noon at the Hoima Hotel.

"One other thing," I added. "Remember the other family I was telling you about that is also here in Uganda?"

"The family with all the *J* names?"

"Exactly. They would like to come too. We've told them all about you and your family, and they want to meet you. Is that okay?"

"It is very okay."

After I hung up, Joline said, "This is going to be a big week—Henry's test results, his possible admission to school, and our Hoima adventure— all within a few days."

"You're not kidding," I agreed.

"Tango is driving us to Hoima, right?"

"He is. He secured a van large enough for us and the Gregstons."

"Good thing he's from Hoima," she mused. "You're *really* going to need him on Sunday."

"Definitely. I'm not sure what I'd do without him."

"You haven't yet told Henry about your surprise plan, have you?"

"It was pretty difficult, but I've kept everything under wraps. I did tell Tango so he could call ahead and make some inquiries, but I haven't told Henry anything. I'll tell him Saturday, though, because I want him to come with us on Sunday."

"This is such a Bob Goff thing to do," she said with a knowing smile. "He'll be proud of you if you can pull this off."

Three days later, I sat across the desk from Martyrs' headmaster trying to muster as much charm as I could. Henry's national exam scores had been delivered to Restore the day before, and Niemeyer had immediately texted them to me and Henry. They were excellent, placing him in the top 5 percent in the country. But they weren't quite good enough for Martyrs.

"I have spoken to many parents in the past few days eager to have their children admitted here," Father Kasasa said as he leaned forward in his chair. "My phone is constantly ringing, and you saw the line outside waiting to speak with me."

"I understand, and I'm grateful to you for meeting with me today," I said. The relationship I'd developed with his support staff had paid off; they ushered me in shortly after I arrived, jumping the lengthy queue.

"We are grateful to Pepperdine for admitting our former student George Kakuru, and we hope to develop a deeper relationship with your fine school," he said.

"I would like that very much, and I hope Henry has the opportunity to study at *your* fine school," I replied.

"Remind me, what subjects is he hoping to study here at Martyrs?"

"He wants to go to medical school, so he's hoping to study PCB," I said, using the common acronym for the physics, chemistry, and biology track.

"That is our most competitive track," he said with a note of seriousness. After a short pause, he said, "So . . . how were his scores?"

"Excellent," I said with more confidence than I felt. "He scored in the top 5 percent."

"That is a good score," he said as he leaned back and clasped his hands behind his head. While his words were promising, his body language betrayed his true feelings. "The limit for our PCB students is the top 2 percent." He leaned forward again and raised his hands, palms up.

"I realize that," I said as I leaned forward myself, "but he scored in the top 1 percent in chemistry and the top 2 percent in physics."

"Wow." His demeanor shifted from resignation to mild interest. "Those are excellent—exactly the scores we look for in these subjects. And biology?"

I anticipated this and needed to nail the answer if Henry had a prayer of getting in. "As you know, he attended school in Gulu and not in Kampala. They didn't have the lab equipment and resources to prepare him sufficiently."

I filled my lungs to capacity before continuing so I could get out all I wanted to say in one pleading breath. "In biology, he scored in the tenth percentile, but just think how well he could've done if he'd been here at Martyrs for his O Level. His chemistry and physics scores show how smart he is—he would've scored just as well in biology if he were studying under the brilliant teachers you've assembled here."

He beamed with pride. "We do indeed have outstanding teachers," he said before pausing and folding his hands. "But none of our students scored that low in biology. If I admitted him, he would start off way behind the others and would have a very hard time catching up."

I nodded as he spoke, signaling to him that none of this was news to me. When he finished, I tried not to pressure him, aware that if I forced him to decide now, Henry wouldn't be admitted. "I understand you have difficult decisions to make over the next few days," I said. "I know you'll consider Henry's situation carefully, and I'm confident you'll make the right decision. I hope you decide to admit him, but I'll understand if you decide you cannot."

"Thank you," he said, seemingly surprised I didn't either continue to push for admission or offer him a bribe.

"In the meantime, can you recommend another strong school for PCB? I want him to get the best education possible. *Your* school is the best; what school is second best?" My passion to secure the best for Henry involuntarily shined through as tears rimmed my eyelids.

"The headmaster at Seeta is the former headmaster here. It is excellent and not far from here."

"Would you be willing to give me his phone number?"

He paused and studied me. He apparently noticed how much it meant to me to have Henry admitted to a good school because he offered, "I will call him for you myself . . . if it comes to that."

"Shall I come back next week?" A ray of hope had broken through the clouds of doubt.

"No need to come all the way to the school. Just call me next Thursday. We are making our initial admissions decisions next Wednesday."

"I will. And just to clarify, I should wait to contact Seeta?"

"Yes, they will be making their decisions the following week, and I can call then on the boy's behalf."

We shook hands, and I promised to call him the next week.

✳   ✳   ✳

Henry dismounted the boda boda and jogged over to where Joline and I were waiting at the entrance to the Hoima Hotel. "You are most welcome!" he said as we embraced. "Is this your madam?"

"Hello, Henry! It's so nice to finally meet you in person," Joline said as she hugged him. She'd joined me on numerous phone calls with Henry over the preceding two years, and they'd seen each other twice on Skype.

A few minutes later, the Gashes, Gregstons, and Henry all piled into Tango's van. As we drove toward Henry's house, he pointed out the Hoima market where Imanriho had initially been captured and then we continued along the path of Imanriho's final journey.

"That is the school where I was arrested," Henry said as we passed by.

"We must be close to your home," I said.

"Yes, it is just there," he responded as he motioned to Tango.

It was surreal seeing firsthand where it had all happened—where Imanriho died, where he'd been temporarily laid to rest, and where Henry's father had been arrested.

As we pulled up to the small concrete box that served as their home,

Henry's family streamed out. I recognized his parents from Henry's graduation. I thought the tall, attractive woman in her early twenties must be his sister, Doreen, and the two other males had to be his older brother, Kegan, and younger brother, Herbert. Joseph had already returned to Restore to begin the new term.

After we all greeted each other, they invited us into the house through the curtained doorway. It was tight, but we all squeezed into chairs or found places on the floor in the main living area. Awaiting us was the surprise Henry had alluded to earlier—a feast consisting of two kinds of meat, rice, Irish potatoes, soup, chapattis, carrots, tomatoes, pineapples, bananas, papayas, popcorn, sodas, and bottled water. Knowing how poor they were after having lost everything, I felt guilty about how much they'd sacrificed to prepare this meal for us.

I kicked myself for not telling Henry they didn't need to fix anything for us. It probably wouldn't have mattered, though; Ugandans usually insist on feeding whoever enters their homes.

Henry's brothers and sister easily understood our English, but their parents struggled to decipher our mzungu accent, so they simply nodded and smiled whenever we looked at them. After we finished stuffing ourselves, Tango drove the Gregstons and the rest of my family to the Hoima market for a couple hours of shopping while Henry and I stayed behind to take pictures and capture video at his home and school.

He showed me where the police officer had been hiding before he arrested Henry, and where Henry was when he first heard the alarm and saw the angry mob. As we retraced his path when his mother summoned him after Imanriho's theft, I surprised him with news of what was going to happen the next day. He could barely contain his excitement.

"I cannot believe it. My mom and dad are going to be so happy! Thank you *very, very* much!"

By the time we reached Henry's house, Tango had returned to pick us up. I asked Tango to take us by the Hoima police station.

Big mistake. *Huge* mistake.

As we pulled up to the station, Henry stiffened. "This is where they brought me, Joseph, and my mom after they arrested us."

"Is it okay if we get out and I film you while I ask you a few questions?" I tentatively asked.

"It is okay," he said quietly.

"We'll be back in five minutes," I told Tango. I pulled out my digital video camera and positioned Henry about fifty feet in front of the entrance. I pressed the Record button and said, "Where are we right now, Henry?"

"We are at the Hoima police station where I was taken after—"

"What are you doing here?" growled a gruff man carrying an AK-47. He wore the scowl of someone looking to make an arrest.

"Good afternoon, officer," I said calmly, hoping to defuse whatever situation was developing.

"Who are you?" he said as he pointed his weapon at my feet.

I extended my hand to shake his. "My name is Jim Gash, and I work for the High Court of Uganda." He waived my hand away with his gun.

Over his shoulder, I could see someone who appeared to be his supervisor watching the events unfold. I raised my hands in a show of surrender so the officer standing in front of me appeared in control of the situation. "What seems to be the problem?" I asked.

"It is a crime in Uganda to photograph a police station!" he barked. "Come inside now. We need to question you."

"It is? I'm so sorry. I didn't realize this, and I'm happy to come inside with you." I gave a quick head nod toward Henry, trying to signal to him to go back to the van.

"Who is he?" he said as he motioned to Henry.

"He is a local boy. He did nothing wrong. I'm the one with the camera."

"You are from Hoima?" he said incredulously to Henry. "You should know better. You come inside also."

I'm such an idiot. I brought Henry back to the police station where he had so many bad memories, and now I've gotten him arrested again?

The two officers escorted us into a holding room and had us sit down at a table. Under the table, I inconspicuously switched out the still camera from my pocket with the video camera in my hand. The only pictures on the still camera were those I'd taken of Henry at his house and school. Switching the cameras was the smartest thing I did that day. But that's not saying much.

As I waited for the interrogation to begin, I contemplated my latest in a string of rookie maneuvers. On our way out of Kampala, we'd stopped at a currency exchange dealer to convert just over four thousand dollars into nine million shillings. Around my neck hung a passport holder, the seams of which strained against the bulge of 180 orange, fifty-thousand-shilling notes. Having left in the van the button-up shirt I'd been wearing all day, my thin T-shirt was powerless to hide this four-inch protrusion equal to *three years* of wages for a typical Ugandan police officer.

The officer and his supervisor proceeded to berate us for violating the law. I profusely apologized and once again reminded them I was the one with the camera.

"Show us your passport," the supervisor demanded.

In our family Joline is the keeper of all passports, so I could honestly tell him I didn't have it with me. "It is at the hotel, but I do have a driver's license," I said as I pulled it from my wallet, which was also stuffed with shillings—a fact that didn't go unnoticed by these men.

Fortunately, Henry didn't have any identification with him. "I am called Henry," he simply said.

After closely inspecting my license, the supervisor set it down in front of him. "Why are you taking pictures of the police station?"

I certainly wasn't going to say, "We're here reenacting Henry's bogus arrest two years ago. You guys are playing your part well," but that's precisely what it felt like. Instead, I explained, "This is my first time to

Hoima, and I wanted to be able to show my wife and kids the places I visited. But I didn't actually take any pictures of the police station. I was planning to take pictures, but this officer reacted quickly when he saw the camera, so I didn't have the chance to use it." My flattery scored a direct hit.

"I stopped them as soon as I saw the camera," he said with pride to his boss.

"Let me show you," I said as I turned the back of the camera toward them. "This is Henry at his house. Here he is with his family. Here is my family with his family. Here is Henry in his field. These are of Henry at his school. And here we are back to the picture of Henry at his house. I took no pictures of the police station."

The supervisor took the camera from me and scrolled through the photos one more time, clearly familiar with digital cameras. Apparently satisfied, he handed it back to me. "I need to see your passport before I let you go, unless . . ." His voice trailed off in a manner that clearly communicated I could pay some sort of private fine in absolution.

I'd been leaning forward the entire time in an effort to obscure the bank vault strapped to my chest, but he'd seen my stuffed wallet when I pulled out my driver's license. "Let's make a deal," I said.

"What do you propose?" he replied with anticipation.

"I really need that driver's license you have there in front of you. Why don't you hold on to it while we go to the hotel and retrieve my passport? I am staying just up the road at the Hoima Hotel and will come right back. While I'm gone, you can call Chief Justice Odoki to confirm I'm working for the High Court. I have his number right here." I quickly scrolled through the numbers in my Ugandan phone and slid it to him. I'm not proud of this name dropping, but I was in a bit of a jam.

He looked at the "CJ Odoki" contact, raised his eyebrows, and said, "It is okay. I will keep your license, and you will come back. I do not need to call the Chief Justice." In a sign of surrender, he slid the phone back to me.

By the time we got back into the van, more than twenty minutes had passed. Tango was wide-eyed. "What happened? I saw them take you inside and didn't know what to do."

"Just drive to the hotel. We'll tell you what happened later," I replied, still a bit stunned by the disaster we'd narrowly averted.

Five minutes later I tersely said to Joline, "I need my passport and I need to go back to the police station right now."

"*Back* to the police station? What are you talking about?" she asked nervously.

"Henry will fill you in. He and I were just detained and interrogated, and I need to get back there immediately. Henry needs to stay here with you, though."

"Okay, but before you go, give me all the money you have."

"Oh yeah, good point," I said, once again reminded she was the better half of our partnership. I handed her the passport holder and all the money I had, save for a single pink twenty-thousand-shilling note, which I left in my wallet. Just in case.

Back at the police station, the supervisor was waiting for me outside. "Where is the boy?" he asked as he inspected my passport.

"He is at the hotel," I said casually.

He handed the passport back to me and said, "You are not permitted to take any pictures of the police station without first getting permission."

In retrospect, I can't believe what I actually said next. "Well, can I have your permission to take your picture here now?"

He didn't laugh, but he did give me a crooked grin. "No, but you can go now."

"Um, can I have my license, please?"

Clearly anticipating this question, and obviously hoping for some *quid* for his *pro quo*, he paused to see if I would offer him anything in exchange. I did. I offered him a huge smile.

Eventually he handed me my license. It was his turn to smile when I gave him a vigorous Ugandan friendship handshake. "Have a good day," he said.

That evening, over dinner at the hotel with Henry's entire family, Henry announced he had a big surprise for us tomorrow. For a moment, I thought he was going to spill the beans and tell his parents what we had planned. But I was wrong.

"I spoke to the pastor at our church when I found out you were coming," he said. "You and Joline will be delivering the word to the congregation tomorrow morning."

"The word?" I asked.

"Yes, the pastor said you will preach the message tomorrow instead of him."

That was, indeed, quite a surprise.

CHAPTER 22
NEW BEGINNINGS

WHEN THE GASHES AND GREGSTONS entered Henry's church at 7:30 a.m., the place was hopping. Literally. The song leader, flanked by singers in matching lipstick-red silk shirts and black pencil skirts, bounced up and down on the concrete stage as if on an invisible pogo stick, while imploring the audience through a sputtering microphone to "raise Jesus higher." The congregation ecstatically strove to do just that— their hands stretched toward heaven as they hopped in unison. The keyboard player, dripping with sweat, danced and played and sang as if Jesus Himself were in the audience.

Having grown up in a conservative, hymn-singing church, this jubilation would have jarred my family had we not worshiped at the Watoto (Pentecostal) Church in Kampala the prior Sunday. This gathering felt rather subdued by comparison.

As at Watoto, the ushers shepherded us immediately to the front row. I suspect this gesture was intended to convey honor, but it also served to entertain the other parishioners. To say the Gashes have no rhythm is rather like saying the Sahara Desert has no snow. Thirty minutes later, the aerobic portion of the worship service mercifully concluded.

The pastor leapt to the stage and welcomed the hundred or so assembled for the early-morning service. "Is God moving anyone to share a word of thanksgiving for what He is doing?"

A dozen hands shot up, including Henry's and his mother's. Henry was the third to take the stage. He offered some kind words of gratitude about my family and asked the members of the church to greet his visitors warmly.

"Visitors? What visitors?" the pastor bellowed as he lightheartedly scanned the audience. We all had a good laugh about how much the ten of us stood out from the others—very few mzungus ever come to Hoima.

Henry's mom spoke next and also thanked God for *her* guests, emphasizing the possessive. A few minutes later, it was go-time.

The pastor dragged the podium to the center of the stage and invited Joline, Henry, and me to come forward. Even though this was the "English language service," the pastor wisely tasked Henry with interpreting our mzungu English into Runyoro for the congregation. In fact, I started out with a quick attempt at humor regarding having an interpreter for the mzungu at the English language service. Half the laughter came when I delivered the punch line; the other half followed Henry's translation.

After I introduced my family, Joline brought greetings from the Community Bible Study in Malibu and told them this group of one hundred women had prayed often for Henry, Joseph, and their father while they were in prison. The audience cheered.

Over the next twenty minutes or so, Joline and I alternated as we shared some scriptures and words of encouragement. As had been the case when I presented the captain's jersey to Henry at Ihungu, the periodic pauses necessitated by Henry's translation allowed me to maintain my composure, though only barely. I vividly recalled Henry telling me about his first Sunday back at church after he'd been released—he'd occupied this same stage and poured out his heart with gratitude to God for sustaining him during his two-year imprisonment. Toward the end of the service, the pastor encouraged the congregation to come forward and pray a blessing over our family. Words cannot adequately capture how special it was to have a group of total strangers fervently praying (in

Runyoro) while gently touching our heads, faces, and hands. We won't soon forget this experience.

After church, Tango, Henry, and I split off from the others so we could focus on the surprise I'd been waiting a few months to deliver. We had our work cut out for us over the next six hours. Adrenaline flooded my veins and appreciation filled my heart as I reflected on how the passport holder around my neck came to be filled with cash.

✷ ✷ ✷

Over the course of my fifteen years at Pepperdine, I've had a front-row seat to countless selfless acts by my students. Ten years ago, a student with one semester left teetered on the edge of the minimum grades necessary to graduate. He was wealthy and willing to pay handsomely for a tutor. I connected him with Virginia—a brilliant student and stellar person. What the struggling student later told me warmed my heart: Virginia refused compensation, declaring her payment would be witnessing him walk across the stage at graduation. The young man had his best semester ever, and Virginia—the class valedictorian—cheered louder than anyone when he received his diploma.

Four years ago, a student asked me if he could assign a portion of his academic scholarship to another student he considered in greater need than he was. The only condition he insisted upon was complete anonymity. I honored his sacrificial request. I could tell dozens more stories, but one stands out from the rest.

On the Sunday before Christmas 2011, Holly, a former student, flagged down me and my two oldest kids in the church parking lot on Pepperdine's campus where we worship. Holly and I had become close while she was in school and stayed in contact after graduation. She'd been following our story on my family's throwingstarfish.com blog and periodically inquired about Henry.

Holly handed me a Christmas present the size of a large box of chocolates. I love chocolate, so I hugged her and thanked her for her thoughtfulness.

"You need to open it," Jessica interrupted with a knowing smile.

"Now?" My darting eyes detected a conspiracy. Apparently it wasn't chocolate.

"You should open it *here*, away from other people," Joshua insisted.

That could only mean one thing—I was likely to get emotional, and my kids wanted to spare everyone, especially themselves, the embarrassment. A lump formed in my throat even though I had no idea what was in the box.

I gently removed the wrapping paper and carefully raised the lid. What I saw momentarily perplexed me—a stack of variously sized handwritten notes and cards, on top of which sat a cashier's check payable to me. The amount was over $3,000.

My confusion gave way to grateful tears as Holly explained what I was looking at. "After I read your blog about Henry's family losing all of their cows while Henry was in prison, I decided to try to collect enough money to buy them one cow. I sent out a Facebook message to those I knew who'd had you as a professor, and the money poured in. The cards are from those who contributed, and more money is on the way."

I had no words to describe such thoughtfulness, so I simply hugged Holly again and tried not to make a scene. A few days later, my parents and sister each decided to purchase a cow, giving me enough to restore the entire herd.

I was blown away. And since then, not a day had gone by that I hadn't anticipated the glorious scene when the cows came home.

That day had finally come.

✳ ✳ ✳

Before we left Kampala for Hoima the day before, Tango had called the butcher in his home village outside of Hoima and asked who in the surrounding area had cows for sale. After our brush with the police the day before, Tango had taken Henry and me out to meet a farmer looking to sell his cow.

I'd initially stayed in the van while Tango and Henry discussed a price. In Uganda, most sales of goods and services are negotiated face-to-face. The asking price, however, rises markedly when a mzungu is the purchaser. It's more economic opportunism than racism, but it's quite real. There's the local price, and there's the more substantial mzungu price. Our goal was to get the local price.

When Tango signaled the deal had been struck, I emerged from the van to pay the 750,000 shillings they'd agreed on. Our plan was to buy nine cows, and the $4,000 I'd exchanged netted me nine million shillings, so I was feeling good about the first purchase. But because it didn't make sense to buy and transport one cow on a Saturday evening, we arranged to return the next day to monetize the deal. Before we left, the farmer offered to ask around for others interested in selling cows to a rich mzungu. Interested sellers were to meet us at the butcher's shop at 10:00 a.m. Sunday.

The next morning after church, three eager sellers awaited us, hoping we'd drive to their farms to buy their cows. Initially, I doubted we could buy and deliver all nine cows in one day, but we were off to a good start.

Because my cover had been blown the day before, there was no point in me hiding while Tango and Henry discussed how many cows each farmer had and where they were located. We promised the seller from the previous day that we'd return to conclude the purchase of his cow later.

We had plenty of room in the van for the would-be sellers, so they all piled in. Along the way, we picked up several others who had cows they wanted to show us. Still others came along for the adventure. At one point, the van was full beyond capacity. So was my heart as I watched Henry's excitement grow at the prospect of this new beginning for his family.

The first farm we visited had only one young cow, but Tango and Henry said it looked healthy so *we* began negotiating. My gaze bounced back and forth as if watching a tennis match between Tango and Henry on one side and the would-be seller on the other. As they gestured and verbally jousted in Runyoro, my curiosity finally bubbled over. "Where are we?" I asked.

"We have offered six hundred thousand, and he wants seven hundred thousand," Henry said.

The seller raised his eyebrows and stretched out his arms to signal seven hundred thousand was his final price.

Tango shook his head and said to me, "This morning the farmer we visited yesterday said he now has three cows and wants to sell them all. We should go and buy those cows."

I liked Tango's negotiation style but was eager to get today's buying binge underway. I pulled out six hundred thousand and declared that either we'd pay six hundred thousand right now, or we'd leave to buy other cows.

The onlookers wanted a high baseline price before we negotiated with them, so they lobbied the seller to stand firm at seven hundred thousand.

My experience with car salesmen in the United States suggested it was time to see if he'd buckle if we started to leave. "We need to go," I said as I tapped my watch and pointed to the van.

As Tango turned toward the van, the price turned south. Apparently some negotiation tactics are universal. We had a deal at six hundred thousand.

When I tried to count out the money into the seller's hand—one fifty-thousand note at a time—he waived me off. Tango grinned and took the money. "We count money our own way."

I watched as he counted the money in his own hand and then gave it to the seller, who did the same. Lesson learned.

As soon as the deal was done, those in our growing entourage started dialing and shouting into their phones like traders on a commodities exchange. Tango said something to the seller in Runyoro and then turned to me. "We will pick up this cow in the village center at three o'clock. I have arranged for a big truck to carry the cows back to Henry's house."

"Are you sure he'll bring the cow?" I asked a bit skeptically, wondering if we had paid the owner too soon.

"I am sure."

"*How* are you so sure?" I prodded.

"In Uganda, if you steal a cow, the villagers burn you alive. He will bring the cow."

No further questions, I thought.

Next, we headed way off the beaten path, which is saying something because the path we were on was only lightly trodden to begin with. This farmer had two female cows and one young bull. His asking price was seven hundred thousand each. Because they were young and relatively small, I told him I'd give him 1.1 million for the bigger cow and the young bull.

Henry translated, and after a moment, the man nodded. I counted out the money in my hand and then watched him do the same. The problem, however, was that we were three miles from the village center and on a strict timeline. For twenty thousand more, he agreed to run the cows to the village. Knowing he risked becoming a human torch if he failed to show, I prepaid the delivery fee.

We knew we needed a big bull fond of lady cows so we could grow the herd. One of the guys in the van said his neighbor had such a bull near the village center, so we headed in that direction. At the farm, we first encountered a massive bull the color of the midnight Ugandan sky— pitch-black. "I'll give you one million for this one," I said to the owner.

"I wouldn't even take two million for this one. He is not for sale. That bull is the one for sale," he said in impeccable English as he gestured across the field.

The bull must have sensed our keen interest in his virility because as we approached him, he approached a nearby cow and, well, demonstrated his fondness for procreation. At this, I involuntarily exclaimed, "I'll take him!" My outburst severely undercut my bargaining position, but I didn't care. I got him for nine hundred thousand, and he was worth every shilling. I named him "Big Jim."

We were on a roll. We finally headed back to the original farm where we'd started the day before. When we arrived, four farmers and four cows were waiting for us, including the one we'd already purchased. After some dickering, we had the lot. In fact, one seller asked us to wait while he fetched another cow. This confirmed what I suspected—we were overpaying. But both Tango and Henry were satisfied with the prices, so I didn't feel cheated. It was also clear that the sellers owned virtually nothing other than their cows, so I felt good about them getting a few extra shillings for their families.

Shortly thereafter, we purchased our ninth and final cow; two of our assembled herd were purportedly pregnant.

When the truck arrived for transport, I learned how to load cattle Uganda style. No ramps, just four buff dudes—two in the truck and two on the ground pinning the cow against the back of the vehicle. One guy in the truck wrapped the tail around his wrist and gripped it like an angry boa constrictor while his partner pulled with all his might on a rope tied around the animal's mammoth horns. As the two wranglers in the truck *heaved*, the two weightlifters on the ground *hoed*, boosting the cow until it skidded onto the truck bed on its side. As you'd expect, the cow pitched a fit like a toddler avoiding a car seat.

None threw as big a tantrum as Big Jim. He thrashed, moaned, snorted, and spat for a good three minutes before finally succumbing. But as he struggled to his feet inside the truck, his disposition flipped 180 degrees when he noticed his awaiting harem. Immediately he sought to introduce himself to the others. After a bit of wrestling (and lots of rope), Big Jim was tied to the truck bed on his side.

When all was said and done, I'd spent seven million shillings on two bulls, seven cows, loading, and other commissions and fees necessary to transport cows in Uganda. We stopped along the way to pick up the Gregstons and the rest of my family, and when we arrived at Henry's home, we made sure the cattle truck parked around the corner until we could set up the surprise.

Henry's family eyed us suspiciously as I gathered them together and we got out our cameras. I began by telling them how sorry we were they'd lost their herd of cows and all their chickens when Henry, Joseph, and their father were unjustly imprisoned. I told them I was a big fan of the biblical story of Job, and that our God is a God of redemption.

"I'm a teacher, and one of my students collected money from some of my other students and from members of my family," I remarked. They stared at me blankly.

"After church today, Henry and I went shopping." Their eyes darted toward Henry, then locked back onto me.

I cued the truck.

As it rounded the corner and rumbled and bumped down the narrow, uneven dusty road toward the family's house, all eyes turned toward the noise. When the truck came into view, Henry's mom saw the huge horns over the truck's cab and let out the same type of "alarm" Henry had heard from his school window nearly four years earlier. She has high blood pressure, and Henry later told me he was worried she would faint at the sight. She didn't, but her emotions were on full display. The same was true for the rest of the family—they clapped, shouted, and hugged, rejoicing.

There's nothing more gratifying than being a tool in God's hand as He sculpts a redemption story. We all watched the cattle deboarding expectantly, though the unloading made the loading process look high-tech. This task needed only one man and one rope. The man simply tied the rope around one of the cow's back legs and yanked like he was starting an old lawnmower. This sudden jerk belly-flopped the cow, whereupon the guy would lean and backpedal like the anchorman on a winning tug-o'-war team. Meanwhile, the cow helplessly slid to the precipice of the truck bed until it literally plopped onto the ground from a height of about two and a half feet.

Most popped back up right away, looking for someone to kick. But Big Jim fell harder than the rest and seemed to have the wind knocked out of him. He eventually recovered, but not before he'd been tied to a tree away from the others to prevent any enthusiastic courting.

After the unloading, I brought Henry and his family into the house and explained we still had some money left over.

"In this envelope is two million shillings. If we had time, we would've purchased a couple hundred chickens and all the chicken and cattle feed you need. Henry will assist you with buying these things. I also understand Herbert didn't start Senior One last week with the others because you didn't have the money for the school fees." They nodded expectantly as I continued. "I hope you'll use three hundred thousand of this two million for Herbert's school fees so he can resume school tomorrow."

They were all elated, especially Herbert. Henry's mother insisted on leading a prayer right then and there. I'm not sure if her exuberant words were in English or Runyoro—the only word I recognized was "Jim"—but her gratitude to God came through loud and clear.

Not all heavily anticipated days live up to our expectations. But this day far exceeded them.

FEBRUARY 12, 2012

My family could not believe the surprise Jim and his family had for us. My mom told us she had always believed God would restore what we lost but wasn't sure how. The next day my father registered Herbert for school. A few days later we paid an animal doctor to come to our farm to give the cows injections to keep them from getting sick. The next week, two hundred baby chickens were delivered. They lived inside our house for about two weeks until they were old enough to stay in the chicken house next to our home.

The money Jim gave us was also enough to buy lots of food and other things we needed for the cows and chickens.

One month later the cow called Rosella delivered a baby, so we had ten healthy cows. My father said that these cows and chickens will provide us with everything we need to support ourselves for the future.

"Wow. This is a very big shop!" Henry said as we entered the four-story shopping center where we had arranged to meet when he arrived in Kampala a few days later. "We did not come here during my only other trip to Kampala six years ago."

I needed to deliver Henry's birth certificate to Martyrs as part of the application process and decided to press my luck by showing up with Henry a day before the headmaster asked me to check back. I hoped that if I could introduce him to Father Kasasa, Henry's engaging personality might shift the balance in our favor.

Henry was agape at the amount of food and other items during his first walk through a real grocery store. Because I wanted to get out to Martyrs by early afternoon, we didn't explore the rest of the mall right then. Instead, we headed to my office at the Commercial Court.

He had no idea why we were stepping into a metal box or why I pushed the button marked "3." "Ah! We are moving! Where are we going?" he said in a panic.

"We're going to my office. It's on the third floor."

He was mystified. "This is taking us there?"

When we exited and looked out a window, he laughed heartily at the magic room that had transported us upward. He'd heard of "lifts" before but had never fully understood what they looked like or how they operated.

After picking up a few things from my office, he and I stopped at my family's apartment on the way to Martyrs. There, Henry had his very first shower and changed clothes. I also showed him the first oven, stove, and microwave he'd ever seen, which reminded me how much of daily life I took for granted. I also demonstrated how a digital scanner worked as I copied his birth certificate.

As we entered the front office at Martyrs, Judith and Ruth greeted us warmly. "You must be Henry," Judith said. "We have heard all about you. You are most welcome!"

"Thank you. It is good to meet you. I hope to see you much as a student here."

"We hope so too," Ruth responded.

"Is Father Kasasa around? I'd love to introduce Henry to him," I said.

"Sorry, but he is not around. He and the other administrators are reviewing applications today so they can make their decisions tomorrow. You should call him then."

I left Henry's paperwork with them, and Henry and I explored the campus. He was in awe of the modern building, desks, and equipment. "I hope I get to go to school here," he said somberly as we left.

Henry seemed to enjoy the Garden City Mall so much, I decided to take him to the only other mall in Uganda (at that time), which had just been completed. I laughed so hard I almost fell down during Henry's first encounter with an escalator. Initially we went down, and predictably, he stepped on a seam and lost his balance as soon as the stairs separated. Fortunately, he also laughed heartily. When we headed back up, he found another seam and stumbled down the upward-moving stairs for nearly ten seconds before leaping off, turning around, and remounting the horse that had bucked him.

As we walked through the Walmart-like Nakumatt store, Henry was introduced to a freezer, a coffee maker, a washer and dryer, a frozen kilogram of hamburger, and a cereal box—among many other items—for the first time.

When we arrived back at the apartment, the others had just returned from a mobile medical clinic in a remote village on a peninsula jutting into Lake Victoria. While Henry was enjoying his first-ever pizza slice, Dr. Jay invited him to join the team the next day. Henry eagerly accepted and was thrilled at the prospect of some on-the-job training for his chosen future occupation.

"Can you swim, Henry?" Jay asked.

"I cannot. Why?" Henry responded, missing Jay's verbal cues.

"We have to travel across the water in a boat that's not very stable. We'll have to swim if it tips over," Jay deadpanned.

Henry looked at him and then at me, unsure how to respond. "I . . . I have only been on a boat one time, with Jim when we saw the animals. It was very big and could not overturn."

"This boat is very small and—"

"My dad's just messing with you, Henry," Jay's eldest son, Jake, interrupted. "The boat's pretty small, but you can wear a lifejacket and you'll be fine."

"It's all set then," I said. "By the way, how'd the clinic go today?"

"You'll never guess what I did today, Daddy!" Jessica's eyes positively sparkled.

✶　✶　✶

During my first year of law school, my Torts professor mesmerized my fellow classmates and me with his skill, intellect, and humor. *That's what I want to do when I grow up*, I said to myself. *I want to teach just like Professor Brain.*

Jessica had a similar experience. In 2009, Joshua's surgery to repair a chronic eardrum problem went sideways and left him in pediatric intensive care for three days. Jessica marveled at the nurses' competence and professionalism as they devotedly attended to her little brother. *That's what I want to do when I grow up*, she said to herself. *I want to be a nurse just like those ladies caring for Joshua. But I can't.*

The seemingly insurmountable barrier was Jessica's crippling fear of needles. Hyperventilation, incessant weeping, and gnashing of teeth ensued whenever she got a shot. And it was even worse having her blood drawn. That's why I sat in stunned silence when she told me what she'd done.

"I learned how to draw blood today!" She said this with the same enthusiastic pride as when she'd announced she peed in a grown-up toilet for the first time fourteen years earlier. My jaw dropped almost as far as my eyebrows leapt. "Dr. Andrew taught me and Jake how to do it. We tested the blood for malaria and HIV."

I looked at Joline in disbelief. I don't know if I was more shocked that Jessica had been willing to be trained or that Joline had allowed it to happen.

Sensing my concern about Jessica's safety, Joline shrugged and said, "Well, they needed her help . . . and they wore gloves."

Dr. Jay chimed in, "Andrew is a Ugandan blood lab technician, and he's very careful. Trust me, I wouldn't allow my son to do it unless I was sure it was safe."

I pondered this for a moment, then asked Jessica, "How in the world did you summon the courage to get so close to a needle?"

"It all happened so quickly, I didn't have time to get scared. I just said a prayer and did what Dr. Andrew told me to do."

I was still half expecting everyone to break out into jeering laughter at my expense, but it never came. Instead, Jessica looked at me with deep joy shining through her eyes. "This means I can be a nurse now, Daddy."

To say I was proud of her for overcoming her deepest fears doesn't even come close. This was shaping up to be a monumental week of new beginnings, and it was only Wednesday.

On Thursday morning, I ventured back to Martyrs while Henry nervously clung to the side of a boat on the way to his first medical clinic. He spent the day translating for and assisting Dr. Jay. Jessica and Jake spent their day drawing and testing blood, and I spent my day waiting for them to come home so I could tell them about my visit to Martyrs.

If I'd simply called Father Kasasa and found out Henry wasn't admitted to Martyrs, I would've always wondered if I should've gone out there in person. So I went. Once again, he wasn't in his office. This time, however, Judith called his mobile phone to tell him I was there. After she hung up, she led me to Father Kasasa's on-campus home.

"Welcome, Professor," he said with a smile. Behind him were several of his colleagues sitting around his kitchen table.

I waved to them with one hand and used the other to give a warm friendship handshake to Father Kasasa.

"We are still making admission decisions, so I cannot talk long."

"Of course. Sorry to disturb you."

"It is okay. But I will get straight to the point. Henry doesn't have the scores to be admitted to Martyrs," he said solemnly.

"I understand," I said softly, struggling to mask my dejectedness. "I appreciate—"

"But," he interrupted, "we have decided to take a chance and admit him anyway. With some very hard work, we think he can succeed here."

I can't exactly remember, but I'm pretty sure I hugged him. It was all a blur after the word *admit*. I do remember running back to the office to high-five the three office ladies, who were as happy as I was. I called Niemeyer and told him, but I decided to tell Henry and my family in person.

When they returned that evening, we all celebrated Henry's new beginning at Martyrs.

FEBRUARY 17, 2012

I assisted Dr. Jay all day as he met with sick people. The youngest was a newborn baby, and the oldest was more than eighty. Some had malaria, some had diabetes, a few had AIDS, and many had worms. Most of the patients spoke Luganda, which I also speak, so

I translated. This was the first time I really got to see what doctors do. Before this day, I thought I wanted to be a doctor. After this day, I knew.

On the way back to Kampala, the waves were very high and the boat bounced around so much, I was afraid we would tip over. I was wearing a vest that would help me float, but I was still so scared. When we arrived back at the apartment, Jim was already there and he said he had some very good news. I could not believe it when he told me I was admitted to study at Martyrs. I was so happy. I had been praying very hard that I could go to school there, and God answered my prayers.

A few days later, Joline took me shopping at Garden City. She bought me a mattress, three pairs of shoes, a wash basin, soap, towel, books, folders, and everything else on the list Martyrs had given me after I was admitted.

The following week—the week after Henry's now-postponed appeal hearing was supposed to have occurred—Joline and I checked Henry into his dormitory at Martyrs. When we returned home, Joline poured out her feelings onto our family's blog:

A MOTHER'S HEART

Do you know that empty feeling you get when someone leaves? It might be from a friend moving away, or a child going off to summer camp, or a sibling leaving for college. Well, I have that feeling tonight. When I look around our apartment, nearly everything I see reminds me of Henry. I see the deck of cards scattered on the table where he was teaching the kids card tricks. I see the school supply list that we spent all day Saturday shopping to check off. I see the school calendar from his new boarding school. I see the Rice Krispies treats he made with the kids. I see the leftover pancakes in the refrigerator from breakfast this morning. I see the sewing kit that I used to mend his shirt before church. I see the Band-Aid wrapper in my purse from the cut he got from carrying his heavy metal foot locker into school today. I see his cell phone that we must keep for him because they are not permitted at school.

My heart is sad because we had to say good-bye to Henry today, but my heart is glad because we have been praying for this day for so long. As my husband and I attended the parents meeting today, with Henry sitting between us, we were so proud to act as his guardians. I should not have been surprised that we were the only mzungus (white people) in the room, but we tried to blend in as best as we could. Henry has wonderful parents, but it would have been difficult for them to make the journey to Kampala and take him to school. There were many supplies that needed to be purchased, packed, and delivered to the school. We really felt like we were taking our first child to college. It was great practice for when we will be taking Jessica to college in a couple of years.

If all goes according to plan, Henry will study physics, chemistry, and biology at this school for two years, then go on to study medicine in a university. His dream is to become a doctor, and I believe he will do it. Henry is smart, hard-working, and has wonderful people skills. I think he will be a great doctor someday. It will be hard for us not to be able to see him until March on visitation day, but we will be praying for him daily. I know God has a plan for Henry. I am just happy to get to watch that plan unfold. So the joy that fills my heart is covering that empty feeling I have from saying good-bye.

CHAPTER 23
FULL CIRCLE

"J-FASTER," MUSED JUSTICE MUKASA, the new head of the High Court's Criminal Division, during my first meeting with him. "I like the name, and I like the proposal. It is very ambitious and will require you to work closely with the Department of Public Prosecutions, the Ministry of Gender, UCLF, and the Judiciary. It is not easy in this country to coordinate large projects involving many constituents, but we shall give it a try."

✶ ✶ ✶

By late January of 2012, I'd nearly finished editing a draft proposal to help the Judiciary refine its juvenile justice system and integrate a form of plea bargaining. While my legal background in the United States was entirely in the civil realm, I understood the challenges facing the Ugandan criminal justice system based on my work in the children's prisons and extensive discussions with Ugandan judges. Nevertheless, I harbored serious doubts about my qualifications to design and implement the structural modifications necessary to substantially reduce the backlog in Uganda's prisons.

Providentially, I knew just where to turn for the practical counsel and assistance I needed. In September of 2011, Shane Michael replaced Jeff Wyss as Pepperdine's Nootbaar Fellow in Kampala. During the summer of 2009, Shane had interned for Justice Lugayizi in the Criminal

Division and was thus quite familiar with the court's work. And while Shane's fellowship required him to devote most of his time to Commercial Division mediations, he was eager to assist in the Criminal Division as well. While in law school, he'd worked for the Los Angeles District Attorney's office and aspired to be a criminal prosecutor after completing his yearlong term in Uganda.

During a Skype call a month before I arrived, Shane and I had wrestled with what to call our proposal. "We just need the Judiciary to facilitate speedier trials—we need them to go faster!" I complained. Shane cocked his head, raised his eyebrows, and started writing. As he did, a smile creased his lips. "How about something like 'Judiciary Facilitating Access to Speedy Trial and Efficient Resolution'? Let's call it J-FASTER."

✷ ✷ ✷

We'd just finished summarizing the ten-page J-FASTER proposal and twenty PowerPoint slides we'd delivered to Justice Mukasa the week before. The J-FASTER program divided the juvenile criminal justice system into four phases—Investigation, Evaluation, Resolution, and Resettlement, each of which could be completed within thirty days. If successfully implemented, no juvenile would ever be held on remand for more than four to six months.

"I have asked Sarah to work with you on this project," Justice Mukasa informed us while motioning to the young lady sitting with us. "She has completed her legal studies and is working for the court as a judicial assistant."

In the wake of the successful Pepperdine internship program, the Judiciary had begun hiring some of its own recent law graduates to serve as judicial clerks; Sarah was one of the first. "I will assign a judge in the Criminal Division to hold a juvenile session for this pilot program," he said. "If it goes well, we will expand it."

"Thank you, My Lord," Shane and I said in unison as we stood to shake his hand.

"One more thing I would like you to consider," said the judge. "Our budget for court sessions is a challenge. I understand a private organization paid the court costs for the earlier sessions the Pepperdine team helped with in Masindi and in Kampala. Are those funds still available?"

Shane and I looked at each other with masked disappointment. We'd discussed this extensively before our meeting with Justice Mukasa and felt strongly that for J-FASTER to succeed on a long-term basis, it needed to be sustainable. And to be sustainable, it needed to be internally funded.

"We'll look into that, My Lord," I said. "But the goal of J-FASTER is to fundamentally change the way juveniles are dealt with in Uganda, and not simply to provide a short-term fix for overcrowding." I wanted to remind him about Henry, Bo, Abdul, and all the other kids who languished in remand homes for two years before getting access to justice. I wanted to tell him I moved my family to Uganda so there'd never be another Henry forgotten by the justice system. But I'd probably already been too bold.

Justice Mukasa narrowed his gaze. "I am fully aware of our challenges. These problems will be solved by Ugandans working in partnership with others who seek to help us. I am not asking for a long-term solution but a short-term bridge until we can secure the funds internally. We do not have funding for a pilot program in our budget."

"I understand," I said, "and I think I know just who to ask."

✷ ✷ ✷

One month before my family left Malibu for Uganda, Scott and Joy Harty stopped by our house on their way from the Los Angeles airport to a dinner in Santa Barbara to raise money for Sixty Feet, the Christian organization they and four other couples had started in Atlanta a year earlier. I'd already met the two Sixty Feet interns in Uganda and was eager to learn more about the organization.

Scott explained that the average depth of Uganda's water table is sixty feet beneath the surface. And while Sixty Feet's initial intent had been to drill water wells, it had refocused its attention on providing aid to Uganda's imprisoned children.

"If you ever come across an opportunity for us to partner with you, Pepperdine, or the Judiciary, please let us know," Scott had said. "We're eager to find more ways to serve."

✴ ✴ ✴

Once Sixty Feet's permission to work inside the Ugandan remand homes was suspended, I'd assumed any chance of partnering with them had vanished. But after the meeting with Justice Mukasa, I set up a call with Scott and another Sixty Feet board member, Dan Owens.

Sixty Feet immediately agreed to fund not only the court costs of the J-FASTER pilot program but also those incurred by the Ministry of Gender, Labour, and Social Development. The Ministry's role under J-FASTER was to perform expedited investigations and prepare Pre-Sentence Reports on the front end, and to manage the resettlement of the juveniles into their communities upon release on the back end. Having secured the willing participation of both the Judiciary and the Ministry of Gender, Shane and I turned our attention to the lawyers.

Fortunately, I'd developed a cordial relationship with the director of the Department of Public Prosecutions (DPP) during my earlier work in remand homes. Additionally, Shane had periodically met with the director during the months preceding my arrival. These relationships allowed us to integrate the director's input into the J-FASTER program before it was formally proposed. So once we had the go-ahead from Justice Mukasa, the DPP was on board.

This left only the defense lawyers for the juveniles, and that was the easiest part. UCLF, the Christian lawyers' organization with which we'd been working in the remand homes, was eager to expand its role in delivering justice to vulnerable children. I was encouraged to learn they'd already secured funding for the remainder of the year from various grants, so their participation kept the costs down.

By the middle of March, the J-FASTER bus was rolling.

Meanwhile, the Gashes and Gregstons were morphing into a single family. We exercised together each morning and ate dinner together each night. We played together on Saturdays and worshiped together on Sundays.

Henry wasn't allowed to have his cell phone at Martyrs, so he called from a campus pay phone during his dinner break once a week. We were only allowed to visit him during designated hours on designated weekends every other month. Nevertheless, we were thrilled with how things were going—he'd made many friends and loved school. "They keep us very busy. We wake up at 5:00 a.m. and work until 11:00 p.m. every night. Sometimes I am tired, but everything is very okay. Choir practice is taking up lots of my spare time, but we are doing very well and hope to win the regional competition."

A few weeks earlier, Henry had informed us he had joined the choir. We had no idea he was a singer, but we wanted to support him in whatever he chose to do. A few weeks later, I traveled to the regional championship and was able to celebrate his school's victory with him.

At the end of Henry's first school term, he did something he swore he'd never do, and I couldn't have been more proud of him.

✷   ✶   ✷

While in Uganda, I unexpectedly became involved with several families whose efforts to adopt Ugandan orphans hit legal snags. In early February, I celebrated with the Ribbens family when the Court of Appeals overturned an earlier denial of their guardianship application. In late March, I traveled to Masindi in an effort to assist the Doyle family in a case pending before Justice Ochan. While there, I met up with Mr. William. Over lunch, he reported that Ihungu had again swelled to capacity over the two years since we'd first come.

"Can you arrange another session with the children?" he asked.

I described the J-FASTER program we'd started in Kampala and promised we'd get something going in Masindi if it proved successful.

Back in Kampala, Shane, Sarah, and I lobbied Justice Mukasa to start another pilot J-FASTER session in Masindi before the Kampala pilot was completed. He agreed, but on two conditions. First, we would need to secure funding for this additional session. And second, Justice Ochan would have to agree to adjust his court calendar to make room for such a session.

Providentially, Justice Ochan was in Kampala presiding over a high-profile trial, and Sarah had been assigned to assist him. The next day, Shane, Sarah, Justice Ochan, and I met to discuss our idea. He didn't hesitate. "If I schedule the session for July, will that allow you enough time to prepare the cases?"

"We'd need to get started with the planning right away, but that would work, My Lord," I said.

"Then let's move forward," he replied.

Despite the fact I was appealing his ruling in Henry's case, I had (and still have) the utmost respect and admiration for Justice Ochan, and I looked forward to working with him again.

A month later, Michael, my court-assigned driver, drove me, Joline, and Henry from Kampala to Masindi. As the car wound up the path at Ihungu, Henry stiffened and slowly started to shake his head. Joline and I glanced at each other nervously. "Are you okay, Henry?" I asked. "Are you sure you want to do this?"

"Yes, I am okay," he said softly. "I do want to do this."

Two days earlier, Henry had completed his first of three terms of Senior Five at Martyrs. He felt good about how his exams had gone, but grades wouldn't be released for another few weeks. Only then would we know if we'd made the right choice to put Henry up against the most highly educated and intelligent kids in Uganda.

After Justice Ochan gave the green light, and after Sixty Feet generously agreed to fund the juvenile session in Masindi, planning had begun in earnest.

About six weeks earlier, the Gashes and Gregstons had taken a weekend trip to Jinja to visit our friend Katie and her family, and to go bungee jumping and white-water rafting on the Nile. We had a great time, but Joline brought home with her an unexpected souvenir from the trip. While we noticed her steady decline in energy, it wasn't until she started feeling depressed for the first time in her life that we wondered whether she had contracted something. Fortunately, Joline remembered a conversation we'd had with an American friend over lunch after church one day when he told us about contracting Bilharzia while white-water rafting on the Nile. This parasite lays eggs in the host's body, which hatch after six weeks. Joline's symptoms matched his exactly, including a rash on her back, so Joline took the pills and we said some prayers. Two days later, I had my wife back.

Joline had never been to Masindi and really wanted to see Ihungu firsthand. Because she was now feeling better, I invited her along the following Monday. Just before we left, we said good-bye to Lindsey Doyle, who was finally heading home to Nashville with baby Eden so she could finally have a family for the first time in her life.

We'd picked up Henry from school two days earlier and he'd stayed with us for the weekend. I told him where we were going on Monday and gave him a choice—he could take a bus home to Hoima on Monday, or he could come with us to Masindi and take a matatu home from there.

APRIL 23, 2012

When Jim asked me if I wanted to go to Ihungu with him and Joline or go back home, it was a difficult choice. I asked him if he would be talking with the prisoners. When he said he would, I asked him if I could also. When he said yes, I knew I needed to go. I still remembered how hopeless I felt when I lived there. I knew how hopeless they must feel.

Jim said I didn't need to go if it would be too hard. I told him I wanted to go to bring them hope.

When we arrived, many memories and emotions came back, and I was not sure I had made the right choice. But when Jim asked me if I was okay, I told him I was. I needed to stay strong for the prisoners.

"It is somehow different now," Henry said as he scanned Ihungu. "One of the soccer goals is gone, the steps to the store have been repaired, and the buildings have been painted."

After we got out of the car, Henry walked directly up to a small group of prisoners loitering near the entrance to the custody. Joline and I slowed our pace and watched from a distance as Henry introduced himself and began conversing with them in Swahili. I heard the word *Katikkiro* and then saw a prisoner raise his hand. Henry playfully slapped his arm and seemed to be sharing that he'd also once been the Katikkiro at Ihungu.

While they were talking, Mr. William joined the conversation—we'd picked him up on the way to Ihungu. He and Henry had a sweet moment of reunion and shared a tight embrace. A few minutes later, we were all in the boys' custody with the prisoners—thirty boys and three girls.

"Ah! They have new beds, and the inside of the custody has been cleaned and painted!" Henry said with evident pleasure. "Who did this?"

"An organization called Sixty Feet," I answered.

Henry translated as I explained to the group that some lawyers would be coming back to interview them and prepare their cases. The kids clapped and cheered when Henry finished translating. I told them I needed to meet with each of them briefly today to gather some information.

When I finished, Henry asked to say a few words. The prisoners were transfixed as Henry addressed them in Swahili.

"For two years, I lived here at Ihungu. I was the Katikkiro for most of that time, and I slept right here by the door like your Katikkiro. Near the end, I was losing hope. I kept praying, but I wondered if God was hearing my prayers. I was not sure I would ever be released or whether I would ever go to school again. But one day some lawyers from America came to see us. They looked at our court papers and asked us lots of questions. We told them the truth about our cases and they helped us get released."

When Henry said the word *released*, the custody broke into thunderous applause.

He continued, "Another group of American lawyers is coming here soon, and they will be with some Ugandan lawyers. They are coming to help you. They will ask you questions. You can trust them like I did, and you need to tell them the truth like I did. They will help you get released. I am praying you will be released very soon."

Once again, applause erupted when Henry finished. But this time it was punctuated with a well-practiced clapping pattern I had heard at several remand homes throughout the country: *clap clap clap . . . clap clap clap . . . CLAP.* This was the universal sign of appreciation in juvenile prisons.

I glanced at Mr. William as Henry was concluding and saw in his eyes pride in Henry and empathy for the children.

As we exited the custody, Henry retrieved three chairs, and we wandered over to our tree. "Here we are again where our friendship began," I said wistfully. "We've come full circle, Henry."

"I hoped I would never come back. When I left, I never wanted to see Ihungu again."

"Are you glad you came?"

"Definitely. It is very different being here free and not a prisoner. I am glad I had a chance to encourage them to stay strong."

For the next hour, Joline wrote out the prisoners' names, took their pictures, and then directed them to us one by one. Henry translated as I asked them a few questions about their cases and how long they'd been at Ihungu. To break the ice a bit, I started out each inter-view by asking which soccer team the inmate supported. This always elicited a surprised smile. One responded by telling us he supported the Uganda Cranes national team, but the others all named a team from the English Premier League, with Manchester United narrowly edging out Arsenal.

Over lunch at the Masindi Hotel, Henry caught up with his old friend Jamil, the Chairman, who still lived in Masindi. We said our good-byes to Henry at the matatu stop and headed back to Kampala.

✶ ✶ ✶

It's actually working, I marveled a few weeks later.

As we sat around the conference table in my courthouse office, it was happening in front of my eyes: the Ugandan prosecutors and defense lawyers were engaging in plea bargaining, and most cases were being resolved without a trial.

At the head of the table, Shane, Sarah, and I served as mediators. To our right sat the UCLF lawyers who represented the seventeen juveniles selected to participate in the pilot program in Kampala, along with a private defense lawyer designated to *separately represent* the adults in the three cases where adults were charged alongside the juveniles. (I wasn't about to let the same conflict of interest that happened to Henry repeat itself.) To our left sat two state prosecutors, and at the opposite end of the table were the probation officers who'd investigated the social, educational, and psychological backgrounds of the children and were preparing individual Pre-Sentence Reports.

By the end of the five-hour session, approximately two-thirds of the cases had been resolved. In most of them, the plea agreement set the sentence at "time served." This meant the juveniles would be released and then resettled into their communities as soon as we could get a court order.

Over the next two weeks, all but one of the remaining juvenile cases were also resolved. So when the trials started, only three were left—one against a juvenile and two against adults who'd originally been charged with juveniles. Two days into the remaining juvenile's trial, the prosecution dismissed the charges for lack of witnesses against him.

J-FASTER had been a success.

The following month a team of Pepperdine law students, Pepperdine lawyers, and Ugandan lawyers descended upon Ihungu and feverishly prepared the prisoners' cases for resolution. Joseph had heard about Henry's return to Ihungu and also wanted to come. Not surprisingly, Bob and Niemeyer happily allowed Joseph to skip a few days at Restore so he could serve as a translator for the prisoners.

Two weeks later, in advance of the trials, Sarah and I—along with two Pepperdine students who were interning with the Criminal Division—returned to Masindi for the plea bargaining meeting. By the time Justice Ochan's court session began in mid-July, all of the juvenile cases had been plea bargained. There were no trials. The vast majority of the kids were back with their families before the end of July.

✷   ✷   ✷

Every few weeks I checked in with the Court of Appeals. The hearing date for Henry's appeal, originally scheduled for February of 2012, was postponed numerous times. By the beginning of June, it was clear the case wouldn't be heard while I was still in Uganda. While disappointing, at least it meant I'd be returning to Uganda.

But I already knew that.

My family and I shared a lovely farewell dinner with the justices the week before we left. I presented Chief Justice Odoki with my final report and recommendations, which included immediately expanding J-FASTER to all five remand homes and then eventually implementing plea bargaining in the adult system.

Each of the half dozen justices in attendance gave a speech, and they showered us with gifts and souvenirs, all of which still adorn my house.

✱　✱　✱

Two days later, Father Kasasa granted us special permission to visit Henry one last time at Martyrs to say good-bye. We gathered six chairs into a circle on the lawn and laughed, cried, and prayed together. His first-term grades had fallen short of our hopes and his expectations. Henry was determined, however, to turn things around and vowed to work harder than ever to ensure his advancement to Senior Six at the end of the academic year.

The next day we flew home. Forever changed.

CHAPTER 24
APPEALS

"I JUST WANT TO GO HOME," Jessica lamented a few days later in Malibu.

Joline and I shared a look of dismay. "What do you mean?" I asked curiously. "We are home."

"I know. And I'm not saying I wish I was back in Uganda. That's not home. But this doesn't feel like home either. Everything changed while we were gone. I changed."

Jessica's twelve year-old sister, Jennifer, was struggling with similar sentiments, as she blogged ten days after we landed:

I'm pretty sure I'm not the only one who's thinking this. "So what now?" The truth is I don't know what's next. Ever since I got back, I've been wondering the same thing. I feel like I have this part of me that's screaming at me to go back.

Back where I feel accepted. Where I know that someone loves me. Where I know that there is a little boy who will be so grateful for medical attention that he will stick around the building until we leave just to say thank you. Someone that will run and grab my hand and never ever let go. I want God to hold my hand and never let go. Please, God, don't ever let go.

I know that God is always with me. I know that. Sometimes there are certain places where the signal sort of gets weaker. The signal is the strongest in Uganda. Back "home," or at least what's supposed to be home, I don't feel God with me as much as I want to. I want to feel like God is always sitting right next to me in the car. And I just don't feel that.

When I look outside at the mountains to my left and the ocean to my right, I feel truly blessed. Even though I missed my ocean in Uganda, I still yearn to go back to the place where I left half of my heart. To the Pearl of Africa.

So what now? I know that a part of me will always want to return to Uganda. I'm sure that I will someday, I just don't know when. But for now, I'm stuck in California. I guess I'll just have to see what God has planned for me.

We knew exactly what our girls meant. We'd all changed, and we were only beginning to understand and appreciate how.

Over time, we resumed our old routines. Our house, once again, became Grand Central Station—weekly Bible studies, youth group slumber parties, law school game nights, and an endless stream of guests staying in what was now dubbed "The Bob Goff Room" after Bob took up residence in our guest room on several Wednesday nights of the fall semester because he was teaching a class on Thursday mornings at the law school.

I still talked to Henry every week, and he was working hard in school. But his second-term grades had not improved. He faced the very real prospect of failing out after his third term, which seriously jeopardized his dream of becoming a doctor. A rising sense of dread overtook me every time we talked about his classes during our calls. One thing he told me, however, gave me hope that things would work out: "Almost half of my classmates have grades lower than mine."

Surely they won't flunk half their students, I told myself. The school fees were quite high by Uganda standards—$1,200 per year. Martyrs wouldn't forgo more than $150,000 in annual revenue by failing out 140 Senior Five students, would they? On the other hand, perhaps a high attrition rate explained how they kept their Senior Six national exam scores at the top.

Fortunately, I had an expert in Uganda secondary school education sitting in the second row of my Torts class in the fall of 2012, just one month after my family returned from Uganda. I needed to look no further for answers to my questions.

Since the publication of Bob Goff's book entitled *Love Does* four months earlier, more than 100,000 readers knew my new student as "Two-Bunk John," as the final chapter in Bob's *New York Times* best-selling book dubbed him. I simply knew him as John Niemeyer—my friend who'd helped me so much in Uganda.

After full-scale construction on Restore's new campus began in early 2012, Niemeyer finally succumbed to Bob's and my repeated entreaties to come to Pepperdine for law school. During orientation, he swung by my office. "Uganda's elite schools like Martyrs give the students horrible grades for the first two terms to scare the crap out of them. The only grades that ultimately matter are those from term three. Henry is really smart. He should be fine."

He had no idea how much of a gift his reassuring words were. Three weeks later, he handed me another gift—by far the coolest one I've ever received.

Every Wednesday night, Joline and I host a law student Bible study. We sing, pray, and have a speaker share his or her faith journey. Most of the speakers are law faculty or staff, but we occasionally have guest speakers. On the third gathering of the semester, Bob Goff brought the eighty students a wonderful message about living the life God intended. When the applause died down, he invited me to join him at the front. He put his arm around me and said some nice things about my family, and then he said, "I brought you something from Uganda that will help you remember the kids in the prisons you've been visiting."

Right on cue, Niemeyer walked around the corner. He was carrying a door. And not just any door—I recognized it instantly.

"You went to Masindi, Jim, and opened the door to the prison. I decided to rip it off its hinges and bring it home for you."

I was speechless.

That door to the Ihungu Remand Home now hangs in a display case in my house, serving as a reminder that there are more inmates behind prison doors waiting for justice.

✳ ✳ ✳

During an October 2012 trip, I had a warm reunion at Martyrs with Father Kasasa. He was kind and encouraging about Henry, telling me how well behaved and respectful Henry was. "I assume you know, however, his grades need to improve this term. He is not meeting our standards right now," he said gravely. "He assures me he is working very hard, so I believe he will make it."

Because final exams were looming, I took Henry for a quick breakfast and then returned him to campus. Over breakfast, I gave him a pep talk and told him how proud of him I was for working so hard. He explained that in physics, chemistry, and biology, he'd be awarded between zero and five points on his third-term exams. He'd also have an opportunity to earn two points in Subsidiary Math and one point on a General Writing paper. In order to advance to Senior Six, he needed to earn twelve out of a possible eighteen points this term.

DECEMBER 3, 2012

I had studied harder than I thought was possible, so I was ready for my final examinations in November. But they were very difficult; I did not know how well I had done and was afraid I would not receive twelve points.

After our exams, we usually traveled home for three weeks to be with our families before beginning the next term and receiving our report cards when we got back to school. But after the third term, the school had us all stay and wait for our report cards. One week later, the headmaster announced to a gathering of all Senior Five students the required standard had been reduced from twelve points to ten points. I was very relieved to hear this and was sure I had earned at least ten points.

But the headmaster also announced that nearly one hundred of the two hundred and eighty students fell below the mark and would be dismissed from school. That made me very nervous. When the gathering ended, the students lined up outside the office to receive their report cards. I said a prayer before I opened mine. When I saw my scores, I was shocked.

When I hung up the phone with Henry, I was heartsick and confused. He'd given it everything he had. He'd invested all his physical, mental, emotional, and spiritual energy into the third term, but he'd still come up three points short. He was devastated. His voice was quiet, shallow, and defeated. He'd been dismissed from school.

I wanted to climb through the telephone line and hug him, to tell him I was so proud of him for trying, and to assure him everything was going to be okay. But I didn't know if everything would be okay.

I chastised myself for zeroing in on Martyrs to the exclusion of other schools. What if he'd simply gone to Seeta, or to any of the lower-ranked science schools in the country? Why had I insisted on aiming so high? What had I done to his dream to attend university? *WHERE ARE YOU RIGHT NOW, GOD? Whatever You're trying to teach me, I'm not learning it, and Henry's caught in the middle.*

I had no idea what the next move would be. Neither did Henry. We agreed to pray about it and then talk the following week. Senior Six wouldn't start until February, so we knew we had some time to look for another school . . . if transferring was even an option. We had no idea.

DECEMBER 4, 2012

I hoped my call with Jim would make me feel better. I hoped he would have answers to my questions. I hoped he knew what I should do next. But after we hung up, I was just as sad and depressed.

He said he loved me and believed in me, but I felt like I had let him and his family down. They had paid lots of money for me to attend Martyrs and I really wanted to make them proud. Once again, my dream of attending university was dying. I started to think about what jobs I could do in Hoima and where I would live. Maybe I could work with my older brother cutting hair and live at home with my mom? I still believed I could succeed at Martyrs if I was given another chance, but I had been dismissed from school.

I prayed hard for something to change, but it was difficult to believe anything would. I also wondered if I would be allowed to go on the Senior Five trip to South Africa at the end of December. Jim's family had paid lots of money for me to go, but I did not know if I would be allowed because I was no longer a student.

"You could appeal the dismissal to the headmaster," Henry's physics teacher, Jonathan Kasibante, suggested to me on the phone.

It had taken a few days for me to reach Jonathan, but Joline's idea to call him had been a good one. Two weeks before we left Uganda, Jonathan had arranged for my family to speak to the entire graduating class of Senior Six students. They asked us many questions about the United States, ranging from the differences in culture to the differences in the educational institutions and structures. A few months earlier, Joline and Jessica had spoken to Jonathan's Senior Five Physics class about science education in the United States.

It'd been clear to us that Jonathan liked Henry and appreciated our friendship with him and with Martyrs. We hoped he'd have some good advice for us.

"Wait, we can appeal?" I asked.

"Of course. The headmaster has the final say about each student and can promote students who are dismissed. But I recommend that you ask him to let Henry repeat Senior Five. He will score much higher on the national exam after Senior Six if he learns the subjects better in Senior Five." I thanked him for his advice and called Henry.

"But I don't want to repeat Senior Five," Henry insisted. "I learned the subjects very well. I know I can succeed in Senior Six."

"I understand, but if given the choice between repeating Senior Five or being dismissed, which would you choose?" I pressed.

"I guess I would repeat Senior Five, but we should see if Father Kasasa will advance me to Senior Six."

I promised to try.

Father Kasasa was noncommittal in his response to my e-mail but agreed to meet with Henry on December 24. Providentially, Henry was scheduled to leave for South Africa early Christmas morning, so he caught a bus from Hoima to Kampala on December 23.

Just minutes before this meeting, I gave Henry a pep talk. "Sit up straight, speak confidently, and maintain eye contact." I didn't know what else to say, other than I'd be praying for him. We agreed I would call one hour later to find out how the meeting went.

At the end of that excruciating and prayerful hour, *déjà vu* enveloped me as I dialed. While Henry's fate once again hung in the balance, the risks of defeat weren't nearly as grave this time around. Before I dialed, I thought about how far Henry and I had come together. Henry had gone from a hopeless and forgotten prisoner to a student at a top school; I'd gone from someone who needed to control everything in my own little world to someone who was learning to see beyond myself and to trust in God's providence in a very big world. There was nothing left to do other than to dive deeper into that trust.

After three suspenseful rings, Henry answered in a quiet and subdued voice. *Oh no.* My heart sank to my feet.

"What happened? What did he say?"

"We are still talking. Please call again in fifteen minutes."

Are you kidding me?

"Well, what happened?" Joline asked as she and the kids waited for the verdict.

"Still waiting," I said. "Let's pray together again."

The next fifteen minutes felt like fifteen hours. My family was as nervous as I was. I strained to trust, but only partially succeeded. Precisely fifteen minutes later, I dialed again. Joline and the kids huddled with me.

"I am praising God!" Henry shouted after the first ring. My family cheered loud enough for Henry to hear.

Henry's determination and confidence had convinced the headmaster to advance him to Senior Six. The next day, Henry stepped onto an airplane for the first time in his life. He had a wonderful time in South Africa. But more importantly, he now had a passport and was beginning to develop a track record of leaving and returning to Uganda—a critical step toward my eventual goal of securing a visa for Henry to visit the United States.

✶   ✶   ✶

In late January of 2013, I returned to Uganda to continue working on the J-FASTER program. Sadly, time didn't permit me to visit Henry and his new little brother in Hoima. Just before Christmas, Henry's mother surprised him by revealing she was pregnant. A month later, the family surprised me by insisting he be named after me—James Josiah.

A much more haunting surprise also awaited me on that trip.

One of the many images I couldn't shake from my initial January 2010 trip to Masindi was that of Katwe, sitting in the dirt on the periphery, giggling every time one of us looked at her or tried to talk to her. She was then fourteen years old, the same age as Jessica. My heart broke for her lost innocence and mourned her seemingly bleak future.

I was overjoyed to learn later, though, that Niemeyer had gotten her admitted into a Christian vocational program after her release. A few months after that, however, I learned she'd dropped out and run away. Every month or two, a memory of Katwe resurfaced. But those memories came crashing back when I returned to Ihungu in January of 2013.

"How many girls do you have here now?" I asked the new matron who was caring for the Ihungu inmates.

"There are two—one on remand, and one who is being released on Sunday."

"Where is she going Sunday?"

"She was released by the court earlier this week, and we are taking her to Kampala to go back to school," she said.

"Why is she going to Kampala for school? Why not here in Masindi?"

"She cannot afford to go to school, but she has a sponsor who has admitted her into a program," she said with a smile.

"Who's sponsoring her?"

"The same organization that is paying my salary—Sixty Feet."

God bless you, Sixty Feet!

I told the matron I needed to talk to each of those on remand so we could get them lawyers and move their cases forward. Out of the corner of my eye, I saw one of the two female prisoners. She looked about seventeen, and I felt like I'd seen her before. *But where?*

"I'll start with her," I said as I motioned toward the girl.

As she approached, my breath caught as the nickel dropped. Her barely smiling eyes met mine. "You are Katwe," I whispered, because a whisper spent all I had in reserve.

"And you are Jim Gas," she said with a grin.

Close enough.

"How have you been? It's been three years. I thought I'd never see you again," I said.

Over the next ten minutes, we talked about what she'd been doing (not much) and why she was back at Ihungu (theft). I pulled up pictures of her and the others on my computer, and we laughed together.

"Where is John Niemeyer? Can he come visit me?" she asked hopefully.

"He's in America. He is one of my students now."

"When can he visit me?" she asked, still not comprehending.

But she wasn't the only one grasping for comprehension. I couldn't decide whether I was glad to see her or whether I would've rather not known her life was again in shambles. The difference between her life and my daughter's couldn't have been more profound. Katwe would likely be released right about the time Jessica started her freshman year at Pepperdine.

As I write this more than a year later, none of this is yet okay with me, but I'm learning that what's bigger than me belongs to God. I'm also learning just how small I am.

During this trip, I also checked with the Court of Appeals about the status of Henry's case. What I learned set my heart racing.

"A criminal session has been scheduled in Kampala, and it will definitely happen," the registrar said. "It will begin mid-February and conclude mid-March. Which date would you like to select for your hearing?"

It's finally happening. I couldn't believe it. I chose Tuesday, March 12, which was during my spring break.

✷ ✷ ✷

No one at Martyrs knew about Henry's prior life at Ihungu. I didn't want to lie to Father Kasasa, but I didn't want to tell him the whole truth either. So the Friday before the court hearing, I called him and asked if Henry could accompany me to a meeting I had on Tuesday. I knew he'd say yes, but I did feel a twinge of guilt about not being entirely forthcoming.

Over the weekend and on Monday, I practiced and practiced and practiced some more. The day I'd been praying about and anticipating for three years had finally arrived, and I was ready.

Or so I thought.

✶ ✶ ✶

Tuesday morning I awoke at 2:00 a.m. to the kind of thunderstorms I've only experienced in Africa—biblical in proportion. In addition to the bunker-busting thunder strikes, I could hear the showers ricocheting off the roof, the side of the Sixty Feet house where I was staying, the window, and . . . pieces of paper? After a few moments, I remembered the screens above the windows weren't covered by glass, so the sidewinding, cloud-borne sprinkler system pelting the side of the house was also penetrating the screen . . . onto the papers I'd foolishly left by the window. I scampered out of bed and moved the court papers I needed later that morning. Fortunately, nothing important was damaged, and I was soon back in bed.

As I lay there listening to the thunder and rain, I wondered whether this was the final, angry gasp of a three-year storm, or whether it was the opening of another, darker chapter. I dozed off and on until 4:00 a.m. and then got up to run through my notes again.

My driver and I picked up Henry from Martyrs before dawn and then went to my office at the Commercial Court. We sat and reflected on our three-year journey together up to this point. Because Joline wasn't able to come to Uganda for the hearing, she had insisted that I bring along a video camera and film as much as I could. We still had three hours before the hearing, so I interviewed Henry for a few minutes to capture the moment for Joline.

Henry then turned the camera on me and said it was my turn to answer questions. "I want to make sure we never forget how we are *both* feeling before the hearing," he said as he pushed the Record button.

Because the Court of Appeals doesn't video the arguments, I decided to record myself doing one last run-through with Henry at my side so he could hear what I was about to say on his behalf. It went reasonably well, but I still stumbled and fumbled more than I'd like.

Over breakfast a little while later, we prayed together. Henry prayed that God would give me the right words to say, and I prayed for total and complete exoneration for Henry.

As we walked into the courtroom at 9:00 a.m., thirty minutes before the scheduled time, I felt much calmer than I'd expected, partially because it wasn't entirely clear that the hearing would take place that day. When the three-judge panel was announced two weeks earlier, the acting Deputy Chief Justice had been among the justices, but she was rather sick and had been inconsistently appearing in court. Whenever she didn't appear, the cases were adjourned until the next session—six months later. Compounding this problem, her brother, Uganda's Deputy Prime Minister, had died the week before. His funeral was scheduled for the day of Henry's hearing in a town far from Kampala, creating the additional risk that she wouldn't show up. But thirty minutes before the hearing, the court clerk confirmed that a three-judge panel—one that didn't include the Deputy Chief Justice—was ready to hear the case.

Fifteen minutes before the argument was scheduled to begin, Edward Sekabanja arrived and helped me put on the neck scarf and robe Ugandan advocates wear in court. I looked around for the prosecutor, but there was no sign of her. I did see, however, another lawyer with whom I'd worked on the juvenile justice projects—he was arguing another case on the calendar that day. What he told me sent my pulse racing. He said he'd spoken with the prosecutor in my case the day before, and she was seriously considering not even contesting Henry's appeal. Part of me felt immense relief at the prospect of not having to argue the case, but a larger part of me wanted to explain in open court why Henry's conviction should not stand. I wanted this case to end with a bang of victory *over* the prosecution, rather than with a whimper of surrender *by* the prosecution.

Fifteen minutes after the hearing was supposed to have begun, the prosecutor finally arrived, apparently knowing much better than I when such hearings usually started. I introduced myself and tried to make small talk, hoping she'd tip her hand. *No dice.* Edward had a little more luck, but my heart sank when he reported what he'd learned: "She will be asking the court to adjourn the case."

"What? Why?" I was stunned.

"She didn't think the hearing would happen today, so she didn't prepare."

"Wait. What? How long does she want to the delay the hearing?"

"Until she has time to prepare."

I knew this thirty-day session ended in two days, so I feared the worst. She was seeking to kick the can down the road. Again.

Just before ten o'clock, a loud *boom* echoed as the court clerk banged once on the door, as was customary to announce the justices' entry into the courtroom.

This is it.

As they sat, I became a magnet for the six judicial eyes. They apparently hadn't expected a mzungu to be among the robed advocates.

On the day's docket were four cases. We were third in line, and the fourth case involved six codefendants whose families had all come to watch. The first two cases were summarily handled and were quickly remanded to the trial court for further proceedings.

Game time.

When our case was called, Henry was led to the prisoner dock in front of the judges, and I stood to address the court. As had been done in the prior two cases, I introduced myself, my co-counsel, and the prosecuting attorney. As soon as I introduced the prosecutor, she asked to be heard on a motion. Edward gently pulled on my robe. Apparently they have a one-lawyer-standing-at-a-time rule.

She requested an adjournment, exactly as Edward had said she would, announcing she wasn't prepared to proceed that day. The justices stared at her blankly. After several uncomfortable seconds, Justice Kavuma asked from the middle seat, "Why not?"

She said she knew the acting Deputy Chief Justice wouldn't be there, and no one called to tell her the hearing would proceed anyway.

They weren't impressed, to put it mildly. Justice Arach on the left side of the bench retorted, "So you are asking us to adjourn because we are not the panel you wanted?" The prosecutor wisely didn't reply to this rhetorical question.

The justices looked at each other, shook their heads, and then Justice Kavuma asked when she could be ready to proceed. She hemmed and hawed and ultimately agreed she could make her argument the next day, if necessary, but preferred a longer adjournment. She bowed and sat down meekly. All eyes turned to me.

I stood and calmly but unapologetically requested that we proceed today. I explained I'd provided the court and prosecution with extensive briefing well in advance of the hearing, and that it was very difficult and disruptive to Henry's studies to be taken out of school. I bowed, sat, and prayed.

The justices conferred among themselves for about a minute. Then Justice Kavuma began writing. Three minutes later, he was still writing. Justice Kasule, who had been leafing through the court record, turned to Henry and warmly said, "How old are you?"

Are you kidding me? Are we going down this path again?

"I am nineteen."

"I see you will be twenty very soon."

"Sir?"

"When were you born?"

"I was born on the eighteenth of March, 1993."

The judge nodded and smiled widely back at Henry.

"It was a Friday. At 7:00 p.m.," Henry said with an even bigger smile.

The audience erupted in laughter.

"How do you know that?" the justice lightheartedly responded.

"My mum told me."

More laughter.

This back-and-forth cut through the heavy tension in the room and convinced me the justice's questions were nothing more than playful banter. When the laughter died down, Justice Kavuma read his ruling. He reiterated the prosecution's request and the supporting reasoning . . . then denied the motion. The hearing would proceed.

Now both energized by the ruling and relaxed by the banter, I stood again and reintroduced myself, explaining I was appearing pursuant to a special practicing certificate and was ready to proceed whenever directed to do so.

"Where is your certificate?" Justice Kavuma asked.

"Right here." I handed it to the clerk.

Justice Kavuma inspected it, nodded ever so slightly, and handed it to Justice Arach. She inspected it, nodded approvingly, and passed it to Justice Kasule. He squinted, frowned, and then pointed to one portion of it as he handed it back to Justice Kavuma. He squinted as well, shook his head, and then passed it back to Justice Arach.

I knew exactly what they were looking at. The certificate had my name, the date, and the necessary signature. But the space for the identification of the single case in which I was authorized to appear was blank.

"Why is the case not indicated?" Justice Kavuma asked.

The one-lawyer-standing-at-a-time rule transformed my seat into a gravitational field that sucked my butt straight down. Up popped Edward, who explained the difficulties he encountered securing the certificate in the first place, which is why his office hadn't gone back to the law council to fix the mistake. That argument struck me as about as compelling as the prosecution's motion to adjourn the case. And from the justices' reactions, it appeared doomed to meet the same fate.

The justices again conferred, and Justice Kavuma again started writing. My heart pounded as I awaited his ruling. Two excruciating minutes later, he declared that because the special practicing certificate did not contain the name of the case, it would be deemed to be a general practicing certificate, which contained no limitations on my advocacy.

Thank You, God.

After a pregnant pause, which I took as my cue to proceed, I stood and said, "Thank you, My Lords. I will proceed when you are ready."

"Yes."

"At the outset, I would like to reserve thirty minutes of argument time. I will try to keep it briefer than that, if possible."

"Twenty will be fine," came Justice Kavuma's response.

"Twenty? Okay. I will be happy to do so," I replied with more confidence than I felt after this slight rebuke.

During my time as a judicial clerk on the Federal Court of Appeals, and during my tenure at Kirkland & Ellis, I'd seen a handful of stellar advocates argue before the Court of Appeals and the United States Supreme Court. I could easily imagine someone who saw my argument say, "I know Ken Starr; Ken Starr is a friend of mine. You are no Ken Starr." And I would agree. Without reservation.

That being said, I truly felt like things went as well as I could've asked or imagined in my opening argument. Whatever level my potential is, I reached it. And I could ask for nothing more. I mostly overcame my tendency to speak quickly, and I didn't feel nervous even for a moment. *Prayer and preparation.*

The justices didn't ask a single question. As I sat, I glanced over at the prosecutor and noticed she had scribbled several pages of notes while I spoke. She wouldn't be conceding after all. Over the next fifteen minutes, she made all the points I would've made in response to my argument, and she made them well, even citing specific pages in the record. She'd been prepared after all. *Why had she sandbagged?*

On rebuttal, I addressed about six different points over the course of about six minutes. I felt like I hit back hard on each of her strongest arguments. And then it was over.

Court adjourned.

Relief washed over me. The case was now where it had always been—in God's hands. He had entrusted it, however, at least for the time being, to the Ugandan Court of Appeals.

For the next half hour, still on an adrenaline rush, Edward, Henry, and I replayed the action outside with David Nary, who had replaced Shane Michael as the Nootbaar Fellow in Uganda a few months earlier. Edward felt good about the likely outcome. The other lawyer I knew who had been at the hearing said he thought the court could go either way.

Only time would tell.

We took some photos, hugged, and then I put Henry into a taxi and sent him back to school, where he would continue his education and wait for the court's decision. David and I proceeded directly to the Katojo Prison five hours west in Fort Portal to explore the possibility of bringing the J-FASTER program to the adult population of Uganda.

✳   ✳   ✳

Two months later, Jessica graduated from high school. Two days after that, Joline, Jessica, and I landed in Uganda. Joshua and Jennifer decided to skip this early-June, twenty-five-day trip and stay in California with their cousins. Waiting for us at the airport were the Gregstons—they had already been in Uganda for two weeks. The next day, Joline and Jessica joined them for a ten-day mobile medical trip to southern Uganda while David Nary and I finalized plans for the first-ever adult J-FASTER pilot program in Fort Portal.

Since the argument date, I'd checked my e-mail every morning, hoping for notification from the Court of Appeals that it had reached a decision on Henry's case. *Still no word.*

The next two weeks were as intense as any I'd spent in Uganda. Ten Pepperdine students, six Pepperdine lawyers, five UCLF lawyers, and four UCU law students invaded Katojo Prison to prepare more than seventy cases for resolution. Our efforts to reduce the adult prison population through plea bargaining were underway.

As we gathered for a final group photo with the adult prisoners involved in this project, I thought back on how much had changed. Henry was doing better at Martyrs, and there was no doubt he'd graduate in November. He would study hard for the national examinations that followed, and then he'd apply for medical school, hopefully enrolling in August of 2014.

Henry's life had been transformed. Because of his case, Uganda's criminal justice system was being transformed.

And I was transformed.

✷ ✷ ✷

Even now, as I think back to "The Starfish Story" five years after meeting Henry, I can picture myself in the story. As the boy picks up a stranded starfish and throws it back into the ocean, I can hear him say, "I made a difference for that one, didn't I?"

I initially pictured myself as the boy, reaching down to pick up Henry and help him get back to the life God intended for him. I am now convinced, however, that I am not the boy in that story after all.

I am the starfish.

EPILOGUE

IN THE SPRING OF 2015, Tango drove me six hours west from Kampala to visit Henry on my sixteenth trip to Uganda. Henry and I had spent the prior summer on pins and needles as we awaited the decision about whether Henry's excellent Senior Six national exam results were sufficient to get him admitted to Uganda's version of medical school—a six-year degree program immediately following secondary school.

We were ecstatic when on July 18, 2014, Henry was admitted into Kampala International University. Joline and I could not have been more proud of him for his perseverance and determination. He started one month later and, at the time of this publication, is now in his second year of study.

★ ★ ★

Two days after Joline and I celebrated our twenty-fifth anniversary, an e-mail arrived that nearly stopped my heart. It was from Betty Khisa—the prosecutor against whom I'd argued Henry's appeal twenty-seven months earlier. It was short and to the point: "Hello, Jim. The long-awaited judgment is ready for delivery tomorrow, 19 June 2015, at the Court of Appeal. Hoping for the best, Betty."

I stared at the screen, mesmerized for a full minute. Was Henry's nightmare really almost over? Or was this simply the precursor to another appeal, this time to Uganda's Supreme Court?

I was touched by Betty's well wishes—she truly wanted the best for Henry. While we had initially reconnected at a plea bargaining workshop nearly a year after the hearing, a close friendship had developed when we traveled together to neighboring Rwanda to introduce plea bargaining to the Rwandan judiciary. Betty had taken over a leadership role in implementing plea bargaining in Uganda after her colleague Joan Kagezi was assassinated by comrades of the Somali terrorists whom Joan was prosecuting in conjunction with the 2010 World Cup bombing in Kampala. Joan had been among the Ugandan delegation who had come to Pepperdine for an early 2014 plea bargaining study tour and is greatly missed. During our time in Rwanda, Betty had asked about Henry and told me she hoped his name would ultimately be cleared.

I knew full well I couldn't get to Uganda in time for the live reading of the ruling, so I called Edward Sekabanja and confirmed he would be there. He promised to scan and send me the ruling as soon as possible.

In the wake of my being presented with the Warren Christopher Award as California's International Lawyer of the Year in the fall of 2013, a documentary film crew had followed our team of students and lawyers around to chronicle our 2014 summer prison project at the Luzira Maximum Security Prison. They had also traveled to Hoima to film Henry and his family at their home, and to Masindi to film at Ihungu.

Because the film crew was returning to Uganda in a few weeks to show the impact of our work one year later, I called one of the crew members, Craig Detweiler, to see if he was interested in capturing Henry and I reading the ruling for the first time. He was.

The rest of the day passed as slowly as any I can remember. Before I went to bed, I called Henry to tell him that we would have the ruling in about ten hours and that I'd call him after I read it. I considered asking Edward to send it directly to Henry, but decided against it because I wanted to share the moment with him—whether we won or lost. As I lay in bed that night, I couldn't shake the feeling that the reason the court had taken so long with the ruling was to ensure their upholding his conviction wouldn't be overturned by the Supreme Court. What finally allowed me to fall asleep, however, was the realization that no matter what happened the next day, Henry was still free and was still pursuing his dream.

JUNE 19, 2015

Jim called me in the morning to tell me that the ruling was going to be issued later that day. It was late at night for him, and he said he would call me after he woke up to tell me what happened. I was sure we had won. I was not guilty and believed the court would dismiss the case against me.

I studied all day for my final examinations in biochemistry, physiology, human anatomy, environmental health, nutritional disorders, and nursing practices that would start in a few weeks. I was determined to get very good grades again, like those I had received my first semester in biology, physics, chemistry, entrepreneurship, behavioral science, ethics, research methods, communication skills, epidemiology, biostatistics, computer science, mathematics, and first aid.

At about 8:00 p.m., my phone rang. It was Jim, and he asked me to turn on my computer so we could Skype in ten minutes. He said he was about to read the ruling. I prayed until he called.

At 10:00 a.m., Craig and another camera operator shooting from a second angle pressed Record just before I doubled-clicked the PDF attachment in Edward's e-mail to read through the ruling myself before calling Henry.

When the ten-page document opened, "Criminal Appeal No. 85 of

2010" jumped out at me from the top of the page, punctuating the fact that Henry had been waiting more than five years for justice. *Is the wait finally over?*

I tried to remain calm as I began reading what was printed just below "JUDGMENT OF THE COURT."

> The appellant and Rose Mpairwe were both convicted of murder of one Innocent Kirungi by the High Court of Uganda at Masindi.
>
> Rose Mpairwe, who was an adult at the time of the offence, was convicted and sentenced to 10 years imprisonment. She did not appeal. The appellant was a minor at the time of the commission of the offense, was placed on 12 months probation, but was released from the remand home before the hearing of this appeal.

Unlike American courts, which almost always state the ruling up front and then explain the rationale later, Ugandan courts usually do just the opposite, and this was clearly not going to be an exception.

The court next restated our grounds for appeal and then proceeded to summarize the "facts" that gave rise to the appeal. My blood pressure started to climb as I read what the court deemed the "facts"—the evidence submitted to the court at trial, which definitely were *not* the real facts. I started to feel heavier and heavier in my chair as I scrolled through two pages of inaccuracies.

That feeling magnified when the court dismissed on procedural grounds our contention that there was insufficient evidence to convict Henry. Only the conflict of interest ground remained.

At this point, my anxiety compelled me to start skimming, and what I was reading sounded actually quite good for a change:

> . . . the appellant was not permitted by his advocate to testify to rebut the evidence his very own advocate elicited from his

co-accused implicating him . . . inherent and inescapable conflict of interest . . . since each one's defense implicated the other of having committed the offense charged.

This was precisely what I had argued to the court, and when the court quoted in bold on page six an earlier Ugandan case I had urged them to follow at the hearing, my confidence soared.

In the next moment, however, my wings melted and I plummeted toward earth. Page seven started with, "In reply, the learned Assistant Director of Public Prosecutions, Ms. Betty Khisa, submitted that no evidence had been adduced to show that there was a conflict of interest in respect of the advocate who represented both the appellant and the co-accused, Rose Mpairwe."

It was then I realized that everything encouraging I had just read was simply a summary of the arguments I had made *to* the court, rather than conclusions reached *by* the court. *No wonder it all sounded so good.*

The suspense was killing me, but I knew the end was near—a box in the upper left of my computer screen told me I was on page seven of ten, and that page closed with what seemed to be an introduction to the payoff, "We have carefully considered the submissions of both counsel, as well as their written submissions and authorities."

My eyes scanned the screen, my finger pumped the down arrow key, my lips mumbled the court's words, and my spirit prayed for exoneration as page eight crept onto the screen.

". . . issue raised in this appeal appears to have been resolved earlier by this court . . . right to a fair hearing is an absolute right that is not subject to the limitations imposed on other rights . . ."

My thundering heart kept pace with my jackhammering finger as page nine climbed into view.

My sanity yo-yoed up as I read, ". . . a person who is not ably represented . . . cannot be said to have been accorded a fair hearing . . ."

But then hurtled toward the floor with, "the appellant . . . opted to remain silent, thereby depriving himself of the opportunity . . . to refute the allegations made against him by his co-accused . . ."

Fortunes seemed to climb yet again midway down page nine with "advocate was more concerned about the case against [Rose Mpairwe] than against the appellant."

This penultimate page closed with, "It was only natural for the defending advocate to concentrate on the case of the adult co-accused, Rose Mpairwe, so as to save her from being convicted and sentenced to death, and to pay less attention to the case of the minor appellant, who stood only to be sentenced to a maximum of three years in case of a conviction."

True, but is this recognition by the court favorable or unfavorable to Henry? One way to find out.

As page ten inched upward, I started reading out loud:

We therefore find that it was not possible, in the circumstances of this case, for the same advocate to have ably and fairly represented both the appellant and the co-accused, Rose Mpairwe, without causing prejudice to the case of one of them.

We find that, in this case, the appellant was not accorded a fair hearing and we so hold . . .

My voice abandoned me before I reached the end of the sentence. Emotion overcame me as more than five years of waiting finally came to end.

We had won. Henry was finally exonerated.

The rest of the ruling made this crystal clear:

. . . the trial and conviction of the appellant contravened Articles 28 and 44 of the Constitution and was therefore a nullity.

On that account, we hereby quash the conviction and set aside the sentence imposed upon the appellant, by the Children's

Court of Masindi, the fact that he has already served the same notwithstanding. For the same reason, we also rule out an order of a re-trial of the appellant.

It was truly over. The conviction was vacated and the case was dismissed.

After a few dumbstruck moments of inaction, I wiped my eyes and clicked Video Call on Skype. Henry answered on the first ring, and I didn't keep him in suspense long.

"The court decided that the conviction was in violation of the constitution and therefore it has been quashed and nullified . . ." My voice misfired, but I reloaded. "It's over . . . you won!"

After the one-second voice lag, a smile exploded onto his face, which he followed with a laugh and some fist pumps.

"So no longer are you someone who has been convicted of a crime—the whole thing was nullified. It's like it never happened," I explained.

"Okay," Henry said as he nodded and wiped his eyes. "Very good! Praise be to God!"

He wanted to see the ruling for himself, so I showed him on the screen what it said. He excitedly read the last page out loud, then pulled out his camera to take a picture of the screen so he could send it to his mother and Mr. William.

Just before we hung up, Henry paused and said, "I want to extend my appreciation for having been represented by a very good, perfect lawyer."

We both laughed.

I shot back, "I had a very good client to represent—someone who was innocent and needed to be proven innocent. I'm glad we had the opportunity to make that happen."

"I didn't know what would happen," he said. "I have been just waiting, praying, waiting, praying—and now our prayers have been answered."

Indeed they have.

$$\star \quad \star \quad \star$$

More prayers were answered over the course of the next three weeks as another team of Pepperdine students, American lawyers, Ugandan law students, and Ugandan lawyers accompanied me to four rural adult prisons. During this project, we prepared over a hundred and fifty cases for resolution by the Ugandan lawyers. Since we started the adult plea bargaining project the prior summer, Ugandans have completed about fifteen hundred cases in our absence, thus expediting justice for juvenile and adult prisoners all over the country.

$$\star \quad \star \quad \star$$

As this book is going to press, Henry's brother Joseph is finishing his Senior Six year and is hoping to attend law school in the fall of 2016. Sadly, Henry's father died after a six-month bout with liver cancer in early 2014, just after James Josiah's first birthday. His death hit Henry's family hard, and we all miss his calm leadership. Shortly thereafter, Henry was appointed head of his clan by his extended family.

Henry still keeps in touch with some of his former fellow inmates at Ihungu. His predecessor as Katikkiro, Sam, works in a sugar factory near

Masindi. Henry's chairman, Jamil, is a motorcycle mechanic in Masindi. Bo, the Ihungu pastor, sells fish at a nearby lake. Nakunda recently relocated to Rwanda to look for work. Mr. William still takes good care of the inmates at Ihungu and talks to Henry about once a month. During their most recent conversation, he told Henry that he recently saw Katwe in Masindi and that she seemed to be doing well.

Tango continues to be my driver when I am in Uganda, which is three or four times a year for about two weeks each visit. During my last trip, he told me his wife recently converted to Christianity from Islam.

The Gregstons take a team of medical professionals to Uganda every summer, and we still keep in close touch with the "twin family" who greatly enriched our family's six months in Uganda.

My oldest daughter, Jessica, is in her junior year at Pepperdine, double-majoring in biology and psychology, with plans to attend medical school in a couple years. She and Henry talk about being doctors together someday. Joshua and Jennifer spent a couple weeks together in Uganda working on a mobile medical clinic team in the summer of 2015 and plan to go back again next summer. Joline continues to be the glue holding our lives together and will always be my personal hero.

During his three years at Pepperdine Law, John Niemeyer served as my research assistant. He graduated in 2015, a few months after I became the godfather of Justice K's son, Mark.

Jay Milbrandt now teaches international business courses at Bethel University in Minnesota, and I direct Pepperdine's Global Justice Program. I will continue to offer my assistance to the country I consider my second home. In fact, I am slated to become an official citizen of Uganda in 2016.

ACKNOWLEDGMENTS

THE FIRST FRUITS of my gratitude belong to Henry, whose unparalleled fortitude and faith have inspired me since the day I met him six years ago. I know him well enough to know that he would rightly insist that God belongs at the top of any list either of us would make—He sits on the throne of both of our lives.

The events depicted in this book would not have happened if not for the persistence of Jay Milbrandt, who wouldn't take no for an answer in his quest to get me to go with him to Uganda. You altered the course of my life, "Dawg," and I will always be grateful to you. We miss you at Pepperdine.

But Jay never would have been in the position to recruit me into his life-changing adventure without the leadership and vision of Dean Ken Starr, whose dream of a global law school gave Jay the room to build Pepperdine's Global Justice Program. Ken, my life is much richer with you as a mentor.

I truly believe, though, that Ken's vision and Jay's persistence would not have been enough to overcome my complacency if it hadn't been for the passion and charisma of Bob Goff and his "Love Docs" speech. It is an honor and a privilege to be your friend and coconspirator, Bob. You constantly amaze me with your huge heart and wonderful whimsy. I look forward to many more capers with you down the road.

A special note of thanks to: Herb and Eleanor Nootbaar for pledging their resources to establish an institute named in their honor; Bob Cochran for welcoming the Global Justice Program into the purview of the Nootbaar Institute; Vice Dean Tim Perrin, Dean Deanell Tacha, and President Andrew Benton for continuing to make the Global Justice Program a priority at Pepperdine; and to Colin and Amy Batchelor and John and Rosella Gash for sacrificially paying Henry's medical school tuition.

If the African proverb "It takes a village to raise a child" is true, then it took multiple villages to bring this book from its birth to maturity. While this five-year project felt to me like raising a fourth child, my wife and three kids would more aptly characterize it as feeding a stray dog. But feed it they did. Their patient understanding and helpful comments nurtured *Divine Collision* from an idea into a reality. I am more grateful to them for the encouragement and space they gave me than I am capable of expressing.

The genesis of this book was a series of daily e-mail updates I shared with a group of friends, family, and colleagues during my first trip to Uganda. I continued writing periodic reports until Henry was released several months later. Not only did reducing these events to writing help me process what I was experiencing, but it also ensured I would have a clear memory of everything that happened. Several of the recipients— who were likely just trying to be nice—encouraged me to turn these reports into a book. And when I eventually tried to do so, many of them were kind enough to read early drafts of the first several chapters. Without their encouragement, I may have given up long ago. So special thanks go to Amy Batchelor, Casey Delaney, Jessie Fahy, and Dave Sugden.

Several others came along at just the right time to spur me on when the writing process revealed itself to be much more difficult than I ever would have imagined. The patience and insight they offered were treasured gifts. Rick Hamlin, without your *Guideposts* story, we never would have met the Gregstons—our twin family who made our six months in Uganda so much more fun and joyful. Jeff Wyss, your clear and honest feedback were immensely helpful as the story took shape. Holly Phillips, your huge heart and selfless concern for Henry, Joseph, and their family restored their herd and allowed Henry's brothers to continue their education. Anna Shea, the direction and guidance you and your middle school class at Quincy Christian School provided were blessings to me and helped me understand how to tell this story for a non-legal audience. And Sienna Hopkins, thanks for grabbing the manuscript off of my sister's coffee table and reading it while you were supposed to be babysitting, and for taking such an interest in this story. The feedback from you and your criminal justice classes at Long Beach State made this book better.

Thanks also to "Two Bunk John" Niemeyer, John Napier, Ray Boucher, and David Barrett, for reading later drafts and ensuring that I got the story right—a story you lived alongside me in the early days.

I owe a huge debt of gratitude to the team of professionals who believed in this project enough to invest vast amounts of time and expertise into turning an unpolished manuscript into a published book. Thank you for meeting with me early in the process, Curtis Yates, and being completely honest with me about what would need to be done to convert what you saw as a "great story" into a published book. Your patience with me over the course of three years was more generous than I had any right to expect. I am grateful that you and the rest of the Yates & Yates team—Matt, Mike, Karen, and Sealy—stuck with me while I struggled to learn how to tell a story rather than simply write a report.

I am amazed by the talent of Kris Bearss, who skillfully and gracefully edited an overlong manuscript into a more concise book. I was sure there wasn't anything that could be edited out without losing an important part of the story; you proved me wrong. I have no doubt that your meticulous edit was critical to attracting the attention of my publisher.

I cannot imagine a better group of professional publishers to work with than the team at Worthy assembled and led by Byron Williamson. Jeana Ledbetter, your passion and determination to tell this story left no doubt that you were the one to whom I wanted to entrust this book. Kyle Olund, your edits and suggestions for additional content enhanced the quality of the book in so many ways. Leeanna, Morgan, Caroline,

Wayne, Betty, Dale, Debbie, Bart, Kelli, and the rest of the team who helped get the book across the finish line and onto the shelves, it has been an honor to work with you.

I am filled with admiration and warmth each time I venture to Uganda and partner with the true heroes of this story—the leaders and reformers in Uganda who are daily overcoming huge obstacles in their quest to deliver justice to their fellow citizens. Thank you for embracing me, my family, our students, and the dream of a more just Uganda: Chief Justice (retired) Benjamin Odoki, Chief Justice Bart Katureebe, Principal Judge (retired) James Ogoola, Principal Judge Yorokamu Bamwine, Justices Geoffrey Kiryabwire, Mike Chibita, Edmund Lugayizi, and Lameck Mukasa, along with others who are leading the charge, Paul Gadenya and Andrew Khaukha.

And finally, to my wife and children—Joline, Jessica, Joshua, and Jennifer; to my parents—John and Rosella; and to the best siblings a guy could ever have—John, Julie, and Jerry: At every point in my life, you have encouraged me, supported me, and showed me what the unconditional love of Jesus looks and feels like here on earth. You are everything to me.

NOTES

1. We later learned that the injured man would make a full recovery and that he likely wouldn't have survived had we not gone back. We also learned that Mohamudu had spent several weeks in jail. He was released once he paid the injured man's medical bills.
2. A video of the entire speech is available at http://www.youtube.com/watch?v=MqaMNlIycKI.
3. Because there's no written transcript or audio recording of the trial, and because I didn't attend the trial proceedings myself, my description of what happened is pieced together from Justice Ochan's scant, handwritten notes and Henry's recollections.
4. The video Joline and the kids created and played for me that day is still available for viewing on Animoto's website: http://animoto.com/play/iFXPPEK2DApt7VjyDGJjig?autostart=true.

ABOUT THE AUTHOR

JIM GASH graduated first in his law school class at Pepperdine in 1993. Over the course of his career, he has clerked with a federal judge on the United States Court of Appeals for the Fifth Circuit, worked at one of the top law firms in the country, and served as dean of students at Pepperdine University School of Law. In 2010, Jim traveled to Uganda on a juvenile justice project, where he met Henry. Since then, he has returned to Uganda more than fifteen times. In 2012, Jim Gash became the Specialist Advisor to the High Court of Uganda and in 2013 became the first American ever to appear as an attorney in Ugandan Court. In recognition of his ongoing work in Uganda, Professor Gash received the 2013 Warren Christopher Award, which is presented to California's International Lawyer of the Year. Today, Jim teaches at Pepperdine Law, directs Perrepdine's Global Justice Program, and is scheduled to become an official citizen of Uganda in 2016. Jim and his family live in Malibu, California. Jim blogs at www.throwingstarfish.com.

GLOBAL JUSTICE PROGRAM

PEPPERDINE | School of Law

The Global Justice Program, a component of the Nootbaar Institute on Law, Religion, and Ethics at Pepperdine School of Law, brings Pepperdine students, professors, and alumni face to face with the most challenging legal problems in the developing world. Through long-standing partnerships with legal institutions in East Africa, Pepperdine law student interns work alongside and are mentored by the leaders of the local judiciary and prosecutorial teams. Pepperdine alumni serving in yearlong fellowships collaborate with professors and students on shorter-term prison projects that bring access to justice for imprisoned juveniles and adults awaiting trial.

The Global Justice Program partners with many of the leading nonprofit organizations around the world to raise awareness, deliver justice, and implement lasting change on behalf of the oppressed. Pepperdine Law also offers semester-length and short courses taught by these world leaders in the fight against global poverty and injustice.

global.justice@pepperdine.edu
www.law.pepperdine.edu/global-justice

Restore International

www.restoreinternational.org

"Our goal is to make a tangible
difference for people and show
the world what it looks like
to love boldly."

Amazima Ministries

www.amazima.org

"To live out the love of Jesus
by educating and empowering
the people of Uganda and
the communities we serve."

Sixty Feet

www.sixtyfeet.org

"Bringing hope and restoration
to the imprisoned children
of Africa in Jesus' name."

International Justice Mission

www.ijm.org

"We are a global organization
that protects the poor
from violence in
the developing world."

IF YOU ENJOYED THIS BOOK, WILL YOU CONSIDER SHARING THE MESSAGE WITH OTHERS?

Mention the book in a blog post or through Facebook, Twitter, Pinterest, or upload a picture through Instagram.

Recommend this book to those in your small group, book club, workplace, and classes.

Head over to facebook.com/worthypublishing, "LIKE" the page, and post a comment as to what you enjoyed the most.

Tweet "I recommend reading #DivineCollision by @Jim_Gash // @worthypub"

Pick up a copy for someone you know who would be challenged and encouraged by this message.

Write a book review online.

Visit us at worthypublishing.com

twitter.com/worthypub

worthypub.tumblr.com

facebook.com/worthypublishing

pinterest.com/worthypub

instagram.com/worthypub

youtube.com/worthypublishing